Praise for
HEAVY HITTER SELLING

"This book will be my sales team's bible going forward."

Rod Hamlin, Vice President, Sales
JRG Software

"I really enjoyed reading the book! An unusual way of looking at sales through perfecting the communications process. I agree—relationships and rapport lead to revenue."

Dr. Shuki Bruck, Gordon Moore Professor of Computation
and Neural Systems and Electrical Engineering,
California Institute of Technology

"During the past twenty years I have seen it all—sales training, motivational sessions, coaching sessions, and workshops. But *Heavy Hitter Selling* has generated the most enthusiastic feedback I have ever seen from a field organization!"

Scott Raskin, Chief Operating Officer, Telelogic

"This practical guide defines sales in an entirely new way and teaches powerful communication skills that can jump-start your sales career."

Laurie Beth Jones, Author, Jesus, CEO;
The Path; *and* Jesus, Life Coach

"I have experienced firsthand Steve Martin's success as a sales leader. It is rare to see someone translate his accomplishments into a well-written book with clear principles and a methodology that others can easily understand. It is a book you prefer your competitors not to have."

Ofir Kedar, Founder and Past CEO, SQRIBE Technologies
Former Chairman, Brio Software

"*Heavy Hitter Selling* isn't another sales process book. *Heavy Hitter Selling* can make the most experienced sales rep more cognizant of managing the human aspects of the sales process and expose junior reps to an experience that normally takes a career to master. I've seen it work in action."

John Schroeder, President, Rainfinity

"Absolutely fascinating. A must-read for the management team of every company. Surviving today's challenging times may depend on it."

Rich Heimsch, President, DEK International

"More than just a book on tips and techniques, *Heavy Hitter Selling* is the sales manager you've always wanted."

Greg Gadbois, Executive Vice President, Sales, Service Net

"Recommended reading for the entire board of directors—especially venture capitalists who need to decipher and approve their portfolio companies' sales strategies."

Dave Pidwell, Venture Partner, Alloy Ventures

"Having trained with Dr. Erickson and after reading this book, I am convinced that Dr. Erickson would be proud."

Dr. Constantine Callas, Founder and Chairman, Medata

"*Heavy Hitter Selling* is a must read for every sales exec in the post-bubble era. It is intuitive, easy to read, practical, and grounded in decades of experience."

M.R. Rangaswami, Founder, Sand Hill Group

HEAVY HITTER SELLING

How Successful Salespeople
Use Language and Intuition
to Persuade Customers to Buy

STEVE W. MARTIN

WILEY

John Wiley & Sons

Published by John Wiley & Sons, Inc., Hoboken, New Jersey.
Published simultaneously in Canada.

For general information on our other products and services or for technical support, please contact our Customer Care Department within the United States at (800) 762-2974, outside the United States at (317) 572-3993 or fax (317) 572-4002.

Wiley also publishes its books in a variety of electronic formats. Some content that appears in print may not be available in electronic books. For more information about Wiley products, visit our web site at www.wiley.com.

Library of Congress Cataloging-in-Publication Data:

Martin, Steve W., 1960-
    Heavy hitter selling : how successful salespeople use language and intuition to persuade customers to buy / Steve W. Martin.
        p. cm.
    Originally published: Rancho Santa Margarita, Calif.: Sand Hill Pub., c2004.
    Includes bibliographical references and index.
    ISBN-13: 978-0-471-78700-6 (pbk. : alk. paper)
    ISBN-10: 0-471-78700-0 (pbk. : alk. paper)
    1. Selling.   2. Business communication.   3. Success in business.   I. Title.
HF5438.25M37366 2006
658.85—dc22   2005056175

Printed in the United States of America.

10   9   8   7   6   5   4   3   2   1

Contents

Why Should You Read This Book?

> Words, of course, are the most powerful drug
> known to mankind.
>
> —RUDYARD KIPLING

GRAB A PENCIL and answer the following question: What tasks are salespeople paid to do?

1. _____
2. _____
3. _____
4. _____

Over the past year, I have asked this question of thousands of people. Perhaps the most popular answer given by people outside the sales field is "SELL!" They write it on all four lines. Meanwhile, salespeople often respond with answers that reflect their company's sales process: close deals, demonstrate products, qualify opportunities, and prospect for leads.

Here are the actual answers given in the order of priority.

1. First and foremost, salespeople build customer relationships.
2. They read customers' minds and know what they are honestly thinking.
3. They predict the future and foretell which deals will actually close.
4. They persuade customers to change their opinions and beliefs.

How many answers did you agree with? More importantly, where do you learn about these four fundamental skills?

A quick search of the Internet using the phrase "sales books" will return more than three million results, so you might ask, "Why read another book about sales?" Most likely, you have already read several books about salesmanship including the well-known classics. You probably found that some had merit and were worth the time and effort to read. However, they all tend to focus on the logical steps of the sales cycle such as prospecting, qualification, and closing techniques. They give limited attention to the less-perceptible aspects of the sales process.

Sales is more than a science—it is an art. The skillful combination of structure and free thinking, process and people, and logic and emotions. Where can you go to learn about this? Unfortunately, most of the popular sales training programs assume salespeople are already capable of building rapport and have an aptitude for establishing trust, that salespeople possess highly developed communication techniques, are proficient in determining what information is important, and can discern when someone is misleading them.

These methodologies do not explain or fully take into account the human characteristics of the people who actually make the purchase decision. They concentrate on the logical and procedural aspects of the sales cycle. In short, they offer frameworks that are limited to the "tangible" processes of the sales cycle. These may include the basic questions a salesperson commits to memory, such as, "What is your budget?" and "What is your time frame?" Or the programs may emphasize the financial justification of a salesperson's solution. They explain how to create a return-on-investment (ROI) model in order to show customers how much money they will save by selecting a product.

CHANGES IN THE WORLD OF SALES

The salesperson's world has changed dramatically in the new millennium. Long gone are the days of "order taking" or closing deals without much effort in a superheated business market. Following a decade of unprecedented economic growth, expenditures by corporations are at a fraction of their previous level.

This situation has only been compounded by a downturn in the overall economy and the terrorist attacks. With so little money available, projects must be continually justified and are constantly being reprioritized. These issues are reflected in the protracted length of today's selection process and the intense scrutiny vendors face daily.

Perhaps most importantly, today's customers are smarter. Information is not only easier to find but also available in greater detail than ever before. For example, the number of magazines available in the United States almost doubled from 1970 to 1999. Today, there are over 10,000 magazines published, each with a very specific audience.[1] For instance, there are magazines for bird watchers, bread makers, and bow hunters. This exemplifies the overall trend of our society toward specialization centered upon very narrow areas of expertise. In some ways, today we know a lot more about a lot less.

SUCCESSFUL SALESPEOPLE

Throughout this book, we'll examine what successful salespeople do and explain their unique ability to acquire information about a customer and discern a deeper level of meaning from what the customer has said. They possess an insight that enables them to develop the optimum account strategy by comparing what they've learned from previous wins and losses with the current situation.

Four major attributes separate successful salespeople from unsuccessful ones. Successful salespeople

1. Are skillful builders of personal relationships. At the foundation of all sales is a relationship between people. Great salespeople have an innate talent to build these relationships by creating rapport. Their presence has an appeal that makes a customer feel at ease. The customer enjoys their company. They build personal alliances based upon understanding individual wants and needs. The customer trusts them.

2. Are masters of language. They are accomplished communicators who know what to say and, equally important, how to say it. Through their mastery of language, they are able to convey and decipher deep underlying messages that less successful salespeople miss. While using the same language as most salespeople, they have developed an uncanny ability to persuade nonbelievers.

3. Are sales cycle experts. The sales cycle is the formalized information exchange between a customer and a salesperson. It consists of a series of steps that are designed to gather information about the customer and present information about the salesperson's solution. While a company has identified these steps for the sales force, successful salespeople enhance this process by drawing upon past sales experiences. They use this reservoir of experience to manage and control their deals. As a result, they close more business.

4. Have highly developed intuition. Successful salespeople are continually cataloging their successes and failures. They store patterns of individual and company behavior and link them to the sales process. From this base of intuitive knowledge they are able to create and execute account strategies. They also use a unique form of highly developed intuition to ensure their message is acted upon by the customer. Through their intuition, they are able to integrate their spoken words with the sales situation based upon their experiences with different types of people and past sales cycles.

HEAVY HITTERS

A successful salesperson is commonly referred to as a "Heavy Hitter." Heavy Hitters have an extraordinarily developed intuition, or deeper level of understanding, about the deals they will close. This understanding is somewhat equivalent to the ability to predict the future or analogous to reading minds. Heavy Hitters have a "feel" for their deals. They can "see" which deals will close this quarter and they can accurately forecast future deals. They not only listen to a customer but also speak the customer's language. This book is about understanding and modeling the Heavy Hitter's behavior. Based upon my personal experience teaching these concepts to salespeople, I believe that almost all salespeople can become Heavy Hitters if they study the concepts presented in this book and put them to use.

From this point on, I will refer to a successful salesperson as a "Heavy Hitter." And, for the sake of simplicity, I will alternate the pronouns "he" and "she" from chapter to chapter.

ABOUT THIS BOOK

The goal of this book is to help you learn how to apply the principles of intangible human behavior to the sales cycle. The behavior is considered intangible because it can't be seen. However, to Heavy Hitters it is quite real. The principles are presented through practical models that can be implemented by anyone. However, you must be willing to take the time to understand and apply the concepts of *Heavy Hitter Selling*.

The book is composed of three sections. In the first section we will examine the layers of communication that occur in every conversation between salespeople and their customers. When I use the term "customer" throughout the book, I specifically mean someone a salesperson is trying to sell something to. This includes suspects who have yet to be introduced to the solution, prospects in the process of evaluation, as well as existing customers who may buy again.

Our quest to understand the human nature of communication continues by studying the structure of dialogue between the customer and salesperson. We will also introduce the fundamentals of neurolinguistics, the study of how the brain uses and interprets language. We will build upon this foundation to examine how the brain and the entire body work in conjunction with language. This is how people are "wired" to communicate. If you know how people think, you can organize your information to have a better impact on their decision-making process. In addition, by scrutinizing how language, the brain, and the body work in combination, you can determine the truthfulness of someone's message.

The second section reviews the strategy of connecting with customers—where to go, whom to connect with, and how to build relationships with them. Heavy Hitters selectively choose the battles they will fight. They create rapport to build relationships by understanding the customer's personal wants, needs, and desires. Building rapport is an art that is achieved by speaking each customer's individual language and communicating both verbally and nonverbally.

One of the Heavy Hitter's most important customers is his sales manager. Your sales manager can make your life enjoyable, tolerable, or miserable, and your mental condition is profoundly influenced by this key relationship. Therefore, it's important to win over this key person.

Another very important customer is you. You probably ended up in sales through a series of unpredicted occurrences or maybe even by happenstance. While you learned that you must be persistent and energetic, who has taught you how to behave as a salesperson? Do you know what really motivates you and how to deal with the ups and downs of this stressful profession? We seek to understand how to live with ourselves given the volatility of our chosen career.

The third section, on the power of persuasion, reveals that there is an additional dimension of meaning and structure within language that can be used to convert skeptics into believers. While Heavy Hitters do this intuitively, we will detail how to not only persuade the rational intellect but more importantly appeal to the emotional subconscious by studying the language of two very well-known Heavy Hitters.

TWO WELL-KNOWN HEAVY HITTERS

The term Heavy Hitter isn't solely applicable to sales. Powerful people who have acquired prominence through their accomplishments, expertise, and reputation are also known as Heavy Hitters. These include politicians, entertainers, lawyers, doctors, sports heroes, and famous businesspeople. The Heavy Hitters in our society create and enforce its rules, determine what we watch and wear, and even influence how we behave.

Over the years, I have mentally recorded the techniques and actions of successful salespeople and witnessed how they are able to change a customer's belief and opinions solely by the words they speak. In order to explain this natural and instinctive phenomenon to other salespeople, I found myself using examples of language from a diverse set of people including Bill Walsh, the famous former football coach; Dear Abby, the advice columnist; and Sun Tzu, the legendary Chinese general who lived more than two and a half thousand years ago. Regardless of the eclectic mix of examples I used, invariably, I *always* used quotations from two very well-known Heavy Hitters, Ronald Reagan and Jesus Christ.

In 2000, Ronald Reagan was ranked as the eighth-best president in U.S. history according to a survey of 78 historians.[2] It's not surprising that he was ranked behind national heroes like Washington, Jefferson, Lincoln, and Franklin Delano Roosevelt. However, the most surprising part of the survey is that he was ranked as the most underrated president of all time. What made this president so unique was his ability to communicate and persuade. In fact, Reagan is known in the annals of history as "The Great Communicator."

Historians consistently rank Jesus Christ as one of the most influential persons of all time. The fact that over six billion copies of the Bible have been printed and one-third of the world's population follows his teachings is direct proof of his impact. His legacy continues to affect people all around the world daily. Obviously, the communication methods of Reagan and Jesus are well worth studying today.

While thousands of books have been written from a theological and political perspective about both of these men, studying them from a business perspective teaches powerful lessons that apply specifically to salesmanship. For our purposes, we are more interested in how something is said and why it was said, rather than what was actually said. Therefore, we want to study and understand the purpose, content, and structure of their language usage to help us learn how to become more convincing. For our pursuits in this book, we are not interested in their political ideology or religious theology.

AN HONORABLE PROFESSION

Unfortunately, our society holds the sales profession in very low esteem, and a recent survey by the Gallup Organization confirms this attitude.[3] When the most honest and ethical professionals were ranked, those in occupations based upon selfless service, such as doctors, nurses, teachers, judges, firemen, and police officers, were ranked the highest. Meanwhile, vocations that involve selling dominate the bottom of the list, as it is perceived they are based solely upon serving self-interests.

Is this stereotype honestly deserved? Based upon my experience, I don't think so. The overwhelming majority of salespeople that I have worked with through the years have been ethical, intelligent, hardworking, and friendly. During the past year alone, I conducted training sessions with more than 1,000 salespeople. Frankly, I liked them all and enjoyed their company. I suspect the ratio of bad salespeople to good is no different from the ratio of bad to good people in our society as a whole.

USING THIS BOOK

This book is a textbook as well as a reference book. I encourage you to write in it while you are reading. Have a pencil handy to make notations. Underline key concepts and important terms to help you remember their significance. This book is intended to be a continual resource and an ongoing reference that you can consult over and over again like an encyclopedia or dictionary. Throughout this book, real-world case studies are presented to illustrate the practical application of these concepts. These examples, known as "cultural transmissions," are true and based on my personal experience. A cultural transmission is the method of learning a behavioral technique by emulating a successful practitioner. Learning by example is the most effective way to learn.

In addition to the concepts of neurolinguistics, I will also use various established psychological theories to explain the behavior of the Heavy Hitter and the customer, theories that I have adopted and use as a framework to explain the specific behavior I have observed.

As salespeople, we are much more concerned with reaching the destination rather than experiencing the journey. Since you have been conditioned to achieve your objectives as quickly as possible, your natural tendency will be to read quickly through this book a chapter at a time regardless of whether you are really paying attention to what you have read. If you try to "power read" this book, you might feel overwhelmed, as there is a lifetime of experiences on the following pages. Read this book differently. Read it only when you want to and read it in very small chunks of a dozen pages or so at a time. Stop when you are tired and pick it up again later when you feel like it. By doing so, your mind will absorb the information and interpret the message in ways that are more meaningful to you.

Think of all the tools you use to complete your job. You use your car, cell phone, and computer, to name just a few. Each of these tools comes with a user manual to help you to understand how the product works and teach you how to get the most use from it. Since you basically talk for a living, the most important tool you use every day is language and the words you speak. *Heavy Hitter Selling* is the owner's manual for your mouth.

PART ONE

The Human Nature of Communication

WITHOUT LANGUAGE you really wouldn't exist. You wouldn't be able to share your ideas, display your personality, and express yourself to the world. You couldn't communicate your needs and desires to others, and the never-ending dialogue within your mind would stop. The words we speak truly define who we are. However, since we are talking all the time, we underestimate the complexity of communication and take the process for granted.

The conversations we have with customers are quite complex. They consist of verbal and nonverbal messages that are sent consciously and subconsciously. Successful customer communication is the foundation of all sales, and in this section we explain how Heavy Hitters speak the language of customers.

CHAPTER 1

The Heavy Hitter

After hundreds of hours of intensive research and a rigorous product evaluation, the day had arrived for the customer to publicly announce which product the company would purchase. The customer opened the meeting in a solemn voice, causing the salesperson's heart to skip a beat. "Well, I guess you know why we asked you to come in today," she said. Then her expression suddenly changed to a happy grin. "We have submitted our recommendation to management to purchase your product!" The salesperson exhaled a sigh of relief and laughter filled the room. In the festive atmosphere that followed, congratulations and many thanks were exchanged between these new friends.

If you ask a salesperson in a company, "How do you sell your product?" you will most likely get a less-than-accurate answer, if any answer at all. The salesperson may recite an oversimplification of the sales process, such as "I get a lead. I meet with the potential customer to determine if my product fits. They evaluate my product against others, and if they like it, they buy it." Or, the salesperson may not answer at all by subtly changing the topic of conversation. By providing these superficial answers, salespeople are not trying to be evasive or condescending. Rather, to try to explain all the complexities and the intricacies of the sales process would be an exhausting, time-consuming project. Frankly, they may not even know the real answer because most successful salespeople are simply doing what comes naturally.

However, not all salespeople are successful. Given the same sales tools, level of education, and propensity to work, why do some salespeople succeed where others fail? Is one better suited to sell the product because of his or her technical background? Is one more charming or luckier? Or is one able to utilize past sales cycle experiences and adapt them to the current sales environment? Does one better understand the human nature of sales?

THE INTANGIBLE SIDE OF SALES

The sales process has an entirely intangible, human side. And mastery of the intangible, intuitive, human element of the sales process is what separates Heavy Hitters from other salespeople.

The art of mastering the intangible side of the sales process can be found in the field of neurolinguistics, the study of how the human brain uses and interprets language. I first began studying this field while I was attending college and working part-time at a medical billing company as a computer programmer.

As a programmer, I became knowledgeable about the fundamentals of how computers work. I learned the importance of the structure of language and how to build a "model." Models are the descriptions and representations of how a system works. Understand a model and you can re-create a system. Models enable repeatable, predictable experiences.

Computers also taught me about the preciseness of language. After becoming versed in the workings of operating systems, I began programming. Programming requires great discipline, and I began to realize the importance of maintaining logic along with the construction of words. Order is just as critical as precision. Because a program has layers of complexity, I also began to recognize the interrelation among two or three separate concurrent streams of logic. In other words, I began to train myself to maintain multiple states of thought at the same time.

Fortunately, Dr. Constantine Callas, the owner of the medical billing company, took a personal interest in my career and introduced me to the works of Dr. Milton Erickson. A leading originator and practitioner of psychiatric hypnosis, Dr. Erickson had an uncanny ability to help people with severe medical problems. Both psychiatrists and neurolinguists have studied his language strategies for changing patient behavior. Dr. Callas had trained under Dr. Erickson and had successfully utilized Dr. Erickson's techniques in his own practice. Learning the Ericksonian approach to neurolinguistics dramatically changed my life.

I have been practicing neurolinguistics for over 20 years. During this time, I have extended the concepts Dr. Erickson used, as well as created many entirely new paradigms. Most importantly, I have specifically applied all of these concepts and paradigms to the sales process.

Before he died in 1980, Dr. Erickson published hundreds of professional articles. Within the medical community, he was both respected and considered controversial. His works and teachings have been painstakingly analyzed, documented, and recorded. He wanted the world to understand the formal methodologies he used to communicate with his patients. These methodologies are also directly applicable to communicating with potential customers. The following passage by Dr. Erickson is from *Advanced Techniques of Hypnosis and Therapy: Selected Papers of Milton H. Erickson, M.D.*[1]

> I had a polio attack when I was seventeen years old and I lay in bed without a sense of body awareness. I couldn't even tell the position of my arms or legs in bed. So I spent hours trying to locate my hand or foot or toes by a sense of feeling, and I became acutely aware of what movements were.
>
> People use little telltale movements, those adjustive movements that are so revealing if one can notice them. So much communication is in our bodily movements, not in our speech. So much is communicated by the way a person speaks. My tone deafness has forced me to pay attention to inflections in the voice. This means I'm less distracted by the content of what people say. Many patterns of behavior are

reflected in the way a person says something rather than in what he says.

Most people recognize someone's spoken words as the most significant element of communication. However, the language a person uses is composed of both verbal and nonverbal communication. Through the use of this "whole" language, we express our needs, wants, desires, and experiences to the outside world. The verbal and nonverbal language you use is a complete representation of your personality and yourself.

As I began to read more about Dr. Erickson's work, I gained an entirely new understanding of how language is directly related to predicting human behavior. I observed that if you understood how a person used language, you could build a model of expected behavior. I also became acutely interested in hypnosis. Normally, you communicate with people's conscious minds. You rely on their conscious minds to forward your message to their subconscious minds. The subconscious mind is where information is validated and decisions are ultimately made. Hypnosis enables a person to bypass this forwarding process and communicate directly with the subconscious mind.

THE TRUTH ABOUT HYPNOSIS

People have different perceptions about hypnosis. Some think of a swinging pocket watch and a soft voice repeating, "You are getting sleepy." Others think of a stage hypnotist making unsuspecting subjects perform embarrassing acts for laughs. Every day, newspaper advertisements stress the benefits of using hypnosis to help provide the willpower to lose weight or stop smoking. Meanwhile, some people strongly believe that hypnosis does not exist. To some extent, each of these observations is correct.

In fact, each and every communication between people has hypnotic qualities, but in varying degrees. Some conversations have a lot of hypnotic qualities and others almost none. Therefore, if you are staring intensely at an object while being told you are getting tired, you will probably accept the suggestion since your eyes will become fatigued. This communication interaction has multiple dimensions—the physical aspect of your eyes getting tired coupled with the verbal suggestion being given. Conversely, if you are having a brief conversation with a colleague at the copy machine, the discussion is more likely to be more superficial (or one-dimensional) and lack hypnotic qualities.

Hypnosis is about influencing another person's behavior with suggestions that correspond to their values and beliefs; it is not about making someone fall asleep or dance the "funky chicken" on a stage in front of strangers. Dr. Erickson also thought of it as "intellectual learning by the unconscious."[2] In reality, Heavy Hitters are hypnotists who use hypnosis all the time, in every conversation. Therefore, one could argue it is just a normal part of their conversation and doesn't really exist. It's merely an additional dimension of language.

Heavy Hitters influence their customers with a fantasy. The fantasy is that their product will make the customer's life easier, happier, less expensive or enable the customer to make more money. Although Heavy Hitters are competing against similar fantasies being told by competitors, their message reigns supreme, and their product is accepted by their customers as being superior.

Heavy Hitters want to influence potential customers to buy their solution. They accomplish this through their natural ability to communicate with customers and make them feel at ease. By analyzing and modeling their communication strategy and tactics, we can learn how they persuade customers to buy. However, this requires understanding how each individual uses his or her own unique language to communicate.

Intuitively, Heavy Hitters have learned the fundamentals of neurolinguistics, and they apply the concepts naturally and automatically. Somehow, they know that if they speak in a certain way, in a particular style, a customer will respond positively. They also recognize that the style they use changes from customer to customer naturally.

Persuading people to change their minds takes more than a promise that their fantasies will be fulfilled. It takes meaningful communication, and this requires speaking each customer's unique language. This skill set can be learned by thoroughly understanding the mechanics of communication and the way the brain works in conjunction with the entire body to communicate. We will study this further starting in the next chapter.

A BREED APART

Salespeople are a different breed of people in society. Stereotypes about their gregariousness, tenacious drive, and money-based motivation show how the rest of the world (including their own companies) views them. While Heavy Hitters may share these characteristics, they have additional superior qualities that separate them from their peers. Clearly, they understand that one of their key responsibilities is building and managing relationships.

They have to manage a tremendous number of relationships externally with customers and partners and internally within their companies. To accomplish this, they have developed an extraordinary ability to communicate and influence people while making them feel safe and comfortable.

Building relationships requires rapport. Building rapport requires the complex process of human communication, so we will examine the different layers of communication that occur in every conversation between Heavy Hitters and customers.

Members of another exotic profession share some of the same qualities as salespeople—professional poker players. Like sales, their profession is about strategy, knowing human nature, and winning. Poker players have acquired an uncanny ability to read their opponents' unintentional mannerisms and predict the cards they are holding. Meanwhile, professional poker players are masters of their own emotions who are as comfortable matching the pot on a bluff as they are when they hold four aces.

Poker players know that any novice can have a lucky streak. However, it's the serious players who make money in the long run. They study the game and constantly seek to improve their skills. Seasoned gamblers have encountered every card combination. They always remember which cards have been dealt and measure their bets carefully in accordance with their odds of winning. They select their strategy based upon the latest information; in this case, it is the last card dealt facing up.

THE IMPORTANCE OF RAPPORT

Heavy Hitters know that the value of information depends upon its accuracy, timeliness, and confidentiality. So, how do they get privileged intelligence about the deal they're working on? By building a deep relationship with someone within the customer's organization. This is one of the fundamental premises of the sales cycle. For many years, the term "coach" has been used by all types of salespeople, selling every conceivable product, to define the person who provides this data.

All sales involve a salesperson being "coached" through the evaluation process. Why would someone coach one salesperson versus another? To establish a relationship with a coach, Heavy Hitters build different types of rapport with a customer. At the foundation is a special relationship, a personal rapport between two individuals. Although powerful, this personal rapport is meaningless unless technical rapport is present. Technical rapport is achieved when a product's features satisfy the customer's requirements. Finally, there must be a business rapport between the two companies to consummate the deal.

Heavy Hitters' secret to survival is being able to qualify an opportunity. Every company has competitors. Today's enemy may seem to be the company that is twice your size and invading your market space. It could also be the little company with an exciting new product. But the real enemy is time.

Heavy Hitters manage their time by qualifying people. They are trying to find one fundamental truth, "Will I win the deal?" They will use their intuition to validate every piece of information in order to find the answer to this question as soon as possible. Most importantly, once they determine they can win a deal, they are able to persuade the customer to choose their product. Persuasion is a key distinguisher between Heavy Hitters and other salespeople.

There are two schools of thought about Heavy Hitters. The first is that persuasive people are born that way. You either have that quality or you don't. Conversely, others feel that you can learn to be a Heavy Hitter. After meeting thousands of salespeople of all ages and from every conceivable background, I have made my decision about this controversial subject. Yes, some people are naturally gifted. However, almost any salesperson can learn to be a Heavy Hitter. I have personally witnessed the most unlikely individuals succeed when everyone else thought they would fail. But here's the important point: Each of us becomes a Heavy Hitter using our own particular style, in our own individual way. Even though an underdog salesperson may not have the bravado and charisma we typically expect of salespeople, she can be equally successful and a Heavy Hitter just the same.

Qualifying a deal is a complex process. The qualification occurs most simply at the business level. Do the customers have a budget? What is their time frame to buy? This type of qualification is fairly straightforward. However, qualifying the political environment requires intuition. We want to know if the customer is giving us truthful answers, and we use our intuition to form our personal judgments by reading the customer.

Heavy Hitters have developed an intense intuition. They uncover important information by analyzing their prospect's words, actions, and behavior. They know when they are being told the truth. Anyone can acquire this skill by understanding how language, the brain, and the body work in combination. Interestingly, they don't always say the same thing. Being able to decipher truthful communication is critical to Heavy Hitters' success. Just as poker players know when an opponent is bluffing, Heavy Hitters have the ability to read each of the individuals involved in a deal.

Heavy Hitters intimately understand that selling is a process as well as a specific result. The sales process starts with the creation of a relationship between people who understand each other's needs.

Heavy Hitters are always trying to determine what a customer wants and to create an environment that encourages the customer to be receptive to their message. They will decide where they should spend their time and where they shouldn't waste resources.

During the early 1990s, the term "win-win relationship" was being used everywhere to explain how to successfully negotiate your position while still enabling the other party to achieve its goal. However, the concept of win-win relationships does not go far enough in characterizing human relationships. Relationships are created when people share the same activities or when they are motivated to achieve the same goals. Goals can be defined into very personal prioritized desires, called "benefactions," where a personal benefit is gained from taking an action. Heavy Hitters strive to understand the benefactions of each member of the selection team, the people who will decide whether or not to buy the Hitter's product.

INTEGRITY

At the foundation of Heavy Hitters' success are credibility and integrity. Heavy Hitters know their environment will influence their behavior and their behavior will influence the environment. A president of a company once rationalized, "If the truth is better served by a lie, then it's okay to lie." This attitude is wrong. When fundamental benefactions do not match or when one party takes advantage of another, buyer's remorse and resentment will break up the current relationship and ruin all potential future partnerships. Heavy Hitters exhibit a morally sound code of conduct in all their dealings with customers.

At some point during your career, you will jealously listen to unscrupulous colleagues brag about a deal they just won and the size of their commission check. These salespeople are not Heavy Hitters. In the end, a strong moral compass will result in more relationships and therefore more sales.

Integrity also provides an additional psychological benefit you may not have thought of. It protects our fragile psyches when we lose a deal. Knowing that we did everything ethically possible to win helps us handle our hostility, funnel our frustration, and recover more quickly from losing. Instead of unproductive second-guessing, we correctly rationalize that this deal simply wasn't meant to be and we move on to the next one. Integrity gives us inner strength and comfort with ourselves.

Heavy Hitters know they probably will be selling products for several different companies during the next 10 years. They understand that technical innovation is moving at an unimaginable, accelerated rate. This, in turn, is compressing the life cycles of companies and their products, which succeed or fail in a shortened time frame.

Heavy Hitters can return to a company they have previously sold to and be perceived as credible. With that being said, the key asset Heavy Hitters bring to their next job is not the contacts in their PalmPilots or laptops. The main reason for hiring an established Heavy Hitter is that he or she has demonstrated success at building and managing relationships, and this process can be repeated infinitely, resulting in consistent sales performance.

THE NATURE OF ENTERPRISE SALES

The primary goal of a sales organization is to deliver revenue to the company by winning business. This goal is accomplished mainly by adding new customers or by creating new opportunities with existing customers. In every company, each department has its own customers.

For example, marketing defines a product for engineering, engineering builds a product for sales, and accounting provides the funds for marketing. With the exception of the sales department and support-related functions, each department's customers are mainly internal to the company, both physically and culturally. The sales department is unique. Its focus is on external customers, geographic and cultural outsiders to the organization. Just as gamblers traveling from town to town must be aware of the local laws and customs, salespeople who journey from customer to customer must adapt their behavior to each customer's particular environment.

The nature of enterprise sales is that the deals are large, the decision process is complex, and great personal rewards are possible for individuals who can close deals. But what exactly is an "enterprise" sale? It has three major characteristics. Obviously, the first characteristic is the size and complexity of the product. If you sell big-ticket products such as computers, machinery, commercial real estate, telecommunications, or planes, you are involved in enterprise sales.

The second characteristic is the complex nature of the sales cycle. It is a process that involves multiple people, or multiple groups of people, who in varying degrees make the purchase decision. The decision is made over a period of time that is typically measured in weeks or months.

Finally, the size of the purchase is large. A deal can be either one large single purchase or a steady stream of future revenue. These sales may involve material items such as electronics and equipment or the creation of new ideas, license agreements, and partnerships.

The concepts and principles of this book apply to a wide range of sales segments that share these characteristics. They also apply to any product that is typically evaluated and purchased by a committee. This may vary from the purchase of a building or selection of an advertising firm to the acquisition of a company. However, the case studies and examples in this book are based upon my personal experience, which happens to be in the computer industry.

MENTORS

A sales organization is typically a mentor-based environment. Inexperienced salespeople don't know what they haven't seen for themselves. Usually, it's through the "school of hard knocks" that they gain their experience. Unfortunately, this takes time. By emulating how Heavy Hitters view the sales cycle, this time frame can be shortened, and the predictability of results can be improved.

In a typical sales organization, role modeling occurs very informally and irregularly. However, through nonstructured interactions, salespeople learn tactics to help close deals. All organizations include both good and bad salespeople. Obviously, we want to model the successful ones. We want to understand how they have mastered rapport, language, and the sales cycle and developed their intuition. Equally important, we want to understand what doesn't work and shouldn't be modeled.

BUSH LEAGUERS

Professional baseball players who continually make mistakes are demoted to teams in the minor leagues. These obscure teams play in small towns across America. In the slang of baseball, the players are called "bush leaguers." Sales also has its share of bush leaguers, who make the following common mistakes:

- They talk too much on a sales call and don't listen to the customer enough.
- They present the same pitch in the same way to every customer.
- They don't know their customer or product well enough to drive account strategy.
- They assume information they don't know, thereby taking the wrong action.
- They fidget with many accounts and don't focus on the winnable ones.
- They don't put themselves in the position of being their own customer.
- They don't take the time to continually analyze their performance.
- They don't understand how to marshal their resources or use their manager.
- They set unrealistic customer expectations or make commitments that their product or company can't fulfill.
- They expect to win the deal without a coach or think they have a coach when they don't.

Most importantly, bush leaguers don't consistently close business. Compared to Hitters, their wins take longer, require more resources, and are less predictable. Bush leaguers need to model Heavy Hitters most of all.

OPPORTUNITY COSTS

If this is a weekday and you happen to be reading this book on an airplane, chances are the majority of the passengers on your flight are salespeople on their way to customer meetings. You have to wonder how many will be successful and how many of these trips are unnecessary. Travel is one of the largest sales-related expenses in any company. Inexperienced salespeople are infamous for "chasing bad deals," or pursuing business they can't win. The opportunity expense of doing this is just as big. Spending time on deals you can't win means you are not spending time on deals you can.

Just as Heavy Hitters will only spend their time on winnable deals, they will only be part of a winnable sales environment. They know that their manager plays a key role in their success. The manager is responsible for the infrastructure that supports their efforts. Heavy Hitters also manage their managers. In other words, they understand their manager's style and act accordingly.

The concept of the sales force has changed dramatically during the past decade. The days of command-and-control military-style sales organizations are over. Heavy Hitters want to be part of an interactive sales democracy. They want their opinions heard and their recommendations acted upon. Most of all, they want to make an impact.

CONCLUSION

Heavy Hitters understand how to build personal relationships and have mastered the art of communication and persuasion. They have accumulated a reservoir of experience working with customers during the sales process and possess a highly developed intuition that drives their choice of strategy and persuades a customer to buy.

If you are in sales, you make your living by talking. If you were a pilot, you would attend years of flight training school and many hours of simulator training before you were allowed in the cockpit of a jumbo jet. If you were a lawyer, you would intensely study law for several years and have to pass your state's bar exam to ensure your proficiency. If you are in sales, you need to understand the use and interpretation of language. You need to understand the process of communication and how it determines the level of rapport that is established between people. You must be able to adapt your use of language to a customer's thought process and personality. Language can be directly linked to a person's behavior. It can be deciphered to predict future behavior and truthfulness or used proactively to influence a person's thinking or opinions.

Different assumptions can be made about why you are reading this book. You may be relatively new to sales and want to improve your base level of knowledge. You may already be an experienced salesperson seeking to expand your sales skills with additional techniques. Or you may work completely outside of sales and desire to discover what the field is all about. Regardless of your motivation, you can summarize almost everything regarding sales in a single sentence: Sales is about speaking the language of the customer.

However, an invisible boundary exists between the seller and buyer. Both the seller and buyer edit their language and hide their true feelings or try to keep the conversation at a nonpersonal level. It's the salesperson's job to remove this boundary and create a friendship.

At the beginning of this chapter, I told a true story of a customer who played a practical joke on a salesperson. The customer's prank is the main point of the story. You would only play a joke like this on someone you liked and knew very well. It's evidence of great rapport and true friendship.

The story contains another important truth. As a salesperson, you have the chance to start relationships with exceptional people who will become your customers and friends. And you have been given unique abilities to accomplish this worthy goal. Perhaps a new attitude is in order. Instead of trying to be so cunning and calculating, perhaps you should try being a little more caring. Instead of solely focusing on revenue, maybe you should concentrate more on relationships. Finally, successful communication is at the foundation of all long-term relationships, as we'll see in the next chapter.

CHAPTER 2

How People Communicate

After some initial introductions, the sales presentation was about to start. The sales rep was visibly nervous and with good reason. He was speaking to the biggest potential customer in his company's history, seeking the opportunity to install his product in 325 different locations. He presented the company's background and product suite as he had done many times before.

Bart, the manager in charge of all of the servers and the key decision maker for this project, sat with his arms and legs crossed and leaned back in his chair. He seemed disinterested. The atmosphere was tense and no questions were asked. Following the sales rep's presentation, the system engineer began an interactive demonstration of the product. Bart moved his left hand and held it by his ear. The system engineer continued the presentation. A few minutes later, Bart put his left hand on his chin and leaned forward slightly. Soon, he put both arms on the table and was finally engaged in the demonstration.

Why do people get married? A recent survey asking men and women this same question yielded these results: Seventy percent of women between the ages of 17 and 23 responded that money, not love, was the main motivator. Meanwhile, 90 percent of the women over 26 responded that love was the main reason. On the other hand, 90 percent of the men between the ages of 17 and 23 responded that love was most important while only 10 percent of the men over age

30 said it was the key reason.[1] The survey results suggest that as women get older, they actually become more romantic and as men become older, they think unemotionally.

This survey provides two very important lessons for salespeople. First, the way you ask a question will determine the response you get. Look at the question again. "Why do *people* get married?" The question is not directed at the individual but asks for his or her opinion on why "others" get married. If the men over 30 were asked, "Why would *you* get married?" most assuredly, the responses would have been different. One way to think of it is that the respondents were giving the answer they thought they were supposed to give. Similarly, when you ask customers, "Do you have the authority to make the decision?" you are going to get the answer they think they should give. They'll say, "Yes." This may or may not be the truth.

The second lesson is that peer pressure plays a powerful role during the decision-making process. People naturally don't want to look stupid or embarrass themselves in public. Therefore, a teenage girl will give the same answer as other teenage girls, and women over 30 will answer "Love" even if they really think the security of money is more important. Peer pressure is a part of every sales call, as selection team members constantly monitor the attitudes of others. Therefore, when you ask at the end of your presentation, "Does everyone believe we are the best solution?" even though everyone nods, the audience probably includes objectors who will try to sabotage your deal later on.

A sales call is a scheduled communication event. However, each party participating in this event has different goals. Heavy Hitters' main goal is to gain continued access to the prospect. They will accomplish this by explaining their product's features and the merits of their company and demonstrating the quality of its people as represented by the sales team on the call. If the team members' performance meets with the customer's approval, they will be given the chance to have additional meetings or granted the privilege of studying the customer's operation. They may be given the opportunity to

install an evaluation copy of their product. If each step is successful, the customer may grant them the highest level of continued
access, making a sale. A Heavy Hitter is a suitor, trying to court a
customer into forming a long-term relationship, akin to a marriage.

The customer has a different set of goals. Relationships are expensive and involve investments of valuable time. Customers have to
spend time to determine whether a product's characteristics are as they
have been represented. They have to spend time evaluating other suit-
ors to determine whether they are picking the best possible partner to
solve their company's business problem. They will have to spend time
learning to use the new products they select, implementing them, and
most likely, debugging or fixing product problems.

These relationships also cost money. The customers will have to
acquire the product and pay ongoing maintenance fees to keep the
technology current. They may have to pay for professional services
or hire additional staff to help implement a solution. And they may
need to buy additional products or technology in order to make the
solution work. Customers want to make sure they are selecting the
best partner and have found their soul mate.

Heavy Hitters create long-term relationships between companies
based upon the process of communication between people. This
process is very complex. However, since we are communicating all the
time, we may underestimate the complexity of communication and
take the process for granted. We tend to ignore the subtleties and, for
the most part, become preoccupied with our side of a conversation.

The communication process is also very efficient. We have the
flexibility to send the same message structure with distinctly different meanings. Take the following example:

- Mary, could you please send the report.
- Mary, could you *please* send the report.
- MARY, COULD YOU PLEASE SEND THE REPORT.

All these sentences use the same words but result in very different
interpretations. When Mary reads the first sentence, she will feel a low

Phonetic	The enunciation of the words you are speaking
Content	The actual words spoken
Purpose	The reason or point you are communicating
Word Catalog	The way the mind uses and interprets language
Internal Dialogue	The never-ending dialogue inside your mind
Physical	The impact the words you are receiving or sending have on your body

Figure 2.1 The Human Communication Model

sense of urgency and receive no indication of any unhappiness that the report has not been sent. The other sentences imply a different sense of urgency and even discontent that the report hasn't been sent.

People communicate in layers. These layers are very flexible and can be combined in many different ways. Layers can be entirely eliminated or they can be fused together to form entirely new meanings. The layers of the human communication model are shown in Figure 2.1.

The human communication model layers are like piano keys. Different sounds, or meanings, are created by pressing particular keys together in patterns or repetitions. Piano keys may be depressed forcefully or softly, just as communication may be explicit or subtle. The combination of keys may result in a soothing melody or just noise. In order to understand their role in the communication process, let's examine these layers in more detail.

PHONETIC LAYER

The phonetic layer is the enunciation of the actual words we have strung together in the form of a sentence. This layer can alter the meaning of the sentence to convey a completely new and/or sometimes opposite meaning. For example, let's say I tell my wife, "Your hair looks great," but my voice trails off at the end of the sentence. She would immediately be concerned that her hair does not look good. This incongruence would then cause her to ask what I actually meant. Congruence can be thought of as "truth in communication." If I say to her, "Your hair looks great!" and emphasize the word "great," my sentence is aligned (congruent) with the content of the words. Here's an example of how a Heavy Hitter determines if the enunciation of certain words is incongruent with the actual words being spoken.

> We had just finished a grueling two-hour sales presentation. The customer had installed our major competitor's product, albeit not altogether successfully. The company had yet to fully implement the competitor's solution across all the locations it had originally intended to. The installation process was overly complex, and the product didn't perform as expected in the locations where they had it installed.
>
> Bob, the leader of the project, had been through a great deal of pain and frustration during the past 10 months. We had been invited to present our solution and gave a compelling case why our product was technically superior to the competitor's. Bob listened intently to all of our arguments and vigorously questioned each presenter.
>
> The lynchpin of our account strategy was to get the project team to evaluate our product so it could physically compare our ease of installation and performance against the incumbent's product. Following the formal presentation, we closed the meeting by asking Bob to evaluate our product in his company's lab environment. He bowed his head slightly, looked down to the right, and said, "We'll find some time to schedule a lab test." Instead of saying the sentence with excitement and conviction, he said it with a sullen tone and a lack of enthusiasm, bordering on disappointment.

We instinctively knew Bob never would schedule the lab time. Sensing this, we unsuccessfully tried to gain a commitment on a date to start the lab test. Although Bob didn't come right out and say it, we knew the deal was lost. His words didn't match his enunciation, and his unspoken message was more important than what he actually said.

CONTENT LAYER

How did we know we'd lost the deal? Because when Bob said he would "find some time to schedule a lab test," the content layer (the actual words being used) contradicted, or was incongruent with, the phonetic layer. The content layer is what most people think of and listen to when they are having a discussion. However, people usually assume the content words they are using have the same meaning to everyone.

Suppose I go to a fast-food restaurant and order a cheeseburger. Regardless of the way I enunciate the word "cheeseburger," whether enthusiastically, soberly, or abruptly, I will still be served a cheeseburger. The phonetic layer has little impact on the content of my message. I could drive up to the drive-through window and yell, "Cheeseburger!!!" and the server would know what I want. In this example, "cheeseburger" has a specific meaning. A cheeseburger specifically has a bun, cheese, and a beef patty.

Now suppose I decide to go to a pizza parlor. When I am asked for my order, I say, "Pizza." The server will give me a blank stare. Do I want a deep-dish, regular, or thin crust? Do I want toppings? Unless the restaurant only has one pizza on the menu, "pizza" is a general word. A general word requires the use of additional words for the message to be received accurately. These additional words, called "operators," are used in conjunction with the general word to change the meaning.

When I introduced the concept of ordering a pizza, the first picture to enter your mind may have been a thin-crust cheese pizza. This would have been your own specific interpretation of the word "pizza."

Let's say I was imagining biting into a deep-dish pepperoni pizza. This would have been my specific meaning of the word "pizza." Obviously, they are not quite the same, as shown in Figure 2.2.

Unless I add more operators to the word "pizza," the server won't know what type of pizza I really want. Also, in this case I can place the operators in any order and still have my message be correctly understood. I could order by saying, "I'll have a large, deep-dish, pepperoni and olive" or "I'll have a pepperoni and olive, deep-dish, large." They both mean the same thing. However, sometimes the order of the operators can change the meaning. Going to the lumberyard and ordering a six-foot-long two-by-four board is very different from asking for a board that is a four-foot-long two-by-six. Since the interpretation of a general word's meaning is up to the receiver of the message, such words have been used by psychics, fortune-tellers, and astrologers for centuries. Look at the following examples with the general words in italics. Try to determine if any of these apply specifically to you and whether the astrological sign is yours.

- Astrological sign: Members of this sign are admired for their *generosity* and *sensitive* nature. They often make excellent businesspeople or salespeople because of their *honesty, skill,* and *genuine* communication.
- Psychic hot line: Someone you know is having *troubles.*
- Fortune cookie: You will *soon* receive *good* news from a *faraway place.*

General Word: Pizza

First-level operator	Regular, deep-dish, or thin crust
Second-level operator	Pepperoni, mushroom, olives, and so on
Third-level operator	Large, medium, or small

Figure 2.2 Examples of General Word with Operators

What happened? When you were reading these sentences, you most likely added your own operators to gain some personal meaning. As you read about the astrological sign, did you think it was your sign? Nearly everyone wants to be admired for his or her generosity and honesty. You may have even thought of a specific person (spouse, child, or friend) or an event (giving a donation) to validate the idea that you are generous and honest.

The psychic understands that everyone knows someone who is having troubles. "Troubles" could be anything ranging from a flat tire to a life-threatening disease. The fortune cookie leaves you to interpret what "soon" means. Is it hours, days, or months? What is considered "good" news? How far is the faraway place? Basically, it is impossible to prove these statements to be false since they apply to almost any situation!

So why are pizza, horoscopes, and fortune cookies important to Heavy Hitters? They show that general words used by themselves are, in fact, meaningless. If you tell a customer your solution is "fast and reliable," what have you communicated? It's through the use of operators that specific meanings are added and meaningful communication is completed. If you tell a customer your solution is "fast and reliable, will print 200 pages per minute, and has a 99.99 percent uptime rate," you have communicated something meaningful.

It's important to recognize the difference between general and specific words. In sales, general words are used predominantly to describe and market product advantages. Probably three of the most regularly used terms are "performance," "reliability," and "scalability."

The following phrases were taken from the web site home pages of three prominent high-technology companies.

- "ABC Company enables organizations to exceed performance and reliability expectations."
- "DEF Company combines power and scalability to meet your business needs."
- "XYZ Solutions automatically and intelligently delivers the best possible performance and availability."

Other popular general terms include "new and improved," "flexibility," "manageability," "powerful," and "price performance." Little meaning can be derived from these product claims unless operators are added. Here's the point: Heavy Hitters always validate the general claims about their products with specific features or specific examples to give credence and meaning to their statements.

USING OPERATORS

A good rule of thumb is to always assume the salesperson you are competing against is as friendly, professional, and knowledgeable as you. Like you, he will be trying to win over the customer with his product and his personality. To the customer, the claims you both make will sound identical. It requires operators to take these generic claims and translate them into proof points the customer understands and believes.

Here's how to incorporate operators into the structure of your conversation. It starts with a high-level statement and continues to define the statement into meaningful terms and proof points.

We	Help save you money.
	Increase your revenues.
	Provide better technology.
	Offer a more comprehensive solution.
	Provide better functionality or ease of use.
Because of our	Superior technology or functionality.
	Quality, people, or support.
	Ease of use or breakthrough paradigm.
In comparison to	The way you conduct business today.
	How the competitor's product operates.
	Your existing process or environment.
As a benefit, you	Will increase revenues by XX%.
	Will save XX% in your implementation.
	Will improve your output by XX units.
	Will process or achieve XX.

For example	The ABC Company implemented our solution and has saved $XXX,XXX in the first six months.
	The DEF Company increased revenues by $XXX,XXX in the first year.
	The XYZ Company improved production by XXX units daily.
Final proof point	I would be delighted to introduce you to John Smith at ABC Company.
	If you like, I could arrange a visit to DEF Company.
	Here's the case study on XYZ Company for further reading.

Here's a real-world example that shows how operators can be used to add a tangible meaning to generic marketing claims. In this scenario, the Heavy Hitter is presenting his network performance product to a group of network engineers who work for a major financial institution in a large city. This example provides the basic thought process and technique the Heavy Hitter uses to drive his point home to a customer. He is building a believable business case for selecting his product. Finally, it is more important to understand the structure of the language in these examples than the technical terms being used.

"We offer superior performance because our architecture is based upon virtual processes, and that is more efficient than our competitor's architecture, which uses a single-machine address." The Heavy Hitter always presents his arguments with operators. The general word "performance" is being operated on by the descriptor "architecture based upon virtual processes." The term "more efficient" is being operated on by the phrase "uses a single-machine address." The purpose of this statement is to differentiate the Hitter's architecture from his competitor's.

"While the single-machine address solution redundantly broadcasts all messages, our solution sends specific information packets to the applicable computer. This results in less traffic and faster performance of the network." After introducing the competitor's architecture, the Hitter must explain his claim in technical terms the audience understands. He describes how the single-machine address solution works in comparison to his. He also introduces the differentiation between the two architectures, which is less traffic and faster performance. In essence, the first sentence is a general sentence that is operated on by the second and third sentences.

The Heavy Hitter continues to explain why his solution is better. "In your four-system implementation, this would result in 75 percent less network traffic." Up to this point, all of the arguments have been theoretical, and you can assume they have been received logically by the network engineers. From previous discussions, the Heavy Hitter knows they have a technical environment that consists of a network of four computer systems. He then makes a specific claim about the impact of his product in their environment. He ties both direct benefits of the generic term "performance" to the engineers' specific technical implementation. He wants them to understand the distinct advantage that his product would bring to their environment.

"For example, the ABC Company recently switched from a single-machine address architecture and improved their network performance by over 60 percent. I would be delighted to set up a conference call for you to talk with John Smith, the manager in charge of their project implementation." To further validate his argument, the Heavy Hitter offers a specific customer example to illustrate his claims. Equally important, to have his claim accepted as the truth, he offers to introduce the existing customer to the prospect. In other words, he says, "Don't take only my word on this, talk to my customers!"

Customer anecdotes and references are a powerful operator and a way to add credibility to his product claims. Think for a moment about the last major personal purchase you made, such as a car, a boat, or even a vacation. Most likely, you wanted to talk to someone who already owned the product or had been to the destination you were considering.

USING CUSTOMER EXAMPLES

Salespeople love to tell stories. Of all the stories we tell, none are more important than the metaphors (or examples) about the customers that are successfully using our products and services. The personal connection between the customer example and its relevancy to the prospect's experiences will determine to what extent the Hitter's claims are accepted. Therefore, the pertinence of the example chosen is very important. Presenting a company that closely mirrors the prospect's business or technical environment will make the statements more powerful. Presenting a company that the prospects don't recognize will have less impact. In reality, it may actually hinder the argument because the prospect might think the product is not pervasive or popular.

At the lowest level of relevance, the example used could be a well-known organization, such as Coca-Cola or Shell Oil. Certainly, these are companies that would be known by the customer. The level of relevance improves when the example company is known for its past innovations such as Federal Express or Intel, or is well respected for its quality and brand, such as Mercedes-Benz or Nordstrom. By providing examples of customers that have a dominant position in an unrelated business, such as Microsoft, Amazon, or Starbucks, you also receive an implicit approval since it is highly likely the prospects have successfully used the services or products of these companies personally. Therefore, they make the logical assumption that the Heavy Hitter's product works successfully.

The company example could also have a technical environment similar to the customer's. In this case, the company's name or business is deemphasized while its technical environment is highlighted. Let's assume the prospect is using Sun computers and Cisco network equipment. By providing a customer example that identically matches this combination, the Heavy Hitter is able to validate his technical claims that his product works in the prospect's exact technical environment.

Geographic proximity is a very compelling attribute of a reference. If the customer's company is based in New York, a reference to a company that is based in Los Angeles is not nearly as strong as a reference to one that is based in New York.

The ideal reference is a customer's direct competitor. This example provides the highest level of relevance and the most persuasive argument to use the Heavy Hitter's product. The best customer reference of all is a company in the same business, in close geographic proximity, and with the same business initiatives.

The Heavy Hitter is careful with name-dropping. He knows that once he offers a customer's name, he has obligated himself to give the contact information should it be asked for, and he has given the prospect the right to call the customer as a reference. He knows that once he extends any customer's name he is offering that company as a reference. Anytime he inserts another person into the sales cycle on his behalf, it adds an element of risk.

One exception to this rule is when he gives a prospect the name of a company that is its direct competitor. The rule of thumb is that they will not call the rival company, and the Heavy Hitter does not have to provide contact information. In fact, two direct competitors almost never share information about a critical project. That's what makes these customer examples so useful. The Hitter is able to validate the product claims without adding risk to the sales cycle. In the final chapter, we will talk about the power of metaphors and their subconscious impact in much greater detail.

TECHNICAL SPECIFICATION LANGUAGE

Every industry has developed its own language to facilitate mutual understanding of terminology and an exact meaning of the content of words. This unique language is called the "technical specification language." These abbreviations, acronyms, and words form one of the primary languages your customer speaks. Whether you are selling airplanes, computer chips, telephone equipment, or real estate, you need to know the terms and nomenclature of your industry. For example, if you sell telephone systems to businesses you need to understand what PBX, PDC, and ACD mean.

Technical specification languages have four major characteristics. First, unlike normal day-to-day language, words within a technical specification language have very narrow meanings. The language is precise and exact. For example, "100 Mbps" means "100 megabits per second," not 99 or 101. Second, the meaning of general words can be completely changed by the addition of operators. For example, a general term like "car" completely changes in meaning when "sports" or "luxury" is added in front of it and keeps changing meaning when additional operators such as "BMW" or "Jaguar" are added. Third, the language is completely androgynous. In general, no reference is made to feminine or masculine characteristics. Finally, the language is usually nonpersonal. After all, it's referring to products, not people.

Unfortunately for salespeople, the technical specification language usually is adopted by customers as the default standard for all of their communication. This presents salespeople with a significant problem. They are trying to create a personal relationship with the buyer. However, the buyer is communicating in an androgynous, nonpersonal, technical language. More importantly, given the use of this unusual language, salespeople must somehow decipher the underlying meaning and intent of what the customer is actually saying.

In addition, the technical content of the language is the yardstick by which a customer's technical peer group (the team selecting a product) measures a person's relevant knowledge. Outside of formal titles, it's another way members of the peer group will establish a hierarchy. It's also how they will validate the sales team's value to them. Conversely, it is how the sales team members will present their product's features and the technical reasons for selecting their product.

So how do you determine if your technical arguments are actually being understood? Obviously, you can ask a content-level question, such as, "Do you understand?" However, most technical people are very reluctant to publicly admit they don't understand something. Peer pressure prevents them from doing so. Doing so could affect their position within the group, particularly in a presentation environment that includes their peers and management.

More importantly, how can you determine if a customer really agrees with your arguments? In the story earlier about the grueling two-hour sales meeting, at the end of the presentation Bob said he would find some lab time to evaluate the product. However, he didn't mean it. The salesperson determined that the content layer of his words was incompatible with the phonetic layer of his communication. The layers didn't match, and Bob was at odds with himself. Heavy Hitters are constantly trying to determine if any of the layers of the human communication model disagree with one another. They want to get a "read" on the customer.

PURPOSE LAYER

So far we have discussed the phonetic and content layers of the human communication model. The third layer involves the purpose of communication. Words are assembled to communicate an idea or experience. Every sentence of every conversation between Heavy Hitters and customers is purpose driven. One way to think of this is that they have an ulterior motive for everything they say. Of course, you and I have been communicating with selfish interests all of our lives.

For example, before my children were old enough to talk, they would cry to let the world know of their unhappiness. As parents, we would then proceed down our mental checklist of what they might be crying about. Through the process of elimination, we determined whether they were hungry, wet or cold, or just needed to be held.

As my children were learning how to talk, their language capability was limited to labeling. They would see a dog and say, "Doggie." My wife and I would excitedly confirm, "Yes, doggie!" Soon thereafter, they learned they could use words to get things they wanted. They were able to grasp that if they said, "Cookie?" with a certain enunciation, they would frequently receive a cookie. They were able to communicate with a self-centered purpose.

Heavy Hitters and customers are just as self-centered in their communications. Each is constantly trying to extract information from the other. Heavy Hitters will collect this information to create their account strategy, the long-term plan to win a deal. They are trying to uncover technical, political, and personal information in order to assess their current position and continually refine their strategy. To implement the strategy, they will determine a tactical plan and the daily tasks that are required.

Meanwhile, customers are trying to obtain information about the Heavy Hitter's company, products, and customers. Their main goal is information assessment. Whether formally or informally, they have developed and prioritized their needs. They need information in order to measure the fit of the Heavy Hitter's solution.

The Heavy Hitter and the customer have two different purposes for communicating. This results in interactions between customers and Hitters that can be thought of as circular "vignettes." These vignettes are small dramas, short interactions between the customer and the Heavy Hitter. Usually they are about one topic or one conversational theme. They are considered circular because every vignette will come to an end and close as the topic of conversation is exhausted. See Figure 2.3.

These vignettes are not static models. Rather, they are very fluid and dynamic. The customer and the Heavy Hitter can be thought of almost like two boxers who are constantly punching and counterpunching based on their opponent's last movement.

Each vignette is composed of a series of actions the Heavy Hitter or the customer may execute. Each party can *gather* additional

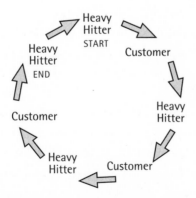

Figure 2.3 Customer Interaction Vignette

information, make an *assessment* as to what a question means, put forth a *response* to information, *present* additional information, or use *persuasion* to influence the other party's thinking.

Gathering is how one party tries to find out information about the other. It usually involves a question, but it can be done in a variety of ways, such as drawing on a whiteboard, presenting a slide, or acquiring a picture of the customer's environment (building floor plan, accounts payable process, or chip design drawing). Basically, gathering is the passing of any knowledge about a specific subject.

Assessments are done when both parties analyze a question (or any other information that has been gathered) prior to making a response. Assessment is the filtering process to find the "right" answer. An assessment can be as straightforward as trying to determine the right words to use to construct the best response to the question. Or it could be a calculated editing process to limit or camouflage a response. The assessment may or may not result in a truthful answer. How long it takes for a customer to complete an assessment is a good indication of the amount of editing needed to produce an answer (and how true it is). Customers may give untruthful information because they simply do not know the answer, aren't in a political position to answer, don't want to answer, or don't understand the question.

Meanwhile, Hitters do their own mental assessment of all the different potential answers to a customer's question. They will present the response they feel will help strengthen their position the most. The Hitter's response is very calculated. Amazingly, it requires a series of complex comparisons to be carried out in a fraction of a second, which makes it seem natural to the customer. Heavy Hitters are like chess players making a move. They are constantly thinking three steps ahead and beyond.

After each customer response, a Heavy Hitter assesses whether he should gather further information, present a solution or feature, or use persuasion. The persuasion he uses will be either visible or transparent to the customer. Visible persuasion is based upon something that physically exists. Examples are product demonstrations, performance metrics, and stories about existing customers. Transparent persuasion, on the other hand, uses logic, reasoning, or examples that cannot be seen, such as hypothetical arguments on why your company is easier to do business with than the competition.

A sales call is a collection of these circular vignettes. A typical sales presentation will begin with individual vignettes about the company's history, milestones, and customer references before moving into vignettes explaining specific technical features of the product.

Vignettes typically change when the subject changes or when an implied agreement on the current topic of discussion is reached. The implied agreement may or may not mean that the issue or discussion point is resolved. Often, it is an agreement to move on for the sake of time. During each vignette you are either on the offensive position in control or defensive position trying to regain control.

Every sales call will have several critical vignettes that will determine whether the call is a success or failure. While every vignette will close, the issues associated with some vignettes will remain open. Heavy Hitters know that unresolved issues will come up again later in the sales cycle, usually when they least want an objection. Therefore, they always try to address these awkward points early. They want them out in the open. They want to know whether an issue will inhibit the purchase of the product, and they want to know as soon as possible.

Although the conversation seems natural and free flowing, the Heavy Hitter is guiding the interaction to the topics he feels will influence the customer's perception of his solution. A vignette could consist of only two interactions or two hundred. The vignette could involve only the salesperson and a single meeting participant or include everyone in the room. Since the use of PowerPoint is so pervasive in sales presentations today, most vignettes last as long as one slide or a series of several slides.

The complexity of a vignette is also directly related to the number of participants. For example, the two types of assessments are external and internal. In meetings involving teams of people, the assessments are frequently external. During a sales call, the customer's team members may have a discussion in front of the vendor to determine what their response should be. When this happens, Heavy Hitters listen intently. They recognize this as a valuable opportunity to learn about the dynamics of the decision process and get a better understanding of a person's knowledge, credibility, and importance in the decision process.

The Heavy Hitter's sales team may also perform external assessments. He and his technical engineer may have a conversation about a technical detail associated with a response from the customer. Together, they use the vignette to make their points. Most importantly, the Heavy Hitter will manage all the vignettes as part of his tactical plan to complete his strategy for the call.

In internal assessments, information is analyzed solely within one person's mind. The Heavy Hitter listens to the customer's response and determines the next course of action in his mind. Likewise, the customer listens to the Hitter's response and determines privately what to say next. The decision of what words are selected and how they are said is intimately linked to the next layer of the human communication model, the word catalog.

WORD CATALOG LAYER

Your word catalog is more than the dictionary inside your mind that determines a word's meaning. It is also the methodology by which you ascertain correct interpretations of a message and associate complex psychological meanings.

You have developed a lifetime of experiences that are unique. These experiences, both good and bad, have shaped your perception of the world. Through your senses, you are constantly adding to your cumulative knowledge of how your world functions. As you accumulate new experiences, they are edited and influenced by your history. As a result, it is accurate to say every person functions in his or her own unique world. Your world is your own personal reality. You use your "word catalogs" to catalog your experiences and describe your world to others. See Figure 2.4.

Reality	Sensors	Influences	My Reality
As it is	Sight, sound, touch, taste, smell	Family, money, work, friends, schooling, spirituality	Experiences cataloged

Figure 2.4 Cataloging Reality

Through language we represent our thoughts and experiences. We use words to represent the sensory experiences of sight, sound, touch, smell, and taste. The map we use to describe and interpret an experience is based upon one of three word catalogs—visual, auditory, and kinesthetic. Visual refers to pictures and imagery, auditory to sounds, and kinesthetic refers to touch and internal feelings.

Most people use one word catalog more frequently than the others. This word catalog has become their default, or "primary," mode of communication. You can identify someone's primary word catalog by listening to the adjectives, adverbs, and nouns they use in conversation.

People whose primary word catalog is based on sight will describe their experiences in visual terms. They are likely to say, "I see what you mean," "Looks good to me," or "Show me what to do." People with a primary word catalog based on sound will say, "Sounds great," "Talk to you later," or "Tell me what to do." People with a primary word catalog based on feeling might say, "I've got it handled," "We'll touch base later," or "I don't grasp what you mean."

Great benefits in communication and persuasion are gained if you understand your customer's primary word catalog and adjust your communication to fit their world. This is an extremely important concept for salespeople to recognize. From this point forward, this book will refer to a person with a sight-based primary word catalog as a Visual (or in the plural as Visuals). Similarly, people with sound-based or feelings-based primary word catalogs will be referred to as Auditory(ies) or Kinesthetic(s).

There's also an additional level of psychological meaning that the word catalog is responsible for deriving. The word catalog attaches a psychological interpretation to words. Let's think about fire for a moment. We easily recognize the difference between the flames from a burner on a stove and a raging fire consuming a high-rise building. Although they are both fires, they each create different mental and emotional interpretations. When we think of a stovetop fire, we might picture warming a can of soup or creating a culinary feast for friends. When we think about a terrifying high-rise fire, the impact on our emotional state is quite different. Your word catalog not only created the mind's-eye picture of both fires but also pulled forward the psychological meaning associated with each usage.

Chapter 5 is dedicated to understanding and communicating with a customer's word catalog. In the final section of the book we will also review persuasion strategies that influence your customer's word catalog. The word catalog is directly related and inseparably linked to the next layer of the human communication model, the internal dialogue.

INTERNAL DIALOGUE LAYER

Every waking hour, a stream of communication is going on inside your mind. You are always talking to yourself. This conversation is an unedited, honest discussion that represents your deepest feelings. This is the fifth layer of the human communication model—the internal dialogue layer or simply the "internal dialogue."

Let's pretend you are at a party and you accidentally meet a person whom you despise. Since you don't want to create a scene, you exchange pleasantries with this person. Your internal dialogue may be cursing at this person, but your spoken dialogue is polite and well mannered.

Usually these internal conversations remain internal. Occasionally, they'll slip out. We are all familiar with the term "Freudian slip." A Freudian slip happens when you say one thing but mean another. Freudian slips often occur because you are having two simultaneous dialogues—the words you are speaking externally to others and the internal dialogue within your mind. Sometimes you accidentally sub-

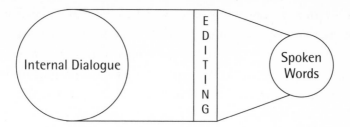

Figure 2.5 Spoken Words as a Subset of the Internal Dialogue after the Editing Process

stitute a word from your internal dialogue into your external dialogue. In other cases, you get confused between the two. You may create a new word that is a combination of the first syllable of your content word and the last syllable of your internal dialogue word. In either case, these slips can be very embarrassing.

Usually, the words being spoken externally are a subset of the internal dialogue. In between is an editing process to filter the precise statement. The Heavy Hitter's editing process is very well developed and so refined through repetitive use that it is automatic. See Figure 2.5.

When people are being totally honest, they repeat their internal voice word for word without editing. People also abandon the editing process during times of great emotions: when they're very sad, extremely mad, ecstatic, or experiencing any other intense feelings. When you are consumed with your emotions, you don't have the wherewithal to plan what you are going to say. The words are spoken in the same instant that they are created within the mind.

PHYSICAL LAYER

Everyone is well aware of the final layer of the human communication model, the physical layer. You were introduced to this layer as a baby. When you were two days old, you were able to distinguish a happy face from a sad face. Soon thereafter, you naturally understood that a smile, hug, or kiss is to be interpreted as something very good.

The physical layer is also known as body language. Body language can be very subtle or more powerful than the actual words being spoken. Let's go back to the party in the previous example. Suppose the person you despise sees you first at the party. This person gives you a glare and starts pushing people out of the way to get to you. Those actions probably communicate one idea to you—run!

Body language is unique in that it is a three-dimensional language. One form of body language is sign language, which is a physical re-creation of the content layer of communication. Sign language is the third most common language in the United States behind English and Spanish. Contrary to popular belief, sign language is not a universal language. Like spoken language, different countries have entirely different sign languages.

A sign is created by combining four different hand parameters—hand shape, palm orientation, hand location, and hand movement. The meaning of a sign changes based on the use of each of the parameters. Like the spoken word, sign language has grammatical structures, syntax, and rules. Essentially, anything you can communicate in the spoken word can be communicated in sign language.

Just as you can communicate any word in sign language, other forms of body language can communicate meaning. Heavy Hitters are masters at reading body language and using their own bodies to communicate. When considered in conjunction with the other layers of the human communication model, body language plays an important role.

With or without conscious effort, you most likely have mastered each of the six layers of the human communication model. However, the *interaction* between the layers is of particular interest to Heavy Hitters. When people speak, the layers are totally interactive. Any layer can communicate with any other layer. The layers can also be combined to form complex statements that can convey additional or different meanings to content-level words.

It's truly a remarkable, flexible model. By combining or eliminating layers, greater efficiencies and a wide range of communication are possible, as shown in Figure 2.6.

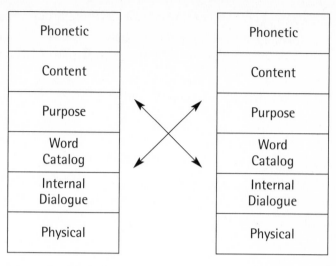

Figure 2.6 Human Communication

Here's an example of how the various layers can be combined, using the example of asking Mary for a report. Suppose Mary is coming to my desk to give me the report. As I see her coming, my internal dialogue assesses what my response will be. Here are some of the ways I could respond to her.

- Physical. I could give her a big smile and a "high-five." She would obviously interpret this to mean I was pleased. My communication is congruent because my facial expression and hand slapping are communicating the same message.

- Physical. I could do absolutely nothing. When she comes to my desk I could continue to do whatever I was doing. How would Mary interpret this? Would she think I was too busy with my tasks to notice her? Or wonder if the report was really not important after all? Maybe she would ask herself if I was ignoring her and communicating my displeasure about the report. Mary truly wouldn't know what I was communicating. However, if my established behavior had always been congenial, then this response would be incongruent with our prior interactions.

- Content plus phonetic plus physical. I could say "Thanks" in my normal tone of voice but present a very forced, fake smile. Mary would have to do some internal assessment as to what I was trying to communicate. Why was my communication incongruent?

- Physical plus content plus phonetic. I could plan and mentally rehearse how I would embarrass Mary when she finally gave me the report. Holding my arms over my head, I could say at the top of my voice, "I see I *finally* have my report!" This would definitely get the point across about my unhappiness and would surely elicit a response. This response requires planning after an internal assessment and some extra effort and energy commensurate with the level of frustration I experienced. My desire is to convey this frustration to Mary.

CONCLUSION

In this chapter, we introduced the six unique layers of the human communication model. These layers are the fundamental building blocks that we will continually refer to throughout the book. They help explain how Heavy Hitters structure their message and discern when they are being misled. As we'll examine later, they also determine the intensity of the Hitter's intuition.

We also reviewed the concept of the technical specification language. Customers speak the technical language of their industry and unfortunately have adopted the attributes of this language for all their communications. They are also judged by their peer group based upon their personal knowledge and command of this language.

The content layer represents only a fraction of the total communication spectrum that is being presented during any conversation. Additional layers can be added on top of each other to convey even greater meaning. They can be aligned to create holistic, congruent communication. The layers can be used selectively to abbreviate our thoughts and speed up communication while still preserving the original message. For example, we shrug our shoulders instead of saying,

"I don't know." Heavy Hitters interpret congruent messages as being honest and true. However, if the layers are at odds with each other, or incongruent, further investigation is required.

Finally, to further complicate the process, human communication is always occurring in several different forms and on several different levels. An immense amount of information is being conveyed, phonetically, verbally, physically, consciously, and subconsciously.

The dark continent of the human communication model is the subconscious mind. It has the ability to permeate each layer. As it seeps through, it sends out signals about a speaker's honest intent. While we will discuss this in much further detail in the book's final section, one important rule needs to be discussed now. If your fundamental concern is fortune, power, and fame, each of the various layers of your communication will reek of it, regardless of how well you think you have your motives concealed or camouflaged. On the flip side of the coin, if you honestly put others' interests before yours, this important statement about relationships will be sent subliminally. You can still be aggressive, competitive, fearless, and forceful, so long as you're acting in the customer's best interests.

Heavy Hitters have developed the ability to listen and sense all of the information a customer is projecting, regardless of whether it is being delivered consciously or subconsciously. They evaluate each layer's message to determine its meaning. Another term for this ability is "sales intuition." Heavy Hitters will use their intuition to create the strategy that gives them the highest likelihood of winning a deal. Based upon their intuition, they will invest more time, develop individual relationships further, and select a plan of action. This is why Heavy Hitters are successful.

Ensuring you have received the correct message isn't as easy as it seems. Even the elite scientists at NASA make embarrassing mistakes. "Clearly something is wrong, and we have to understand it," NASA administrator Daniel Goldin pronounced in 1999 after the loss of the $165 million Mars Polar Lander. "These failures in the Mars program have given us a wake-up call and we are going to respond to it,"[2] said Edward Weiler, deputy director of NASA's Office of Space

Sciences. The Mars climate orbiter burned up in the Martian atmosphere because technicians at Lockheed-Martin and at the Jet Propulsion Laboratory (JPL) used different units of measurement for navigation. Lockheed-Martin transmitted English units to JPL engineers, who thought they were getting metric units.

Sometimes it takes the loss of millions of dollars to understand that people aren't necessarily speaking the same language. In sales, failure is a lot less expensive. We simply lose the deal.

CHAPTER 3

How People Are Wired

After initial introductions, the salesperson started her standard presentation. As usual, she planned to introduce the company, describe how it was formed, and give a brief overview of the success it had enjoyed. She planned on highlighting a few prominent installations to illustrate her product's benefits. She would close the presentation by outlining the key features of her product.

However, after the first slide, she was interrupted by the prospective customer, who said, "Could you tell me how your product manages large numbers of users?"

The salesperson responded, "I have a slide that shows our benchmark performance later in the presentation," and continued. A couple of slides later, she was interrupted again.

"Could you explain how your product performs in an environment with 10,000 users?"

The salesperson jumped forward a few slides to show a high-level profile of one of her largest accounts. After showing the slide, she went back to her planned presentation.

The customer was growing frustrated. "I heard your product doesn't work well when there are large numbers of users. Is this true?"

Fifteen minutes into the sales presentation, the meeting was at a complete standstill and any hope of a personal connection between the salesperson and the customer had vanished.

After professional golfer Mike Weir won the 2003 Masters Tournament, one of the congratulatory letters he received was from golf legend Jack Nicklaus. It wasn't the first time Nicklaus had sent him a letter. Twenty years earlier, 13-year-old Weir had written Nicklaus seeking advice on whether to use a left-handed or right-handed golf swing. He explained to Nicklaus that he wrote with his right hand but threw with his left hand. Nicklaus wrote back telling him to do what came naturally and not to change it. Fortunately, Weir followed his advice and became the first left-hander to win the Masters since 1963. Weir was "wired" to be a left-hander.

Each of us is wired in our own particular way. Our wiring is the result not only of our genetics but also of the experiences we have accumulated during our lifetime. Because our pasts are unique, our views of the same situation may be very different. For example, you and I may have grown up in the same town and even gone to the same schools. However, our recollection of our childhoods will be distinct since we both have a unique ability to interpret, classify, store, and retrieve information in our brains.

In the last chapter, we introduced the concept that everyone lives in his or her own world. The world you experience is not the real world but rather your perception of the world. The way in which you perceive your world is intricately connected to the language you use. You use your senses to define everyday experiences for storage in your brain. Your word catalogs are the storage-and-retrieval mechanisms used to access these experiences. They are also responsible for the words you select to communicate your world to others.

Every day, you receive an infinite amount of information. This information constantly influences the decisions you make. Think about the first few minutes after you awoke today. You got out of bed. You may have casually glanced outside to determine what would be appropriate to wear. Perhaps you went to the bathroom and proceeded to take a shower.

We experience the world through three main word catalogs: feelings (touch, taste, and smell), sound, and sight. We continuously process information from our senses. The senses can't be turned off, and the large amount of information they gather can overwhelm our conscious mind's ability to process and catalog it. Therefore, not all information is treated equally. Some information is ignored, some information is misinterpreted, and some information is generalized.

Let's take another look at your morning experience with this in mind. We process kinesthetic information from all parts of our bodies at all times. Our skin alone is a 16-square-foot sensory blanket. When you awoke, were your feet cold? Was the weight of the blankets heavy or light? What was the temperature under versus above the blankets? How did the floor feel as you walked to the shower? Was the shower handle cold? Was it easy or hard to move? What was the taste in your mouth?

We also process auditory information continuously. Was the clock radio alarm set to play music or to buzz? Were sounds coming from outside your window? Were sounds coming from other parts of your house? What sound did the water make as it came through the shower head? Our ears have the ability to hear an infinite number of diverse sounds.

What visual information did you receive? Was the room light or dark? What was the time on the clock? What color were the numbers on the clock? Was sunlight beaming through the window? Did you notice anything on the floor in your path to the shower? Was it bright or dark in the shower? Did the steam vapors fog the bathroom? Our eyes can see stars millions of light-years away, as well as a speck of dust on a computer screen.

In the first few minutes of your day, you were exposed to thousands of pieces of information. It would be very inefficient if you had to process each piece of information and catalog it. You therefore process the minimal amount of information you need to accomplish the task at hand. The other information is tuned out or ignored, deleted from your conscious mind. However, the subconscious mind still collects all the information, just in case it is needed later.

By retrieving information from past experiences, you can extrapolate what to do in an entirely new situation. For example, let's pretend I gave you car keys and placed you in a parking lot with a hundred different cars. You would know what to do with the keys based upon your knowledge of how cars work. You would be able to open the car door, start the car, and drive it away, even though you may have never driven or seen this type of car before. You have developed a model based upon your cumulative experience of driving and being in cars. Now suppose a hundred different kinds of tractors are in the same parking lot. Your model may or may not work, depending on how close a particular tractor's operation mirrors that of a car.

TRIANGULATION

Up to this point, we have learned that we all operate in our own world, which is our perception of reality. We also filter information all the time. While most salespeople operate in a world of incomplete or incorrect customer information, Heavy Hitters have a different strategy, called "triangulation."

Triangulation is the process of identifying your position by using three or more data points. If you are sailing across the ocean, you can calculate your latitude and longitude by forming an imaginary triangle with certain stars. In sales, we do the same, with the stars being the members of our project team assembled to win an account. In most cases, the team consists of a Hitter, a presales engineer, an inside sales team, and a sales manager.

Sailors continually take readings from different stars to ensure their position is accurate. In the same way, Heavy Hitters may even talk about a deal with someone who has never met the customer or isn't even in sales, such as a spouse or friend. Heavy Hitters constantly try to triangulate their position by answering these questions: Is there a deal? Am I winning? Who do I have to watch out for, and what can ruin this deal?

In sales, triangulation is the process of checking all information that has been gathered about a customer with other people. Through triangulation, Heavy Hitters try to identify the pieces of information that their word catalog may have ignored, generalized, or misinterpreted. It's a calibration technique for finding "reality."

You should think of triangulation as the "rule of three." When you're working a hot deal, you would like important information validated independently by three different sources. When strategizing about a deal, three minds are better than one. When cold-calling an unfamiliar company, make a new rule whereby it takes three "not interesteds" from three different people within the company before you cross the company's name off your prospect list. You want three independent points of validation to ensure you know the truth.

Before we take an in-depth look at triangulation, we should identify the main participants involved in a Hitter's triangulation process.

Heavy Hitter or Salesperson

The Heavy Hitter is the customer's main point of contact for all customer communication. The Hitter coordinates all meetings and events, such as presentations and technical evaluations. She is in charge of all the company resources that are assembled to win the account, regardless of their departmental origin. In essence, she is the project manager. The project is to win the account. To accomplish this, she can pull from any department in the company, including management, engineering, support, consulting, marketing, and product management. The project team may also include partners from outside the company.

The Heavy Hitter is responsible for creating a proposed solution and ensuring that the solution matches the customer's needs. As the team leader, she confirms the customer is qualified from a business and technical perspective to the rest of her project team, motivates the team, and takes responsibility for the overall relationship with the customer and ongoing account satisfaction.

Presales Engineer or System Engineer

The presales engineer is mainly responsible for understanding the customer's technical profile and presenting the company's technical solution. The system engineer conducts the process that determines the level of technical fit between the vendor's product and the customer's technical environment. The system engineer is also responsible for the solution design, product evaluation, and implementation of the project. Members from other departments, such as consulting or support, may also perform certain tasks at the system engineer's direction. Most importantly, the system engineer is responsible for the technical relationship with the customer and the ongoing technical satisfaction with the product. In this role of a customer advocate, the system engineer will represent the customer and facilitate meetings with the technical support department.

Inside Sales Team—Telesales or Telemarketing

The inside sales group will play a different role depending upon the complexity of the Hitter's product. With technically complex products that require longer implementations, the inside sales team members generate leads by making cold calls or sending e-mails and direct mail. They also provide the Heavy Hitter with a support system at the corporate office. The support functions may be administrative, such as sending marketing collateral, providing order follow-up, or tracking down specific information the Hitter may need. In any case, members of the inside sales group work at the direction of the Heavy Hitter, even though they may have an immediate supervisor.

If the products are less complicated to install and sell, the inside sales team will be able to perform a telesales function. In this case, the inside sales team is made up of salespeople with a quota who close new business and search their customer base for additional sales. Depending on the nature of the product, the team members may be closely integrated with the Hitter's territory, or they could work independently on smaller deals, freeing the Heavy Hitter to pursue major accounts. Most likely, the inside sales team will be involved in the triangulation process at the beginning of the sales cycle. Once their information has been passed on to the Heavy Hitter, their role is less active.

Sales Manager

The final person involved in triangulation is the Hitter's sales manager. Sales managers have been involved in more sales cycles and have experienced a more diverse set of sales scenarios than most salespeople. Therefore, they can draw upon these experiences and compare them to the existing sales cycle.

The various members of the customer's evaluation team are going to give contradictory information. Since we all have our own perception of reality, this isn't surprising. Disagreements will occur, and as the saying goes, "When two men in business always agree, one of them is unnecessary." The intent of the triangulation process is to identify these subtle or obvious differences. Areas of contention or contradiction require further analysis, so the issue is assigned to a member of the Hitter's team to investigate.

TRIANGULATION DIAMOND

The following discussion and Figure 3.1 show how Heavy Hitters carry out the triangulation process. It is based on the analogy of a baseball diamond. (After all, Heavy Hitters are trying to score a home run!)

First Base

On the triangulation diamond, first base is the "What" base. What are the content-level words being spoken by the prospects? What specifically do they mean? The Heavy Hitter is trying to determine as specifically as possible what the customers mean when they speak. The Heavy Hitter will do this by asking specifically what they mean. Questions asked on first base include the following:

- Specifically, what are you trying to accomplish?

- Specifically, what business problem are you trying to solve?

- Specifically, what technical problem are you trying to solve?

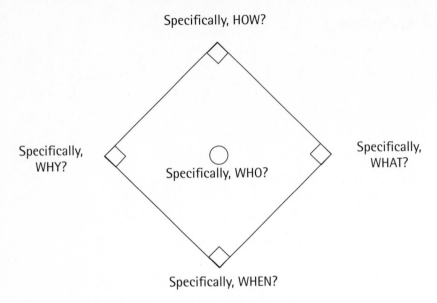

Figure 3.1 The Triangulation Diamond

As the customers answer these questions, the Heavy Hitter is trying to decipher their high-level requirements into very specific targeted needs. For example, let's say a Heavy Hitter sells a financial application and is meeting with prospects who are unhappy with their company's accounting system. She will help them define exactly what is making them unhappy. Is it functionality, performance, ease of use, support, or flexibility? Suppose it's functionality. Is it accounts payable, accounts receivable, human resources, or integration? Suppose it's accounts receivable. Is it customer creation, payment application, or delinquent accounts reporting?

The Heavy Hitter is trying to get to the very specific cause of pain or dissatisfaction. Members of the triangulation team will each have their own prioritized list of the customer's pain points. Once the Heavy Hitter has triangulated with the group about the pain points, she can determine whether her product can solve that pain, particularly in comparison with other solutions being evaluated.

Second Base

Second base is the "How" base. The Heavy Hitter uses second base to understand how the customers will take action. Again, she is trying to determine in as much detail as possible how the sales process will happen. She does this by asking specifically how the customers will accomplish a task. Questions asked on second base include the following:

- Specifically, how will you make a decision?

- Specifically, how will you implement the solution?

- Specifically, how will you determine if it is successful?

Suppose the prospects have decided to evaluate the Heavy Hitter's financial application. She will want to know the prospects' evaluation criteria, the steps of the evaluation, and how they will determine if the evaluation is successful. Members of her triangulation team will gather this information from their respective contacts. Together, they will assimilate the results. From this exercise, the Heavy Hitter will identify areas of product strength, weakness, and information she doesn't know.

Third Base

Now that the Heavy Hitter knows specifically what the customers are planning and how they intend to accomplish their goal, she needs to understand why. Third base is the "Why" base. Hitters want to understand "Why" from the company's perspective.

- Specifically, why is the company evaluating a new financial system?
- Specifically, why is our product a better fit than our competitor's?
- Specifically, why would the company select our product?

The second element of "Why" is the personal agendas of the individuals involved with the initiative. Items on these agendas are called "benefactions," personal benefits that come from taking a particular action. The dictionary definition of "benefaction" is "the act of doing good or helping others, especially by giving money."[1] Clearly, the Heavy Hitter wants customers to feel good about giving her money when they buy her product. Nonetheless, the Heavy Hitter's definition is more intricate: "To derive an advantage that contributes to one's well-being, such as happiness, esteem, power, or wealth, that results in influencing the way the person behaves during the sales cycle." We will explore benefactions in more detail later in the chapter. At the personal level, the Heavy Hitter will ask the following questions about each participant in the customer's selection process:

- Specifically, why is this particular person on the evaluation team?

- Specifically, why would this person endorse our product?

- Specifically, why would this person oppose our product?

Home Plate

After rounding third base, you are headed for home plate. Home is the "When" base. Even if you reach third base every time you hit the ball, you don't score until you reach home. All the work the Heavy Hitter has done on the account is moot if the customer doesn't have a time frame to evaluate, decide, and purchase. On home plate, the questions include the following:

- Specifically, when will the evaluation start and finish?

- Specifically, when will a decision be made?

- Specifically, when will the customer buy?

The Pitcher

In baseball, the pitcher can throw the ball to any base at any time. The pitcher's position represents "Who." "Who" can be applied to each base. The Heavy Hitter will determine who decided on the criteria, who will perform the evaluation, who will make the decision, and who will buy. At each base, triangulation is used to compare the various responses from each of the sales team members. Hitters triangulate incessantly and with everybody.

WHY DO PEOPLE BUY?

I recently opened a sales seminar by asking the audience, "Please raise your hand if you bought something very expensive in the past 90 days." Three hands immediately shot high in the air. I asked each person to stand up. "So, what did you buy and why did you buy it?" I asked the young woman in the front row.

She replied, "I bought a BMW. It's a great car and the 325 was *Road and Track's* car of the year."

"How long did you take to buy it?"

"It took about a month to find exactly what I wanted," she said.

In a skeptical tone I said, "Come on, tell me the truth. When did you decide you wanted the car?"

She sheepishly replied, "I have *always* wanted that car. For years I have dreamed about owning one."

I went on to the next person, a middle-aged man who proudly said, "I bought a brand new Toyota SUV. It's beautiful."

"So, why did you buy it?"

"Well, it has all the latest technology, navigation system, entertainment center, and it's surprisingly fast!"

I pressed him, "No, really, why did you buy it?"

He thought for a moment and said, "Honestly, I bought it for my wife. Got to keep her happy."

Then I moved over to the final person, a young man in his early 20s. He said, "I didn't buy a car. I bought a television that actually cost more than the car I drive."

As laughter from the crowd died down, I asked, "How much did it cost?"

He answered, "$4,000." He went on to justify his extravagant purchase: "I watch a lot of movies. I guess you could call it my hobby, and it's very important to me."

"Have you always liked gadgets?" I asked sympathetically.

"I love gadgets. Ever since I was a kid."

"Who do you watch movies with?" I asked.

"My wife. We like to chill together and forget about the world."

What do these three stories have in common? First, each of these people had made the decision to buy before they went shopping. The young woman had always wanted the car, the middle-aged man is always seeking to make his wife happy, and the young man has always played with toys. Second, the reasons they gave for buying (car of the year, navigation system, important hobby, and so on) weren't actually responsible for motivating their purchase. Instead, they were rationalizations that mentally enabled them to make the expenditure. These reasons allowed them to justify their decision psychologically. Every purchase decision can be traced to one of four psychological roots.

Physical Well-Being

The will to survive is one of our strongest desires. We are wired to maintain our health physically, mentally, and emotionally. We say to ourselves, "I should work out more," "I should go back to school and get that degree," or "I can't believe I did that." When we ignore this drive, we experience guilt, remorse, and the consequences of our denial. Many of our purchase decisions are made to ensure our well-being and the well-being of our close friends and loved ones.

Pain Avoidance

When something is hurting you badly, the desire to eliminate the source of pain is all consuming. Nothing else really matters. Think about the last time you had a painful injury. The pain dominated your thoughts and determined every move you made. We want pain to stop as soon as possible. Therefore, pain avoidance is the greatest purchase motivator because the customer is forced to act quickly and decisively.

Self-Preservation

We naturally seek the approval of others. While we want to be recognized for our unique talents, we still want to be part of a group. We will purchase items that we believe enhance our stature and protect our group position. The desire to be wanted by a group and loved for who we are is a powerful purchase motivator.

Self-Gratification

Everyone's got a selfish ego, and self-gratification is our desire to put our own needs before everyone else's. We'll go to great lengths to purchase something that makes us feel better about ourselves and superior to others. The word "ego" is derived from the Greek word for "I," and egos drive the business world. Someone's ego is the driving force behind the major projects and the grand initiatives that result in the purchase of your product.

Buying a BMW sports car to impress others is very different from buying an SUV to protect the physical well-being of a loved one. The gratification we derive from buying an expensive television is on the other end of the buying spectrum from buying life's necessities. Watching a movie to escape reality helps refresh the mind and spirit. Each of the four psychological purchase motivators creates compelling reasons to make a purchase in order to satisfy a psychological need. It compels us to take an action for our personal benefit.

THE HITTER'S BENEFACTION

Heavy Hitters' goal is to win the deal at hand. In order to win the deal, they form an account strategy based upon information they have accumulated about the account and their knowledge of the products they are selling. Whether formally or informally, they will plan a series of tactics that they believe will give them the best opportunity to win at the least possible expense in terms of precious resources. The most precious resource is their time and the time of their project team. As they continually gather more information about an account, they will adjust their strategy and the associated tactics.

Heavy Hitters have their own personal benefactions associated with winning a deal. Maybe they dream about using the commission to buy a new car. Perhaps they envision themselves driving to the office in a Ferrari or Porsche. Maybe they are eager for the accolades they will garner by winning a large and prestigious customer. Possibly, they can hear the applause as they are handed an award at the next sales meeting. A benefaction is something strongly desired, defined in a personal way, that is important to you.

Professional athletes understand benefactions. Sprinters will visualize an entire race and see themselves on the winner's stand (their benefaction) receiving the gold medal. College basketball coaches will ask their team to mentally rehearse cutting down the net after they win the national championship (their benefaction).

Athletes describe their field of vision narrowing while they are focused on their benefaction. A professional baseball player will see the stitches on a 90-mile-per-hour fastball. Golfers that are surrounded by members of the gallery won't hear or see them while they focus on the next putt.

Understanding your benefaction affects your conscious activities, as well as your subconscious mind. Your conscious mind is obsessed with achieving benefactions. Meanwhile, your subconscious mind is constantly sensing and filtering data that is necessary to achieving important benefactions.

In computer terms, the conscious mind is like a point-to-point model. For example, a salesperson wants to check her e-mail while traveling on the road. Using her laptop, she makes a dial-up connection to the host computer. Her only concern is to get her e-mail, and once she checks it, she disconnects the phone line. This point-to-point connection is similar to the conscious mind focused on a specific benefaction.

The subconscious mind is more like a broadband connection that is always on, such as a cable modem. The modem has a wider band of data and processes at a higher speed than a dial-up connection. The modem is always on, always receiving information. In the e-mail example, the salesperson always receives e-mail in real time. She doesn't have to dial up a connection.

The subconscious mind retains information that the conscious mind doesn't. It simply isn't efficient to store everything in your conscious mind. Remember the last time you misplaced an important item (your keys, wallet, glasses)? At first, you employed a conscious strategy to find it. You may have thought about where you had recently been and gone back to those locations. If you didn't find the item, hours, days, or weeks may have gone by. Then suddenly, without specifically thinking about it, you knew exactly where it was. Your subconscious mind found it. In the same way, when your prospective customers say, "Let me sleep on it," they are actually saying, "Let me see if my subconscious mind has any objections since it has some additional information that I don't have right now."

PERSONAL BENEFACTIONS

Let's assume a Heavy Hitter has a scheduled meeting with a prospective customer. The goal of the meeting is to present her company's product to the customer team. In the process of presenting the product, she expects to collect additional data and further define her account strategy. Obviously, she wants the presentation to go well. Ideally, she wants to have the team members get so excited that they progress to the next step in the sale process, such as a product evaluation or, better yet, a close. Meanwhile, the customers' goal is to limit their investment to a finite number of relationships. They are trying to use the meeting as part of the courting process to determine the quality of the suitor.

To measure the success of the meeting, the Heavy Hitter creates a personal benefaction. It may be to have the key decision maker tell her at the end of the presentation, "It looks great. Send me your final quote!" In this example, the Heavy Hitter may have a picture of the person in her mind. She hears those words being said and perhaps feels the excitement of closing the deal. This is her benefaction for the meeting. She can measure the success of the call based upon what actually happens and how closely that matches her benefaction. In other words, she will know she has achieved her benefaction when the sensory information she has collected confirms it.

Each meeting participant from the customer team also has a benefaction. The manager of the department may view the cost savings of implementing the product as the main goal. His benefaction may be being rewarded with a bonus for reducing the department's expense structure (which he will use to take his family to Hawaii).

The person in charge of implementing the solution may view manageability as the goal. Since she will have to devote less time to managing the new product than the current one, her benefaction may be to have more time to spend on the projects she enjoys (or less time at work and more time at home with her family). Notice all these people's benefactions are personal, regardless of whether they are the buyer or the seller.

The Heavy Hitter uses her word catalogs to determine the benefactions of each individual. And she also uses her word catalogs to determine if her benefaction for the meeting has been achieved.

SURVIVAL, SUCCESS, AND SIGNIFICANCE

Whom would you rather sell to? A person who has been working in a company for 16 years or someone who has been there for only

6 months? The answer depends on what stage the person is at in his or her career and the type of product you sell. Everyone is in one of three career stages: survival, success, or significance. In survival mode, people are struggling to exist. Their career or job is in jeopardy or under an imminent threat. Successful people are competent at their jobs and secure in their positions while significant people want to make their mark on the company and have an impact on the organization.

Over the course of my career, I have naturally gravitated toward selling to significant people. Why? Because they are personally motivated to get something done, and the products I sold required a major shift in the way the company conducted business. Since significant people are the "movers and shakers" of their companies, they are the individuals who are naturally interested in innovation. In fact, the person I most enjoy selling to is a senior executive who has been with his or her company for only a short time. I know that this person is on a mission to make a name for him- or herself.

My second favorite group to sell to is people in survival mode. I like to work with people who must do something or perish. However, if I were selling office products, I would probably want to deal with successful people in successful companies—people who are competent at their jobs and will be there later on when it is time to reorder.

The concept of survival, success, and significance also applies to companies. In this regard, I would rather sell to successful and significant companies. However, since companies in survival mode are extremely motivated, I'll still go after their business, but more cautiously. Therefore, I proactively prospect for successful and significant companies and react to requests from companies in survival mode. Whenever you attend a meeting, always try to classify the stage of the participants' careers and their company.

THE PYRAMID OF MEETING SUCCESS

At the heart of every successful sales call are mutual trust between both parties, the competence of the participants, and the identification of personal benefactions. The pyramid of meeting success (Figure 3.2) illustrates this concept.

All sales calls start with a handshake. The tradition of the handshake started as a way of physically validating that a person wasn't carrying any weapons. Since both sides shook hands freely, it was a mutual event, a ritual that occurred very quickly at the beginning of a meeting. Unfortunately for Heavy Hitters, mutual trust is not achieved as quickly. It is earned over time and not freely granted. Depending on the product you are selling, it may take many meetings or several demonstrations over many months to gain a customer's trust. Once achieved, it can be lost or weakened if commitments given by either party are not honored or if information given is proven false.

The next level of the pyramid is competence. The first aspect of competence is the personal fit between people. Since the sales team members are a direct reflection of their company's competence and culture, the customer wonders if this team will capably manage their long-term relationship. Are they technically competent? Do they understand my problem? Are they pleasant to be around? The sales team, on the other hand, determines if the customer's selection team has the wherewithal to make the decision, purchase the product, and implement it.

The other aspect of competence is the fit between the product and the customer. How well does the product solve the customer's tech-

Figure 3.2 The Pyramid of Meeting Success

nical problem? Will it operate as promised? What features of the product is the customer unsure of? How good is the product's technical support? What is the product's future release schedule? The questions regarding personal and product fit must be answered satisfactorily at the competence level.

At the top of the pyramid are benefactions. Entering into a meeting, each party knows what the overriding goal of the sales team is. It's to sell the product. What's the customer's goal? More specifically, what are the benefactions each participant has for achieving this goal? Decisions are influenced by politics. Politics are based upon self-interests. Hitters will attempt to find out and understand these self-interests. They will incorporate all participants' desires into their strategy to help them achieve their individual benefactions.

A sale will most likely occur when three criteria are met. First, an adequate level of mutual trust must be established. Second, both parties must be assured of the competence of each other. And third, the Hitter's solution must be aligned with the benefactions of the individuals involved in the decision process.

However, one more key part of the formula is needed in order for the equation to actually work. Rapport must be underneath the entire process to actually close the deal. The formula is shown in Figure 3.3.

In the early 1990s, I had the opportunity to work for one of the fastest growing software companies of that time. For five straight years, the company was a darling on Wall Street. For two of those years, it was one of the top five appreciating technology stocks on the NASDAQ. In every office in the company, a plaque with a quote from the president was posted: "Always take the customer's point of

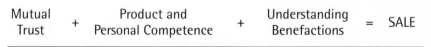

Mutual Trust + Product and Personal Competence + Understanding Benefactions = SALE

RAPPORT

Figure 3.3 The Importance of Rapport

Figure 3.4 The Complete Pyramid of Meeting Success

view." The plaque covered only half the point. It should have read, "Always work to help the customers achieve their benefactions!"

Let's take another look at the pyramid of meeting success. As illustrated in Figure 3.4, with the addition of rapport, it actually is a pyramid, not just a triangle.

WORD CATALOGS AND RAPPORT

How do you establish rapport? By speaking individuals' different languages, understanding their distinct word catalogs (their "wiring"), and relating to them in their world. Most likely, you are being introduced to the details of their word catalogs for the first time. The information may surprise or even startle you.

Why is it important for you to learn and use this information? Understanding a person's word catalog can aid you in achieving your benefaction by helping you create rapport. By being conscious of people's word catalogs and communicating with them in the same meaningful terms they use, you will facilitate mutual trust and help demonstrate your competence. Customers will understand you better and, in fact, like you more because you are speaking the same language.

This chapter includes exercises to help you create rapport with your customers. Remember that learning something new always takes time. By honestly completing the exercises, you will be taking the first step in learning something very powerful.

Some people are left-handed and some are right-handed. The dominant hand you use was not your conscious choice. Your brain was wired to use that hand. In addition, over time you have grown comfortable and proficient in using it more than the other.

Some people also have a more dominant ear (perhaps the one you use when you talk on the telephone), a more dominant eye, and even a more dominant leg. Similarly, people have a dominant or primary word catalog. They also have a weaker secondary catalog and finally, a recessive catalog. People process information with their word catalogs using pictures, feelings, or words according to the strength of each catalog.

However, people do not use one word catalog exclusively. Instead, they use all three word catalogs. Because spoken language is the system we use to communicate our experiences, people will describe their experiences and convey their thoughts in terms that match their word catalog wiring.

You can tell what people's word catalog wiring is by noting the adjectives and verbs they use in their conversations. An adjective is a word used to modify a noun, and a verb is usually an action word. However, some words can be used as either a noun, verb, or adjective, and this usage will significantly change the interpretation of the word catalog. The sentences in the left-hand column represent a visual, auditory, or kinesthetic usage, while those in the right-hand column do not imply any particular word catalog.

Please *outline* your strategy.	He's finished with the *outline*.
Bob will *call* a meeting for tomorrow.	Did you get the phone *call?*
Let's *copy* what they're doing!	Please make me a *copy.*
Please *watch* your mouth.	His *watch* is broken.

The italicized words in the sentences in the left-hand column are verbs that imply a particular word catalog. Although the same words are used in the right-hand column, they are used as nouns. As you know, a noun is a word that describes a person, place, or thing. In general, nouns do not imply any particular word catalog.

For example, people with a primary visual word catalog will use visual keywords more frequently to describe their experiences than they will use auditory or kinesthetic words. Here are some examples of visual keywords:

Beaming	Demonstrate	Frame	Imagine	See
Bleak	Diagram	Gaze	Light	Shine
Bleary	Diffuse	Glance	Look	Show
Blight	Disappear	Glare	Magnify	Sight
Blind	Discern	Glimpse	Map	Snapshot
Bright	Display	Graph	Murky	Spectacle
Brilliant	Distinguish	Hallucinate	Observe	Spot
Chart	Dreary	Hazy	Outlook	Stare
Clarify	Emit	Highlight	Perspective	Survey
Clear	Expose	Illuminate	Preview	View
Cloudy	Fade	Illustrate	Reflect	Viewpoint
Dazzle	Focus	Image	Scan	Watch

People with primary auditory word catalogs will use auditory keywords like these in their conversations:

Accent	Bark	Denounce	Note	Say
Amplify	Berate	Dictate	Paraphrase	Shout
Articulate	Bicker	Digress	Persuade	Slur
Ask	Blare	Discuss	Plead	Snap
Assert	Boast	Drone	Profess	Sound
Attune	Cajole	Edit	Promise	Speak
Audacious	Call	Giggle	Quiet	Spell
Audible	Chime	Hum	Rave	Talk
Backfire	Chord	Implore	Recap	Tell
Back talk	Crunch	Loud	Retract	Vague
Banter	Cry	Noise	Ring	Yell

People with a primary kinesthetic catalog will use kinesthetic keywords like the following:

Ache	Catch	Hard	Pique	Smile
Bash	Chafe	Heart	Plug	Smooth
Bask	Chew	Heavy	Post	Spit
Bat	Choke	Hit	Press	Squash
Bend	Chop	Hold	Pull	Sticky
Bind	Clinch	Impact	Push	Stink
Bit	Cough	Impress	Queasy	Strike
Blink	Crawl	Irritate	Rough	Taste
Boot	Draw	Kick	Rub	Thaw
Bounce	Feel	Leap	Scratch	Throw
Bow	Friction	Mark	Sense	Touch
Breathe	Gnaw	Move	Sharp	Walk
Caress	Grab	Nip	Smell	Weigh

EXERCISE 1: HOW ARE YOU WIRED?

What is your primary word catalog? Here's an exercise that will help you understand how you are wired. Print out the last 10 business e-mails you sent to colleagues within your company and the last 10 personal e-mails you sent to friends or family. Write the letters *V*, *A*, and *K* at the top of a piece of paper. In the left column write "Work," "Personal," and "Total." The chart should look like Figure 3.5.

	V	*A*	*K*
Work			
Personal			
Total			

Figure 3.5 VAK Keyword Count Chart

You are now ready to perform a "VAK keyword count." Examine the e-mails and circle each occurrence of a visual, auditory, or kinesthetic word. Remember to circle the usage of the word only when it is used in the context of an action or description ("you *light* up my life," not "please turn the *light* on"). As you circle the words, add a tally in the appropriate column. The chart may look something like Figure 3.6 when you are done.

Was there a difference between the tallies from the work and personal e-mails? In the example above, the person is primary auditory, secondary kinesthetic, and recessive visual. Most likely, the language in your work e-mails is more androgynous and technical; therefore, the counts will be lower. Were the counts evenly dispersed or clustered under one catalog? You can do a similar exercise with the e-mails you receive to determine a sender's word catalog wiring.

DETERMINING SOMEONE'S WIRING

Although nouns do not usually imply any particular word catalog, there are exceptions to this rule. When a person's communication is dominated by nouns that can be associated with one of the word catalogs, it is a good indication of a person's wiring. For example, if an e-mail had a pervasive or repetitive use of nouns such as "photograph," "picture," or "maps," this would provide additional clues that the person is a Visual.

Other nuances about VAK keywords are helpful. Here are three separate e-mails I received from the same individual. All the VAK keywords are italicized.

	V	A	K
Work	III	ⲧ⺼ I	III
Personal	ⲧ⺼	ⲧ⺼ ⲧ⺼	ⲧ⺼ IIII
Total	ⲧ⺼ III	ⲧ⺼ ⲧ⺼ ⲧ⺼ I	ⲧ⺼ ⲧ⺼ II

Figure 3.6 Sample Results of a VAK Keyword Count

E-MAIL #1

I *saw* Jeff's note on the good news about version eight and our token support. However, I would like to see us run a test to verify that the product is running *smoothly.* Can we do that?

E-MAIL #2

We have this gal *handled.* I called her and updated her with all the appropriate info right away. I have been working with a few folks including her around Q2 & Q3. *Looks* like we will be getting a deal from them. Will verify if it is a new opportunity or the one I have had in the pipeline for a while now.

E-MAIL #3

MAN. . . . I think we are *hearing* it all these days!! I do not even want to know what we will *hear* next!!

If you do a VAK keyword count on these e-mails you will notice that the categories are equal (two visual, two auditory, and two kinesthetic). Since the VAK count is evenly distributed, how can you tell what this person's primary catalog is? The more stressful or tense a situation is, the more likely people will communicate in their primary word catalog. The third e-mail was sent under very distressing circumstances. The sender had just been told he lost a deal in which he had invested a lot of time and effort. This person is wired as primary auditory, secondary visual, and recessive kinesthetic. I have validated this through my many conversations and interactions with him.

Bring a notebook to your next meeting, and perform a VAK count to determine the primary, secondary, and recessive word catalogs of each of the participants. While people are being introduced, write their names down. In the left-hand margin of the paper, conduct a VAK count for each person. You don't have to count for the entire meeting, just until you have a basic understanding of each person's wiring. Better yet, take along your manager or associate and have him or her conduct the counts.

Another trick is to place their business cards inside your binder and write the VAK counts directly on them (in tiny print). Later, you can review the cards and refresh your memory about the people's wiring. The results of your VAK counts will be fascinating. You will begin to be able to identify a person's word catalogs in a very short time. You will also spot patterns and similarities between people who share the same word catalogs.

Your ultimate goal is to become aware of VAK keywords automatically without any handwritten counts. You want the process to become a natural part of listening so that, for example, when a customer is explaining her company's needs, you hear not only her content-level words but also the VAK keywords.

Everyone uses all three word catalogs, just in different increments and priority. You have a primary word catalog, which is your "default" method for accessing your catalog of experiences. It is the catalog used most often. Visuals think in terms of pictures, Auditories in sounds, and Kinesthetics in terms of feelings. Your secondary word catalog is your next strongest method for accessing your catalog. Finally, your recessive catalog is your least used and least developed access method.

Many people make prejudiced generalizations about word catalogs based upon their experiences with a small sample of people. For example, people may associate being kinesthetic with being more emotional. This may or may not be the case. Just because people's primary word catalog is kinesthetic does not mean they are more emotional or temperamental than anyone else. It simply means they catalog experiences and express themselves in terms of their feelings.

Whether people are introverted, extroverted, or emotionally mature is a function of their personality. While your customers' personalities are influenced by their word catalogs, a person's personality is a complex matrix of different traits. In other words, you will meet introverted Visuals, and you will meet extroverted Visuals. You will interact with selfish and unselfish Kinesthetics. In Chapter 9, we will review personality traits in further detail.

VAK KEYWORD COUNT PATTERNS

As you begin to perform VAK keyword counts, you will notice some patterns developing. At a sales meeting, I asked my entire sales force to perform VAK counts for three speakers making 45-minute presentations to the group. Interestingly, their VAK counts (shown in Figure 3.7) were representative of the three major types of VAK count patterns: balanced, strong secondary, and dominating primary.

We found that the president has a visual primary catalog along with strong auditory and kinesthetic catalogs. This is a very balanced pattern. This wiring suits him well in his position. As president, he is responsible for the vision of the company, and it makes sense to have a Visual in that role. Other responsibilities of the president are company communication and consensus building. His well-developed auditory and kinesthetic catalogs help him to naturally accomplish these two tasks with people who are not visually wired.

The vice president of engineering has an auditory primary catalog and a strong secondary visual catalog. His kinesthetic recessive catalog is almost nonexistent. The nature of the vice president of engineering's position is both analytical and visionary. He has to be able to give specific direction to the programming teams in order to build products. Since the communication framework by which this is done is a functional specification (a detailed description of the product in the form of words), having an auditory primary catalog helps.

Meanwhile, he has to chart the product road map; therefore, having a strong visual secondary is desirable. Since the vice president of

Title	Visual	Auditory	Kinesthetic
President/CEO	20	17	14
Vice President of Engineering	16	20	2
Product Manager	5	34	4

Figure 3.7 Sample VAK Keyword Counts

engineering is consumed in the technical specification language (described earlier as precise, androgynous, nonpersonal language that uses technical operators to modify general words), a strong kinesthetic catalog is not necessarily needed in this position and, in fact, could even be a detriment.

The product manager has an overwhelmingly primary catalog that is so dominating that the secondary and recessive catalogs are very rarely used. This pattern is called a "dominating primary." In this example, the person has a dominating auditory primary catalog. A dominating catalog could be visual or kinesthetic just as well. This person's role is primarily technical. One of his main job functions is to create detailed technical collateral, such as white papers, data sheets, and technical content for the company's web site. Having a strong auditory primary catalog is helpful in accomplishing these tasks.

In addition to the VAK keywords, catch phrases, descriptions, and clichés also reveal a speaker's word catalogs. Some individuals use an unusually high number of clichés, for example. These people tend to be strong Auditories, and they actually repeat a cliché to themselves first before repeating it externally. In fact, Auditories actually spend more time listening to themselves speak than Visuals and Kinesthetics because the volume of their internal dialogues is higher.

Sayings, descriptions, and clichés may be used by people from all three catalogs. However, usually a phrase is more often used by people with one particular catalog. For example, "sizzling hot" is most likely to be said by Auditories. They hear the sizzling sound. Upon hearing this phrase, Visuals might picture a grill with something sizzling on it, and Kinesthetics might think of a finger actually touching the grill (particularly if they have burnt themselves in the past).

EXERCISE 2: SAYINGS AND CLICHÉS

Let's do another exercise. Following is a list of sayings and clichés. After each phrase, mark a *V* for visual, *A* for auditory, and *K* for kinesthetic. If you think the phrase has multiple interpretations, write the order of what you believe is the priority usage. Here are some examples:

"music to my ears," A   "from their perspective," V
"windows are opening," V, K   "that's alarming news," A

The answers follow, but don't look at them until you finish the entire list.

"tough nut to crack"   "juggling so many balls"
"balls in the air"   "iron out the problem"
"we'll keep pinging him"   "play it back for me"
"push the deal"   "look them in the eye"
"we'll hammer it out"   "banging the phones"
"coin rattling down the pipe" "see how the smoke clears"
"die a slow death"   "they want to vent"
"level playing field"   "domino effect"
"I'm listening to this feedback" "ear to the ground"
"he's sharp"   "that's a new twist"
"bottom line, in a nutshell" "echos what I say"
"dream state"   "close-knit"
"breathe some life"   "after my own heart"
"talk it through"   "crunch time"
"touch it every day"   "harping on this"
"flying off the shelves"   "newly charted territory"
"recipe in the cookbook"   "talk a little bit about"
"take that to heart"   "carry the flag"
"talk the talk"   "kick them when they're down"
"in the crosshairs"   "that resonates with me"
"from their perspective"   "bubble to the top"

Based on my experience, here are the most likely usage of these phrases matched to the word catalog:

"tough nut to crack," A, K   "juggling so many balls," K, V
"balls in the air," V, K   "iron out the problem," K
"we'll keep pinging him," A   "play it back for me," A
"push the deal," K   "look them in the eye," V, K
"we'll hammer it out," K, A   "banging the phones," A
"coin rattling down the pipe," A "see how the smoke clears," V

"die a slow death," K, V

"level playing field," V, K

"I'm listening to this feedback," A

"he's sharp," K

"bottom line, in a nutshell," K

"dream state," V

"breathe some life," K, V

"talk it through," A

"touch it every day," K

"flying off the shelves," V

"recipe in the cookbook," A, V

"take that to heart," K

"talk the talk," A

"in the crosshairs," V

"from their perspective," V

"they want to vent," A

"domino effect," K, V

"ear to the ground," A

"that's a new twist," K

"echos what I say," A

"close-knit," K

"after my own heart," K

"crunch time," A, K

"harping on this," A

"newly charted territory," V

"talk a little bit about," A

"carry the flag," K

"kick them when they're down," K

"that resonates with me," A

"bubble to the top," V, A

There is another very interesting way to learn about a person's word catalog wiring. To understand this, it is helpful to revisit how computers work. Computer systems store data in two areas, either in short-term random-access memory (RAM chips) or in long-term storage (hard drives). Since RAM has no mechanical parts, it is much quicker to access RAM. However, RAM is more expensive than long-term storage. Therefore, it is impractical to keep all your data in RAM. When you turn off your computer system, you lose the contents of your RAM. However, the information in long-term storage is still stored on the hard drive, regardless of whether the computer is on or off.

If I ask you what you had for dinner last night, you will easily be able to give me an answer. In a way, you can think of this information as being stored in your brain's short-term RAM because of its recent occurrence. However, if I ask you what the most memorable dinner you have ever had was, you will have to access your long-term storage to process and compare different memorable dinners. You would access and remember the dinner using your primary word catalog, whether you think of the appearance of the restaurant, the taste of the food, or the conversation during the meal (pictures, feelings, and sounds). Like a computer, you use your input and output systems (senses) to gather information and form an answer.

You can think of your primary word catalog as the default method of cataloging your experiences. It is your personal search engine for your brain. With an Internet search engine (such as Yahoo!), you start your search based on a topic and receive a list of results. From this list, you can access more detailed information (such as web sites). Similarly, your primary word catalog is the key by which you can retrieve a complete experience (or memory). (See Figure 3.8.)

For example, if you are a Visual, your initial search would be through mental images. Once the correct mental image is found, you could access the auditory and kinesthetic portions of the experience.

Suppose you are asked, "What was the best day of your life?" If your primary catalog is visual, you may search your memory, looking at many stored pictures before finally deciding on the day your first child was born. To make this decision, you retrieved a picture of the hospital room, which then may have triggered the feeling of holding your baby for the first time and being both joyous and nervous. The experience may have been further embellished by hearing the sound of the baby crying in your mind.

Take a minute and think about the best deal you ever closed. Pay close attention and try to follow the path of your word catalogs. What did you experience? Depending on how you are wired (as an

Figure 3.8 Cataloging Experiences

Auditory, Visual, or Kinesthetic), here are examples of what might have happened:

- Auditory—You thought of being told by the customer you won the deal or telling your manager or your spouse you won the deal.

- Visual—You saw a picture of the company's building or the people who bought your products.

- Kinesthetic—You thought of holding the signed contract or your commission check or shaking hands with the customer or your colleagues.

Your brain has a very efficient technique of searching for information using your primary catalog. When compared to your primary catalog, your secondary and recessive catalogs are less developed. Since your recessive catalog is the least used, you may find you have the most difficulty accessing it. However, if you start to incorporate the use of language associated with your secondary and recessive catalogs daily, it becomes easier (as they become more developed), and you will find your use of all three catalogs more balanced. Exercising these other parts of the brain makes them grow, much like exercising any muscle.

Medical evidence supports this line of thinking. One prevalent treatment to revive coma patients is the stimulation of the noninjured portions of the brain.[2] The remedy includes bombarding the patients' senses with sights and sounds, along with moving their limbs and muscles. The treatment is based upon the theory that the brain creates new pathways that work around the damaged areas.

Word catalogs are physically powerful. If you became particularly ill while eating a certain food, the smell or sight of that food may trigger queasiness. To this day, I can barely stand the sight and smell of salmon, artificial bacon bits, or gin because they trigger very bad past experiences. Conversely, the smell of freshly cut grass always reminds me of football and being part of a team.

Even people can be triggers. Think for a moment about someone who has seriously mistreated you or whom you are deeply in love with. Every time you see this person, the corresponding emotion is triggered.

EXERCISE 3: ANCHORS

Let's do another exercise. Think of the best day of your business career. Have a very specific day in your mind. Remember how great you felt on this day. Perhaps it was a day you received an award or were promoted. Whatever it is, try to relive the feelings, hear the sounds, and recreate a picture of it in your mind. Take a minute to do this. While holding these thoughts, take your right hand and pinch the back of your left hand. You have now created an "anchor." An anchor is the process of associating a certain feeling to an object. Unlike triggers, anchors are conscious, premeditated associations.

USING ANCHORS

Here's a personal story about how I use anchors. I had been asked by my sales office in Boston to speak to a group of 100 people at a seminar. I was very apprehensive about this presentation for three reasons. First, the audience was a gathering of very senior technical people. This alone took me out of my comfort zone. Second, I was to give an entirely new presentation based on a subject in which I do not consider myself an expert. And finally, a well-known and widely respected author of several books on this subject would be speaking immediately following my presentation.

The pressure was definitely on. I prepared and rehearsed my presentation many, many times. Although I felt confident I knew the content, I was still nervous. I was very tense when I walked into the meeting room and saw the crowd. Immediately prior to my presentation, I spent a few minutes replaying the tapes in my mind from previous successful presentations. I chose one event in particular and anchored it to my left hand (by pinching the back of it). As the announcer introduced me, I pinched my anchor. I became calm, confident, and relaxed. The presentation was a huge success.

Anchors are valuable tools, and I use them all the time. For example, when someone on my staff did something great, I gently put my hand on his shoulder and let him know how much I appreciated his hard work. Later, perhaps when he was feeling down, I put my hand on his shoulder in the same manner and his spirits changed noticeably. Hitters naturally anchor with their customers in a similar manner. When Heavy Hitters take their clients to play golf or out to dinner, they are actually attempting to anchor themselves to a positive experience in the customer's mind.

You've probably already noticed my name is Steve Martin. When I introduce myself, people almost always smile. I am very lucky to have a name that triggers a positive recollection of such a humorous person.

Over the years, I have noticed an interesting pattern after I am introduced. An Auditory will most likely say, "Excuuuse me!" while a Visual will be more likely to ask where my arrow is. For me, my name is also my personal anchor. I feel good when I say my name, as I hope you do when you say your own. Conversely, I once had a business meeting with a fellow named Jesse James. Sharing the name of a famous outlaw is obviously a lot less desirable way to start a meeting.

In sales, we are frequently placed in uncomfortable situations where rapport is nonexistent. Under these circumstances, the Hitter's job is to create a receptive environment. Using humor is a great way to start the process. When people laugh, at some level they agree with you or they have shared the same experience.

In particular, self-effacing humor, where Heavy Hitters poke fun at themselves, is particularly effective. For example, if my name were Jesse James, I would try to make light of the situation and might say, "Be careful, I'm meaner than a sidewinder in molting season." Being able to turning a negative into a positive is a fundamental part of selling.

EXERCISE 4: IDENTIFYING YOUR CUSTOMER'S WIRING

We are finishing this chapter with another exercise. It is critical that you be able to identify your customer's wiring. Like the earlier exercise, after each phrase write a *V* for visual, *A* for auditory, and *K* for kinesthetic in the order of priority usage:

"what we are shooting for"

"glimpse of the future"

"across the company"

"put our finger on it"

"we're cooking now"

"want to point out"

"they're hooked"

"flowing through"

"humming along"

"tell you what"

"concrete example"

"apples and oranges"

"in a later discussion"

"one thing to mention"

"look at the numbers"

"the question is"

"take a step back"

"through the tunnel"

"what's the angle"

"train left the station"

"hindsight is always 20/20"

"walk through"

"cry on your shoulder"

"weigh the possibilities"

Following are the answers to exercise 4:

"what we are shooting for," V, A, K

"glimpse of the future," V

"across the company," V

"put our finger on it," K

"we're cooking now," K, A

"want to point out," V

"they're hooked," K, A

"flowing through," K, A

"humming along," A

"tell you what," A

"concrete example," K, V

"apples and oranges," V

"in a later discussion," A

"one thing to mention," A

"look at the numbers," V

"the question is," A

"take a step back," K

"through the tunnel," V, K

"what's the angle," V

"train left the station," K, V, A

"hindsight is always 20/20," V

"walk through," K, V

"cry on your shoulder," K

"weigh the possibilities," K

CONCLUSION

We experience the world by receiving constant streams of information from our visual, auditory, and kinesthetic senses. However, this information can overwhelm our conscious mind's ability to process it. Therefore, information is ignored, misinterpreted, or generalized. As a result, our judgment is not 100 percent correct, and we need a strategy to ensure we know our exact position in a deal.

Sailors of old superstitiously believed that if they tattooed a rooster on the bottom of one foot and a pig on the other they wouldn't drown. However, triangulation, the process of navigation by using three or more stars as data points, saved far more lives than any tattoo. Similarly, Heavy Hitters rely on triangulation with the other members of the sales team to ensure they are using the correct data. Through triangulation, they determine their bearings and chart their future strategy.

A key factor in formulating the strategy is identifying the individual benefactions of the customers. A benefaction is the self-centered interest of each person involved in the selection process. When Heavy Hitters meet with a customer, they know they must establish mutual trust and demonstrate competence in order to align themselves with their customer's benefaction. Most importantly, rapport must be present. By understanding how people use their word catalogs, you can help create rapport.

People's word catalogs are responsible for how they process information (in words, sounds, or pictures) and relate to the world. They will always have a primary, secondary, and recessive word catalog. To identify their wiring, you can perform a VAK count of the most frequent descriptive or action words they use. Their sayings, descriptions, and clichés will also reveal their wiring.

People catalog experiences using their primary word catalog. Once cataloged, the primary catalog triggers the retrieval of the other aspects of the experiences. Also, you can use your word catalogs to purposely anchor a past experience. By doing so, you will be able to recreate the total experience on demand.

By storing past experiences, people create personal histories that are used in the decision-making process. Or as Bill Walsh, one of the most successful coaches in the history of professional football, described it, "History is our collective memory. It is our accumulated experiences. It is invoked constantly and unconsciously by every person, every day, to help them make decisions based, to some extent, on what has gone on before in their lives."[3]

We learned that language is a direct reflection of how the brain operates and is organized. In addition to examining a person's language usage, there's another, even more interesting, way to determine how someone is wired. Amazingly, you can actually watch the brain access information. We'll cover this technique in the next chapter.

Finally, everyone's wiring is unique. However, you have far more in common with Leonardo da Vinci, Salvador Dali, and Albert Einstein than you realize. Although most people think of creative genius as inborn talent, noted neurologist Dr. Oliver Sacks provides a slightly different perspective: A key characteristic of creative people is their ability to relentlessly focus on a single goal. He believes "Creators are passionate and sometimes obsessive. Most of us get distracted or lured away; we don't have the mental muscle to hold on that tight."[4] More than almost any other profession, salespeople truly understand the concept of focusing and being obsessed with achieving a single goal, and that goal is called "making quota."

CHAPTER **4**

How People Think

In the last week alone, Darren had made more than two dozen cold calls to the vice president of a prominent bank. Finally, on a Tuesday around 7 P.M. he caught him at his desk.

"This is George," said the vice president as he answered his telephone.

"Hello, George, this is Darren from ABC Company and I have been trying to reach you for some time."

"Oh, you're the one who's been calling me night and day. Do you realize how many calls I get? It's simply impossible to talk to everyone who calls me," lectured George.

"And I wouldn't bother you unless I had something important to say," Darren said sincerely. "Eight of the top ten largest banks use our services. They tell us that we have helped reduce payroll expenses by an average of 25 percent. I have been calling you to schedule a meeting to discuss how we might possibly help you."

"Well, I'm very busy."

"I understand and I promise it will be worth your time."

"Hmmm . . . as long as it is brief. Call my assistant tomorrow to schedule an appointment."

The majority of salespeople I meet tell me they don't like to read because they don't have the time or patience for it. Meanwhile, frustrated marketing and product managers tell me that

their salespeople are too lazy to read their internal announ
and bulletins. This situation doesn't surprise me in the least b.
for the reasons you may be thinking. You see, your brain was buii
talk. It was not designed to read. While speaking comes naturally an
automatically to us, reading is a skill that must be learned. The fact
that one in every five Americans has a reading disability confirms how
difficult reading is.[1] While it requires three different areas of your
brain to work together in close coordination to read, nature has
optimized your mind to speak. Another way to put it is that salespeople are the best talkers!

Every day, you speak and listen to thousands of words. Through
the words you speak, you are able to explain your ideas, recount your
past experiences, and share your personality with others. Since it
comes so naturally, it is easy to take the communication process for
granted. However, its complexity is quickly remembered when you
travel abroad and have to communicate with someone who doesn't
know your language.

You are an expert at conveying information. Since you do it all
the time, you have learned the most efficient way to transmit and
receive a message or several messages at once. You have also mastered
how to conduct simultaneous conversations while performing different physical activities. For example, you are able to drive your car,
listen to the radio, and talk on your cellular telephone at the same
time. Undoubtedly, you have typed an e-mail and conducted a meeting concurrently.

Most of the time, you probably don't think about the specific
meaning of the words you are using. Since they are so integrated
with your being, they just seem to happen. However, your words
represent your attitude, outlook, and perspective about life. For
example, sitting in my backyard on a moonless night, I can describe
the light emanating from a galaxy as a "pinpoint." Looking at the
same stars, an astronomer might talk about the apparent magnitude
of the Horsehead Nebula in the Orion constellation. A physicist
might explain the complex principles of nuclear fusion. Meanwhile,

an astrologer might view the same stars as an apparition of the future. While we are all viewing the same stars, the language we use to describe our viewpoint will reflect our individual orientation.

In the last chapter, we learned how we organize the world according to the information received by our senses (sight, sound, touch, taste, and smell) and that we use language as the method to describe what we have experienced. The language we use is dependent upon an individual's word catalog, and each person has a primary, secondary, and recessive catalog that determines how his or her brain processes and stores information. In this chapter, we are going to take the next step in understanding the connection between the brain and the communication process. You will learn how you can actually "watch" the mechanical movements of the brain as it accesses a particular word catalog and how this enables you to identify a person's wiring. Once the catalog is identified, you can then adjust your communication style to build rapport using the customer's own language. After you have mastered this technique, you will be able to tell when a person's communication is congruent (truthful) or incongruent (misleading). Here's a hint at how it's done. It all starts with looking your customer in the eye!

Ralph Waldo Emerson once said, "Tell me what you know."[2] In my case, I feel I know three subjects very well: people, sales, and computers. Therefore, I tend to use examples from these areas to explain concepts of "how things work." By way of illustration, let's review how a computer works as a logical model to understand how the brain operates.

In the last chapter, we discussed how the slowest parts of a computer have moving or mechanical parts. Storing and retrieving data electronically from RAM is much faster than storing and retrieving data magnetically on a hard drive. Since the hard drive has to position a mechanical arm to a precise spot on a spinning disk and physically manipulate the surface of the disk, it takes more time to read and write information.

Although it weighs only three pounds, our brain is infinitely more complex than any computer. It's an intricate architecture of 100 million neurons (nerve cells) and 100,000 connectors or pathways that control all of our body's components. These components include the nervous system, muscular system, respiratory system, digestive system, and circulatory system. These systems are also responsible for gathering data via our senses.

The brain has three major parts: the cerebrum, cerebellum, and brain stem. From a sales perspective, we are most interested in what is happening within the cerebrum. The cerebrum controls our voluntary actions, such as body sensations, learning, emotions, and pain. Two hemispheres make up the cerebrum. The right side controls the left side of the body. The left side controls the right side of the body. This cross-management occurs because the nerves connecting the brain to the body cross the spinal cord. The cerebellum coordinates our movement and keeps us in balance. The brain stem controls our automatic functions, such as breathing, heartbeat, and circulation.

If you are right-handed, you have a dominant left side of the brain. You are more likely to have a higher proficiency in solving problems, doing math, and using language. If you are left-handed, you have a dominant right side of the brain. You are more likely to have a higher proficiency in the arts, such as music, writing, and drawing. Your brain is wired a certain way. You were born with this wiring and you cannot change or camouflage it.

The brain has an incredible capacity to sort, prioritize, and process information. As you read this book, your lungs are breathing, your food is digesting, and your heart is pumping blood to all parts of your body, without your having to think about it. Meanwhile, you are consciously moving your eyes to the next word to be read and saying that word to yourself. When you reach the bottom of the page, your hand and arm will execute a complex series of muscle movements in response to commands from the brain to turn the page.

While it is interesting to know the parts of the brain and understand their physiological function, Figure 4.1 represents the logical layout or map of the mind.

The innermost circle represents the deep place inside your mind where the real you resides. You are surrounded by your conscious,

Figure 4.1 Logical Layout or Map of the Mind

or controllable, and subconscious, or uncontrollable, minds. Your internal dialogue surrounds your subconscious and conscious minds. It is very dominating. It's always on, always engaged, and always talking to you. It drives the language you speak to others as well as your actions. Your customer's internal voice is equally active. The final circle represents the impact the inner layers have on external communication in terms of the words actually spoken, voluntary or planned body movements in conjunction with the spoken words, and involuntary or unplanned body movements.

It's helpful for a salesperson to think in terms of this diagram. Usually, the subconscious mind is busy managing all the systems of the body (nervous, muscular, respiratory, digestive, and circulatory) without much effort, and it is working independently most of the time. However, during a sales call, the words spoken and actions of the participants can have an immense effect on the subconscious mind, which results in changes to the body. Heavy Hitters monitor all of the sales call participants for these bodily changes. Are they tense or relaxed? Are they breathing faster or slower?

When people are discussing issues they are passionate about, their hearts pump more blood and their skin flushes. The volume of their voices may rise and their speech quickens. Conversely, people who are bored or apathetic will fidget or become lethargic. People who are worried may feel sick to their stomachs, and their bodies will broadcast this. Consequently, Heavy Hitters are astutely aware of the physical communication of the body. The next chapter is devoted to understanding how Heavy Hitters interpret and manage this important channel of communication.

INTERNAL DIALOGUE

You can't turn off your internal dialogue. It's always there, always working consciously. It's also being affected by subconscious memories of past experiences. When you make a sales call, you are not talking to people. You are talking to their internal dialogue. Understanding this is crucial to becoming a Heavy Hitter.

During the sales call, the Hitter's internal dialogue is at its loudest. It is constantly communicating, telling the Hitter what to say next and how to respond to questions. It also monitors the rapport being established with participants. Here's another way to explain this: The words you say and the words other people say to you affect your entire body. As a result, the body is continually transmitting valuable information about a person's mental state.

The airport is a fascinating place to study internal dialogues. If you are in sales, you undoubtedly spend a great deal of time there. The travelers are most likely thinking about where they are going, and their internal dialogue is consumed with the success of their personal benefaction (whether it is going home to family or off to an important meeting). Airports are also stressful places because we are in a situation where we have little control. Our subconscious is always preparing us for bad news (primarily based upon previous experiences). Hence, the internal dialogue of travelers can be very nasty. It also quickly surfaces to reveal itself in their spoken words.

Groups of travelers have a completely different demeanor from that of someone traveling alone. Having someone to share your internal dialogue with reduces the stress (one reason to bring someone along on your next sales call). If you take a moment to stand by the flight arrival and departure monitors, you will notice people traveling alone will be talking to themselves, repeating aloud their flight and gate numbers. Watch them as they walk through the airport. You can almost hear their internal dialogues calculating the time and distance to the gate.

EYE MOVEMENTS

When you sleep, your mind can create vivid dreams. You can be transported back to your childhood to relive an experience that is stored in your long-term memory, or you can replay yesterday's sales call that resides in your short-term memory. Although they are just dreams, they seem equally real.

Similarly, when you are awake, you are constantly accessing your short-term and long-term memory. However, it is much easier to access your short-term memory. Accessing your long-term memory is harder and slower. Much like the computer's disk drive, it requires some "mechanical" movements. Short-term storage is accessed "electronically" and is therefore unobservable. However, access to long-term memory can be seen. Amazingly, by observing people's eye movements, you can follow the mechanical movements of the brain that happen when they access their long-term memory. By watching their eyes move, you can determine if they are making pictures in their mind, listening to themselves speak, or experiencing feelings. From this information, you can determine their word catalog wiring.

When people remember pictures, their eyes will move up. When people remember sounds, they will move their eyes down to the left, straight to the right, or straight to the left. When people remember feelings, their eyes will move down to the right. Take a minute and do the following eye movements. After each movement, make a mental note if it was more comfortable than the others.

Figure 4.2 Visual Word Catalog Eye Movements

- Up and to the right.
- Straight to the right.
- Down and to the right.
- Down and to the left.
- Straight to the left.
- Up and to the left.

What happened? Did some movements feel strained while others were easy? Suppose that in the analysis of your e-mails you performed earlier, your VAK count indicated that you have a visual primary, kinesthetic secondary, and auditory recessive wiring. Most likely, the auditory eye movements were noticeably more uncomfortable to make than the others. If your VAK count indicated you are wired with an auditory primary, kinesthetic secondary, and visual recessive, then the visual movements were most likely harder to do. Eye movements reflect how the brain is processing information.

When remembering pictures, people will move their eyes up to the right, keep their eyes straight while defocusing their pupils, or move them up to the left. (See Figure 4.2.)

When remembering sounds, people will move their eyes straight to the right, down to the left, or straight to the left. (See Figure 4.3.)

Figure 4.3 Auditory Word Catalog Eye Movements

People will move their eyes down to the right when remembering feelings. (See Figure 4.4.)

Recall the earlier example of someone being asked, "What was the best day of your life?" Visuals may start searching their memory by looking for stored pictures before finally deciding on a specific day, such as the day their first child was born. To search their memory bank of pictures, their eyes would move up to the right, move up to the left, or look straight ahead with the pupils defocused. Once retrieved, the picture could then trigger the feeling they had of holding the baby for the first time. Their eyes would move down to the right to get the feeling. Finally, to recreate the entire experience, their eyes may move down to the left or straight to the right or left to actually recall the sound of the baby crying.

Have you ever tried to have conversations with people who would not look at you? Perhaps they tilted their heads down and stared at the ground during the entire discussion. Maybe they turned their heads slightly to the right or left so that it seemed they were looking at something behind you. Or they could have cocked their heads back, as if they were looking at the sky. Each of these scenarios is an example of someone who has an exceptionally strong or dominant primary catalog. These people have a single catalog that is so controlling that their heads become an extension of their eye movements. If their eyes move down and to the right, that indicates they are dominant Kinesthetics, while people who always tilt their heads up are dominant Visuals. When people stare down and to the left or laterally away from you for the majority of your conversation, you can assume they are dominant Auditories. The person you may have thought of as being shifty-eyed, or untrustworthy, may actually just be an Auditory.

Figure 4.4 Kinesthetic Word Catalog Eye Movements

SHORT-TERM AND LONG-TERM MEMORY

Two categories of information are kept in your long-term memory, date-dependent experiences and minutiae. Just like a computer's RAM memory, your short-term memory has a limited amount of space. In comparison to RAM, the computer's disk drive (long-term storage) has much more space available. Similarly, your long-term memory is almost infinite. Therefore, your brain is continually optimizing what is kept in short-term memory and "writing," or transferring, it to your long-term memory. As time goes by following an event, its relevance diminishes, causing it to be reclassified into long-term memory. In addition, your brain will place small details that are considered trivial directly into long-term storage. In this case, the date of the experience has nothing to do with where the experience is stored. It is being stored based solely upon its importance.

Every morning, I read the business section of the local newspaper. While I ignore most of the information, news I consider important is placed into my short-term memory. This morning, for example, I made a mental note that the next Federal Reserve meeting is on the twenty-seventh. If it lowers rates again, I may want to pursue refinancing my home loan. Therefore, I placed this important date in my short-term memory. Once the date passes, this information will become trivial and be moved into long-term storage. However, all the other minutiae from today's business section were immediately placed into my long-term memory. If later in the day someone asked me what I had read that morning, it would require the identical eye movements to access the information as if I read it a year ago. Remember, some information is placed into long-term memory regardless of the date it is experienced.

EXERCISE 5: YOUR EYE MOVEMENTS

At this point, you may still be skeptical about whether eye movements can really explain what is happening in the brain. Try this experiment. However, before you start you will need to find a mirror.

This exercise is much more meaningful when you can watch yourself, so don't proceed until you are in front of a mirror.

Next, you will find a list of questions. All of these questions are intended to make you access your long-term memory. However, it is possible that an answer is actually stored in your short-term memory. Finding answers in short-term memory doesn't require any specific eye movements. For example, if I ask, "When did you wake up this morning?" the answer is available instantaneously without much work. However, if I ask you what time you woke up last Saturday, that answer may require some additional thought.

As you read each question, try to follow your eye movements. Specifically, concentrate on where your eyes move first to "search" for the answer and make a notation of it. Use *UL* to reflect upper left and *UR* for upper right. Write *SL* for straight left, *S* for straight center, *SD* for straight defocused, and *SR* for straight right. Write *DL* for down left, *DR* for down right, and *DC* for down center. Also try to pay specific attention to the exact position of your eyes when you actually "find" the answer.

- What did you have for dinner last Friday?

- What was the name of your third-grade teacher?

- What was your favorite vacation?

- What was the best job you ever had?

- What was the best sports event you ever attended?

- Who is your favorite music group?

- Where were you when you received your first real kiss?

- What was the worst day of your life?

- What was your SAT verbal score?

- What was the color and license plate number of your first car?

What happened? Did you have to look away from your reflection to answer a question? Where did your eyes move first? What was the last position of your eyes when you found an answer?

Let's examine the questions further. They are all date-dependent and designed to access your long-term memory. However, it's possible that some of the answers were in your short-term memory. It depends on you. If you're reading this book on Saturday, it's easy to remember what you had for dinner yesterday. However, if you're reading it on Thursday, the answer may be in long-term memory. If you had Friday's dinner at your favorite restaurant or ate with a classmate you hadn't seen in 10 years, then it would be more likely that the experience would be in short-term memory. If there wasn't anything particularly eventful about the meal, it was probably placed in long-term memory.

I cannot tell you who my third-grade teacher was. However, I do know a person who can name each of her teachers, even though she attended school over 40 years ago. Not surprisingly, she is now a counselor and has dedicated herself to helping others. Obviously, her teachers had a lasting impact on her and this information has been stored to reflect its importance.

If it has been a long time since you took a vacation, you probably had to do a complex mental search to determine your favorite one. If you were on vacation last week, you may have recently performed this comparison, and the results are still in your short-term memory. If all of your vacations have been indistinguishable or you had a problem selecting the correct answer, you may have continued in a "search loop."

It's easy to spot people using their search loop. Their eyes are moving around in a circle, going from catalog to catalog. They'll start in the primary catalog, move to the secondary catalog, then the recessive catalog, and then repeat the process. Someone with a particularly strong dominant primary will get stuck with his eyes in the primary word catalog position. When this happens in the sales call, the Heavy Hitter knows that the customer is trying to "find" the answer. Since the answer wasn't immediately retrievable, most likely it represents the customer's best guess and the answer needs to be validated.

This experiment was intended to make you aware of your own eye movements. This exercise should have helped you understand and validate your own word catalog wiring. Don't be concerned if you were unable to complete every question, as it is hard to track eye movements when you can't look yourself in the eye.

EXERCISE 6: SHORT-TERM MEMORY

Now, let's do another experiment. Look in the mirror and ask yourself these questions:

- What did you have for breakfast today?

- What color is your car?

- What is your birthday?

- What is your ZIP code?

- What is your Social Security number?

Did you notice completely different eye movements or no movement at all? While the first set of questions required you to access your long-term memory, the second set of questions probably didn't. Most likely, the answers were already in your short-term memory because the experience happened recently or you use this information all the time. In computer terms, the answers for the first set of questions required you to access the hard drive, while the second set of answers was already cached (held temporarily) in your RAM.

Now, take the first list of 10 questions to some friends you know very well. Without telling them why, ask them the same questions. However, instruct them not to tell you the answers. Rather, at the instant they know the answer have them say, "Got it!" After each question make two notations—where their eyes went first and where their eyes were when they said, "Got it!" You should get a very consistent pattern. Once again, the direction their eyes consistently move indicates a person's primary word catalog. Most likely, it will also be the same place they find the answer.

CALIBRATING EYE MOVEMENTS

Twenty years ago, it was more common for companies with expensive merchandise to require potential employees to take a polygraph (lie detector) test, and when I joined a large computer firm, I had this requirement imposed on me. The polygraph measures the body's response (breathing, heart rate, and temperature) as you answer questions. At the beginning of the polygraph test, the administrator asks a certain number of questions he knows to be true, such as your name and where you live. These questions calibrate your response of a known answer to the machine's measurements.

Similarly, you can calibrate eye movements of individuals by watching their response to known answers. By doing this, you are establishing a baseline measurement of their truthfulness. For example, you just finished a great meeting with the decision maker who is responsible for buying your product. Based on the presentation, you know he is auditory primary, kinesthetic secondary, and visual recessive.

HITTER: How long have you been evaluating solutions?
DECISION MAKER: (eyes left, momentary pause) Well, we started last . . . November.

Analysis: Since the evaluation started over 10 months ago, this question was a date-dependent event stored in long-term memory.

HITTER: When do you plan to roll out the first systems?
DECISION MAKER: (eyes straight, focused, instantaneous answer) Our plan is to be up and running by the end of Q2.

Analysis: This is another date-dependent question. However, the answer was in short-term memory. This is probably an important project date, and it is always on his mind.

HITTER: Where will the first system be implemented?
DECISION MAKER: (in a search loop, eyes move left, down left, upper right) Probably . . . Los Angeles.

Analysis: This question may have caused him to search for an answer. He was actually making his best guess as the decision is not final.

HITTER: What other companies are you talking to?
DECISION MAKER: (eyes straight, focused) We are looking at Acme, Beta Company, and ABC Company.

Analysis: The answer resided in short-term memory. He's probably talking to all the vendors on a regular basis.

HITTER: Does one of the solutions sound better than the rest?
DECISION MAKER: (eyes up to the right) No, they all sound the same.

Analysis: Incongruence! Or as the robot from the classic television series *Lost in Space* would say, "Danger! Danger!"

In the preceding example, the first four questions established the baseline measurement. The decision maker's eyes moved to the left when he accessed his long-term memory. They were straight center (not defocused) when he accessed his short-term memory. Any eye movements outside these two ranges must be evaluated in context with the answer.

We can assume that the answers to the first three questions were truthful. The third answer was his best guess. Based on the non-political content of the question, this would be an appropriate assumption. The answer to the fourth question, about which companies he is evaluating, should be in short-term memory. If the answers "Acme, Beta Company, and ABC Company" were given extemporaneously at a quick tempo, then you would assume the answer is truthful. If he went into a 30-second search loop to produce the other vendors, he's editing his response, which is another form of incongruence, and this requires further investigation. If you observe very complex eye movements for seemingly simple questions or no eye movement to questions for which you would expect movement, then you need to investigate further to ensure the person is being truthful.

The fifth question is the interesting one. The collection of these five questions represents one vignette as previously described in Chapter 2. The questions from this vignette may seem free flowing, but they were purposely constructed and orchestrated by the Heavy Hitter. He wanted to know if the playing field was level or if there was a favored vendor. His goal was to find the truth. The first four questions established the baseline to set up the fifth question. This is reminiscent of the boxer who throws a series of right jabs in order to land a big left hook. While the first four questions provide valuable content-level information about the sales process, they also give the Heavy Hitter a chance to calibrate the answers to the customer's word catalog. The answer he gave to the fifth question is most likely a lie.

While answering the fifth question, his eyes went up to the right to his visual recessive catalog. This is the first incongruence. Based on the previous questions, we would have expected that his eyes would either go to short-term memory (straight, not defocused) or long-term memory (straight left). Since his eyes went to the visual position instead, it can be assumed he was "imagining" or creating an answer.

The second incongruence is that the visual eye movements do not match the content language he is using. "No, they all sound the same" is an auditory statement. However, when he said this, his eyes were in a visual position. The two incongruencies would suggest that this person is not telling the entire truth. This type of incongruence happens all the time during sales meetings. Most Hitters rely on their intuition to tell them they are being misled. With this methodology, anyone can develop the same skill by tracking eye movements and matching these movements to spoken words.

If you are a salesperson armed with this information, you have two courses of action. First, you could introduce a new round of questioning to further determine the extent of the bias. For example, you could ask, "Has the company used other products from one of the vendors?" "Has anyone on the selection team used products from one of the vendors?" Or you can take a greater risk approach by confronting the customer with your suspicions that one vendor is favored.

Second, you could take this information and incorporate it into your account strategy. You could implement account tactics that would require the customers to make extraordinary commitments, above what is normally required in terms of their time and resources, before you committed any more of your resources. For example, if your product requires a customer questionnaire or preimplementation plan, you could demand the completion of the document before you provided them an evaluation product. Your goal may be to consume as much of their time as possible. Either they will push back and by doing so reveal their bias, or you will have an opportunity to build the relationship.

Before you select any strategy, you need to determine if you can find a coach (friend) within the customer company to help you win the deal. If you can't develop a coach, it does not make sense to invest your time in any account. Also, you should always be gaining momentum with the account, and you need to have tangible evidence that the deal is moving in your direction. Evidence of this includes vendors being eliminated, meetings with upper management or people involved in procurement, and other buying signs. We'll cover more sales cycle strategies in Chapter 6 and discuss how to develop a coach in Chapter 9. Remember, customers want a finite number of relationships. In the evaluation process, they will spend the majority of the time with the person they believe will provide them with the "best" relationship.

SALES CALL MEMORY

In order to become a Heavy Hitter, you must build your personal knowledge base with your own experiences. Obviously, taking insightful notes during sales calls will help you recall the meeting. However, during the next sales call you won't have time to search through your notes to find the "right" answer to a customer's question (nor would it be considered appropriate). You must make information available instantaneously by committing it to memory. Heavy Hitters have the ability to precisely recall events. Here are six principles to help improve your sales call memory:

1. *Sensory information.* During the sales call, consciously gather as much information as possible from your sight, sound, and touch senses. A vivid event is more likely to be memorized than a dull one, and the more sensory information that is incorporated into your memories, the higher your likelihood of recording it.

2. *Association.* Thoughts and experiences are more readily recalled when they are linked to a specific association. A very simple association would be the success or failure of the call. The association may be further defined by the customers' technical and business requirements, their objections to purchasing your product, their prominent personality traits, their word catalog wiring, and so on. Movement or action can also be used to add a third dimension to the memory and help ensure the event's retention—for example, imprinting in your mind that you were writing on a whiteboard when the customer presented a significant objection. How something is remembered will determine how much is remembered.

3. *Specificity.* The persistence of a memory is directly related to the precision of details that are input at the time of the experience. During a sales call, you may even want to tell your internal dialogue that some information is important and is not to be forgotten.

4. *Unique events.* Many sales calls are free-flowing events that lack a strict organization of facts. Therefore, it is easier to remember any unusual and unique aspects of a sales call that stand out from the ordinary and mundane.

5. *First and last.* Most salespeople are quick to remember how a sales call began (the big opening) and how it ended (the grand finale).

This is a natural characteristic of memory, whereby we tend to remember the information that is presented first and last more than the details in between. This particularly applies to longer sales calls, more than an hour. One way to help remember all of the in-between information is to mentally break the sales call into smaller segments (or chunks) either by time, presenter, or topic of discussion.

6. *The good, the bad, and the ugly.* Be forewarned, your brain has been trained to block out unpleasant images. However, it is critical that all information during a sales call, both good and bad, be stored.

Memory plays a fundamental role in determining the strength of a salesperson's intuition. As salespeople, we spend most of our time trying to predict the behavior, intentions, attitudes, and feelings of our customers. To accomplish this, our senses gather information from the words they speak, their gestures, and other sensory perceptive signals.

SALES INTUITION

Sales intuition is the ability to read and anticipate a customer's action beforehand. Four components of sales intuition are recognizing all the elements of a message using word catalog, decoding the meaning, storing the experience and linking like experiences, and finally, retrieving and comparing information. (See Figure 4.5.)

The first component of sales intuition is recognizing all the verbal and nonverbal communication during a sales call. It is being aware of phonetic, content, purpose, word catalog, and physical layers of the human communication model. After the information is

Recognizing all sensory-related information	Decoding the meaning	Storing the experience	Retrieving and comparing

Figure 4.5 Components of Intuition

distinguished, it must be decoded (the second component of intuition). Language is the medium used for interpreting the definitions of words, identifying their value, and finding out their purpose.

People have their own personal dictionaries or lexicons of words. In fact, the average person's vocabulary is about 50,000 words. However, the definitions or semantics of the words vary between people. People who have been blind all of their lives can say "light" exactly the same as people with sight. Not unexpectedly, their lexical definitions of what light is will be very different. Correctly ascertaining the meaning people are actually trying to communicate by the words they select, the order of the words, and the way they are said is necessary for proper decoding. "Does the customer's dictionary definition of a particular word match mine?"

Decoding also requires determining the congruency of people's communication. It's not only making sure the speaker's and listener's dictionaries are the same but also checking if the speaker's verbal and nonverbal communications are in agreement.

Once decoded, the next component of sales intuition is storing the experience. An analogy of how computers operate helps us understand how our memory works. One of the simplest ways to store information on a computer is in a key access file, shown in Figure 4.6.

Let's suppose you had to enter 1,000 names, addresses, and telephone numbers into your computer. The most logical way to enter and access this data is by name. Therefore, you would use

	Key		——— Attributes ———	
Record #1	Anderson	123 Elm	Mayberry	555-1212
Record #2	Andrews	456 Maple	Petticoat Junction	123-4567
Record N	Zigler	689 Fig	Springfield	555-4111

Figure 4.6 A Key Access File

each person's name as the key to access the attributes (address and telephone number) that are associated with it. By using a key, you are able to directly access that record instead of performing a time-consuming sequential search of all the records for a match.

In this example, we would expect numbers in the telephone column, a combination of numbers and letters in the address column, and letters arranged in a certain way for the names and addresses. You wouldn't expect to see a town named "Bob" or see "Petticoat Junction" as someone's last name.

The mind's ability to store information is much more sophisticated and structurally complex than this rudimentary representation. The attributes that are stored in the mind are unstructured objects. The objects are pictures, sounds, feelings, or actions that represent experiences or stored information. In addition, each object has the potential to be a key. Figure 4.7 shows how sales calls would be stored in memory.

The next component of intuition is linking like experiences and similar data. These relations combine attributes from completely different sales calls and help create intuition. In Figure 4.8 are two different sales calls with customers who are strong Visuals. You will notice that the two sales calls resulted in different experiences. However, unlike a key access file where there is only a single key, every attribute has the potential to be a key.

Attributes—Pictures/Sounds/Feelings/Action

	Key	Key	Key	Key
Sales Call #1	Data	Data	Experience	Data
Sales Call #2	Data	Experience	Data	Data

Figure 4.7 Sales Calls Stored in Memory

Attributes—Pictures/Sounds/Feelings/Action

Sales Call #1	Joe Smith	Visual primary	Sales call successful	Open
Sales Call #2	Jane Doe	Rejected trial close	Visual primary	Skeptical
	Key	Key	Key	Key

Figure 4.8 Two Sales Calls and Their Attributes

Retrieving and comparing the individual entries within memory is the final component of intuition. Let's pretend the salesperson from Figure 4.8 is on a new sales call and recognizes the person he is meeting with is a Visual. By recalling past sales calls that contain a visual key, he is able to access the other attributes from these sales calls, which enables him to determine the best course of action for this account. By linking attributes, you are able to search your memory and retrieve one or more records containing information that satisfies your query.

Learning continually occurs through the ongoing accumulation and consolidation of information from sales calls and interactions with people. As shown in Figure 4.9, when the model of intuition is

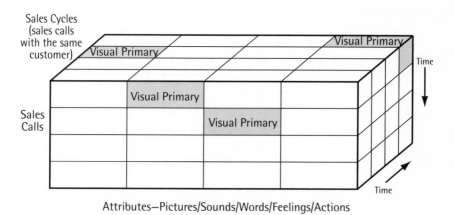

Figure 4.9 Sales Intuition Cube

finally assembled, it is a three-dimensional cube that enables instant matching of previous experiences to the current situation. From this knowledge base, salespeople can predict what will happen and what they should do in light of what they have done in the past.

INTUITION AND THE SALES CALL

How do the components of intuition actually work during a sales call? In order to answer this question we need to revisit the concept of vignettes from Chapter 2. Vignettes are short interactions between a customer and salesperson about a topic or one conversational theme. Each vignette is composed of a series of actions the Heavy Hitter or the customer may execute.

The decision about which response Heavy Hitters will give during a vignette is largely the result of their sales intuition. During a vignette, when they are asked a question or make a statement, they will provide either an "instantaneous answer" or a "calculated answer." The instantaneous answer is available immediately since it is either the recall of a logical fact or the recollection of a "flashbulb episode." Logical facts include details committed to rote memory, such as product specifications, features, and performance details. Flashbulb episodes are emotional, physical, or cerebral experiences that were so overpowering that they are permanently imprinted in short-term memory. For example, the terrorist attacks on the World Trade Center is a flashbulb memory for many people.

Meanwhile, the calculated answer is akin to solving a mathematical equation within your mind by searching and selecting the right answer or creating an appropriate answer based upon a set of rules learned from prior experiences. The vignette answer retrieval diagram (Figure 4.10) helps illustrate these concepts.

Three types of calculated answers are constructed in long-term memory. The first type uses a key attribute of the call to search previous experiences—for example, recalling previous meetings with Visuals to help answer a question asked by a Visual.

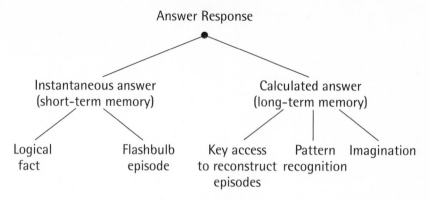

Figure 4.10 Vignette Answer Retrieval

Pattern recognition requires a more complex calculation involving multiple attributes. Let's say you were asked by an Auditory with a skeptical, detail-oriented personality how your product is different from your major competitor's. The creation of your answer would be based on previous encounters with this particular circumstance. Pattern recognition can be thought of as trying to find the what, when, where response—what you should do, when you are in this circumstance, where you need to respond to a question or execute a sales-related action.

Finally, in some instances Heavy Hitters are presented with situations they have never encountered before and they will have to use their imagination to create an answer. Making a best-guess answer requires a pattern recognition search to find closely resembling experiences plus additional hypothetical reasoning to create a new model. Obviously, this process takes the most time.

Since all types of calculated answers require processing in long-term memory, they take longer to produce. Recalling a logical fact that is resident in short-term memory is much easier than figuring out what to do next based on imagination. However, a customer expects you to respond to a question within a certain time frame. If you are face to face, this time is measured in seconds and there is a penalty for delay. The customer will perceive your answer as untruthful if the expected length of time is exceeded. This results in "selection pressure" on Heavy Hitters to produce an answer promptly. (See Figure 4.11.) Quite often, when salespeople lie to a customer it is more likely because of the pressure to produce an instantaneous answer rather than a conscious decision to mislead.

Unfortunately, many companies today are making two common mistakes. First, the majority of sales training time is spent only on memorizing logical facts about the company, product, and competitors. Little or no training is given on the development of sales intuition, when in fact a person's intuition is responsible for saying or doing the right thing at the right time. Sales intuition is responsible for all answers that are calculated from long-term memory and flashbulb episodes from short-term memory.

The second mistake is made during the hiring process. Most companies make previous experience in the same industry their main criterion for hiring. Since experienced people command the logical facts, they are assumed to be qualified candidates. I refer to this as the "trained simian" approach to hiring since even monkeys are capable of simple learning, such as distinguishing colors. A more important

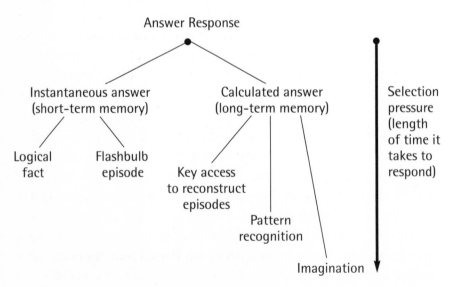

Figure 4.11 Vignette Selection Pressure

hiring criterion is how candidates respond to selection pressure. In other words, how quick-witted or fast on their feet are they, and are they able to solve complex problems in real time?

EXERCISE 7: EYE MOVEMENTS AND VAK COUNTS

You have probably been exposed to something new in this chapter. The interpretation of eye movements and understanding their relationship to word catalogs is a new set of tools to add to your sales survival kit. However, before you use them in the real world with customers and colleagues, you need some additional practice. Your first assignment is to watch four hours of television interview programs.

They could include any interview show, such as *The Tonight Show, Oprah,* or *Larry King Live.* However, watch these shows from a new perspective. Specifically, study the guests' eye movements when they are answering questions. While you are doing this, perform a VAK count and try to correlate keywords with the eye movements.

One night, I watched former secretary of state Colin Powell on a television interview program. He had previously spent his entire career in the military. Most certainly, this molded the way he speaks and his calm, cool, collected demeanor. Most government employees operate in an impersonal, bureaucratic world and their use of language reflects this. They speak with carefully selected words to form their own type of "government specification language."

However, even though they may be able to edit their words, they cannot edit the eye movements of their word catalog. If I had been negotiating a treaty with Colin Powell, knowing he has strong visual and auditory catalogs would help me "tell my story" (auditory) in the "best possible light" (visual).

Several months following the television interview, *Time* magazine published an interview with Colin Powell that confirmed my previous assessment about his wiring. Here are some of the more revealing quotations from the interview.

I would like to see our alliances strengthened. I would like to see NATO expanded. I would like to see us develop a very, very strong relationship with China. I would like to find a solution to the problems of the Middle East and the Persian Gulf . . .

In every administration, there are many voices, but the only voice I really listen to is the voice of President George W. Bush.

Let's just say, if there were another situation that approached the Rwandan level, I think in light of what has happened in the past, we'd have to take a very, very hard look at doing something.[3]

Another famous American statesman, Thomas Jefferson, said, "Knowledge is happiness. . . . Knowledge is power."[4] Learning how to use word catalogs to create rapport and determine the truthfulness of someone's communication is advantageous. Most often, power is associated with the use of physical force and the one-sided domination of someone or something else. However, Heavy Hitters achieve their power by creating a harmonious relationship with a customer and having the confidence in their product and themselves to be honest at all times. After all, it was Jefferson who also declared, "Honesty is the first chapter in the book of wisdom."[5]

CONCLUSION

Upon your birth, your brain was a tiny malleable computer. Even though all the circuitry was in place, the software had yet to be installed so its functions were extremely limited. As you experienced the world, your senses began gathering more information and turning on all the switches inside your mind. Soon you were speaking and a little while later learning to read and write.

Since those early days, you have developed sophisticated ways of cataloging the enormous amount of data you receive daily. And you are able to process and interpret this information into objects in order to catalog their relevant meaning. You can congregate haphazard information and derive meaning from seemingly nonsensical data as in the following example.

> It denos't mtater waht oredr the ltteers in a wrod are, the olny iprmoatnt tihng is taht the frist and lsat ltteer be at the rghit pclae. The rset can be a total mses and you can sitll raed it wouthit porbelm. Tihs is bcuseae the huamn mnid deos not raed ervey lteter by istlef, but the wrod as a wlohe.

Word catalogs play a very important role in how your customer thinks. They are responsible for assembling and interpreting the words they say and hear into objects. These objects consist of four separate elements: the word's lexical meaning, sensory conception, memory recollection, and psychological meaning.

For example, the lexical meaning for the word "dog" is "a four-legged animal that is closely related to a fox or wolf." If I was driving with friends and said, "Watch out! There's a dog in the street!" they would be on the lookout for a furry, four-legged creature and not expect an elephant or giraffe.

Your word catalog also adds additional dimensions of sensory meaning to the word object in the form of pictures, sounds, and feelings. My dog is a 35-pound tan cocker spaniel named Blossom. It's what I personally think of when someone mentions the word "dog."

The word catalog also associates memories and psychological meanings to an object. I still remember the day my children chose Blossom from the litter of puppies. Today, Blossom and I spend a great deal of time together. When I am working in my home office, she'll lie under my desk for hours at a time. When a stranger comes to the door, she alerts the family. When the children are roughhousing, she'll join right in. Our dog is much more than a pet; she is part of the family and in many ways like one of our children. We love her, and she loves us as only a dog can. How strange that a little word like "dog" can carry so much meaning.

CHAPTER 5

Finding the Truth

We were in search of a new vice president of marketing. Since the candidate had worked in the same market segment for the past five years, her background matched our requirements. The interviews had gone well enough with the other members of the management team, but we wanted to be very sure that we were hiring the right person. The previous vice president of marketing had lacked the aptitude to build our brand. More importantly, she had difficulty relating with other members of the company and was not integrated with the management team.

The first portion of the interview went fine. Then the candidate was asked, "What part of marketing do you enjoy?"

She answered, "Hmmm . . . I like to work with the press and analysts . . . I enjoy creating new market awareness programs and collateral . . . and I really enjoy working with the sales force." As she was answering the question she nodded her head up and down until she said, "I really like working with the sales force," when she began to shake it back and forth as if saying no. Something wasn't right.

"What specifically do you like about working with the sales force? " I asked.

She immediately gave me a "deer in the headlights" look. She fumbled for an answer because she honestly didn't have one.

That question led to a lengthy round of questioning about how she worked with others within the company. The discussion left us feeling unsatisfied, and we ultimately passed on the candidate.

My youngest daughter came home from the toy store the other day proudly displaying the "mood ring" she had purchased. She excitedly explained how the ring's color showed whether you were either happy, tense, moody, or sad. She showed me how the stone changed colors when she rubbed it. It seemed like magic to her. What she didn't know is that inside the stone was a heat-sensitive liquid crystal.

I seriously doubt a mood ring is an authentic indicator of a person's emotions since you can easily change the stone's color by standing outside or putting your hand in your pocket. Also, I know I have been happy with both warm and cold hands so temperature doesn't seem to be a dependable indicator of mood. However, it did make me start to think how helpful it would be if there were some type of mood ring you could make customers wear. This ring would change colors according to the truthfulness of their words!

In the short story about the mood ring, three types of information are presented: obvious, interpretive, and calculated. The mood ring is an example of "obvious" information. It is a tangible object that can be seen, touched, and felt. The color of the stone is "interpretative" information because it requires the observer to make a determination of the precise color. For example, what someone might refer to as turquoise, another person may call aquamarine. The cross-reference of the color to a particular emotional state is "calculated" information. If the stone is blue, we calculate that the wearer is happy, and if it is black, the person is sad. Whereas obvious information is concrete and definite, the meaning of calculated and interpreted information is more subtle and subjective.

Most salespeople recognize the obvious information presented to them by a customer during the sales cycle, such as written technical requirements and formal decision milestones. However, it's the ability to correctly recognize and interpret misleading, subtle information that enables the correct account strategy to be created. In particular, the salesperson is searching for false or contradictory information that signals the true intentions of the customer.

Everyone is familiar with the basics of body language, the physical layer of the human communication model. Body language is defined as communicating through gestures or poses. People communicate using many different parts of their bodies. Someone who is smiling at you is assumed to be friendly. Conversely, someone who is approaching you with a very serious look and fists clenched is considered a threat. Children who strike out in baseball may hunch their shoulders with shame and depression. When a home run is hit, there are "high-fives" throughout the dugout. These are just a few of the many ways we communicate nonverbal messages. However, the body language salespeople need to be able to recognize and interpret is much more subtle than these explicit examples.

In Chapter 2, we identified the six different layers of the human communication model. To review, the phonetic layer is the manner in which words are pronounced. The actual words spoken are the content layer. Words are assembled to communicate a particular message or purpose. The word catalog catalogs your life's experiences and influences your communication choices. And all of these processes are the result of a never-ending internal dialogue, or conversation, inside your conscious mind. This leads us to the final layer of the human communication model, the physical layer. In this chapter, we will study the physical layer of communication, more commonly referred to as body language.

Earlier, we learned that each of these layers may communicate knowingly or unknowingly with other layers. For example, a conversation at the content level is a purpose-driven communication that your conscious mind knowingly creates. Phonetics are then consciously applied to spoken words to create greater impact or to clarify the meaning. Telling a customer, "Yeah, we have the feature, too" is different from exclaiming to a customer, "Yes! We have that feature!" The last statement exudes confidence and excitement and was said with a different purpose.

In addition to phonetics, another form of underlying communication occurs in every conversation. It is typically not recognized as part of the communication event except when it becomes so obvious that it changes or contradicts the meaning of the words spoken. For example, the candidate for vice president of marketing was nodding her head up and down as she spoke about what she enjoyed. When she began to speak about working with the sales force, her head began to move back and forth, communicating no. In this chapter, we will review the different types of nonverbal communication and learn how to interpret them.

Your conscious mind is obsessed with benefactions. The most vital benefactions are driven by your physical well-being. If you are hungry at the moment, you may have difficulty concentrating on reading these words. If you haven't eaten for the past 24 hours, you would definitely be more interested in food than any concepts on these pages. The conscious mind is fixated with the avoidance of pain, the preservation of self, and self-gratification.

The conscious mind is on a mission to satisfy the most urgent benefactions first. As a result, it will instruct the senses to collect the relevant data needed to accomplish this urgent sortie. In this regard, typical salespeople and Heavy Hitters share the same desire and sense of urgency to close the deal. However, one of the primary differences between most salespeople and Hitters is the amount and range of data that is collected by the senses. Heavy Hitters gather data from all levels of the human communication model. Armed with this information, they are better able to determine their course of action based upon the data they have collected and past comparable experiences. By doing this, they can determine the sales strategy that offers the highest probability of winning. This process is most commonly referred to as "sales intuition."

Most likely, the Heavy Hitter's process of assimilating all these data points is not formalized. Rather, it is both a conscious and subconscious process. Although the subconscious mind is not actively assertive, it is always vigilant and capable of influencing actions. The ability to effectively send and receive information from each layer of the human communication model is a critical component for developing sales intuition. While it is easy to recognize the communication being sent consciously, the subconscious information being sent is just as expressive, but it's much harder to recognize and interpret. It is important to realize that the subconscious and conscious are communicating at all times, internally within the self and externally to others, as shown in Figure 5.1.

Each of the communication layers can also communicate both consciously and subconsciously between themselves. For example, when people lie, the subconscious mind will affect the phonetic and physical layers of communication. The pitch, tone, and volume of their voice may change along with their posture, demeanor, and skin tone. The subconscious mind is very influential. It is your subconscious mind that keeps you from falling out of your bed at night.

Most people equate physical communication with the term "body language." Unfortunately, this term has been sensationalized over the years in books on everything from dating to cosmetic surgery. However, since it is the more widely recognized term, I use it interchangeably.

Hitters want to communicate with a customer's physical layer in order to develop rapport. They are aware of a customer's body language and analyze it to ensure they are communicating effectively. They also try to understand any communication from the customer's subconscious that may be revealed physically. These unintentional messages will help them determine their chance of closing the deal.

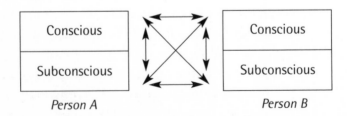

Figure 5.1 Conscious and Subconscious Communication

Heavy Hitters are always trying to understand the physical layer for four reasons:

1. Heavy Hitters know the key to developing long-term successful relationships is rapport. Just as they develop rapport at the content layer by using the customer's language, they also desire to develop rapport at the physical layer. In other words, we want rapport with the customer's body as well as her mind.

2. Heavy Hitters are continually searching for feedback on the prospect's receptivity to their solution. Body language provides another visible checkpoint that can be used to ensure everyone participating in the meeting understands and agrees with the topic of discussion.

3. Heavy Hitters want to "perceptively persuade." They want to win to satisfy not only their own benefaction but the benefaction of the customer as well. They honestly feel their solution serves the best interest of the customer. Therefore, they want to use all of the tools at their disposal to ensure the "right" solution is selected. Perceptive persuasion involves leading another person (the customer) to do something on your behalf (buy your product).

4. Customers will say things they don't mean and mean things they don't say. A survey conducted by UCLA made these startling statements about persuasion.[1] When respondents were asked to judge various speakers' performances, 7 percent said the words they used were most important, 38 percent said it was the quality of their voice, and 55 percent said it was their nonverbal communication. These results suggest that more meaning is derived from the nonverbal communication than from the actual words being said. Therefore it could be argued that it isn't what customers say during the sales call that is important, it's what they don't say.

A CAVEAT

Up to this point, you have been introduced to the fundamentals of how people communicate and how they are wired. In the remainder of the book, you will be introduced to strategies and techniques that will enable you to directly influence another person's behavior. These techniques should be used only when the customer's benefaction is best served by your solution. Heavy Hitters use perceptive persuasion to defeat their competitors because they deem them inferior.

Understanding how to influence another person is powerful knowledge. If you use this to selfishly accomplish your benefaction and not the customer's, there will be consequences. Manipulation results in remorse and vilification. It is the exact opposite of rapport. Remember the old adage that a customer who buys a product and likes it will tell 5 people, while the customer who dislikes it will tell 25.

Heavy Hitters also know their biggest competitor is time. They want to learn as soon as possible if rapport is not present. They want to know immediately if the information being discussed was not understood or agreed to by the customer. At the end of a sales call, many salespeople do not truly understand where they stand in terms of the competition. Often, customers say all the right things but do not follow up with any meaningful action. Heavy Hitters assimilate physical communication as a key part of their decision whether to continue on with the sales process.

PHYSICAL CHANGES

Many physical changes occur while we communicate. Our skin becomes flushed when we are embarrassed or mad. Our breathing becomes slower when we are relaxed and faster when we are excited. Our facial muscles become tight when we are stressed or in disagreement. The response on the outside of our bodies represents what's going on inside our minds. Our body posture indicates our comfort level in any particular situation.

Understanding the nuances of these changes is a tricky proposition. First, you cannot assume that each body movement means the same thing for everybody. For example, I worked with an individual who moves his right foot constantly during every meeting. This is his "rapport posture," or the position he assumes when he is in a receptive state to receive information. This is very different from someone who would be showing impatience by moving in the identical way.

Second, the way to understand the meaning of a physical movement is by observing the movement over time. The time period could be as long as days or as short as a few minutes. The vice president of marketing candidate was vigorously nodding her head up and down and talking enthusiastically about certain aspects of the jobs she liked. She was able to give specific examples instantaneously. She was telling the truth. When she was asked about working with the sales force, her physical behavior shifted completely.

Just like a polygraph examiner, you must establish a "control group" of movements your customer makes. You want to link a specific movement to a known meaning. By doing this, you create the default meaning of the movement. More importantly, you are trying to specifically understand if the default meaning of the movement is in congruence with the words spoken at the content layer. For example, the candidate's head nodding changed in conjunction with her statements about working with the sales force. When a person's physical communication is incongruent with (not matching) their content-level communication, then that person is not telling the truth!

IS IT THE TRUTH?

Over the years, I have had the opportunity to participate in thousands of sales calls with both typical salespeople and Hitters. A key difference between Heavy Hitters and most salespeople is their ability to determine if they are being told the truth. Truth is an interesting concept. Truth is defined as "genuine and authentic in accordance with a person's reality."

For a moment, let's put ourselves in the position of the customer. As the customer, you are going to meet with multiple vendors, watch their presentations, and read their marketing collateral. Each vendor, most likely, has equally talented, friendly, and professional salespeople who come to your office. However, you will select only one product. Given that, how will you behave with each vendor? Will you tell each one the truth? Probably not.

It is basic human nature to want to avoid confrontation. This is particularly true when you are meeting in person, face-to-face. In addition, our society has implicit guidelines of behavior. We are taught at an early age that if we have nothing nice to say, then we shouldn't say anything at all. If you (the prospect) are not interested in the product after the meeting, it is much more comfortable to tell the nonwinning vendors about your decision over the phone or just do nothing. The problem is that all of the vendors may have to continue to spend an equal amount of time and effort to win the business when a decision for one vendor was most likely made early on in the sales cycle.

Our definition of truth also includes the phrase "in accordance with a person's reality." The problem here is that multiple realities are at work. The company reality may be that product sales are disappointing and the economy has slowed. Given this reality, the previously approved project budget may have just been slashed, even though the lower-level personnel working on the project may not know of the cuts or may believe they can work around the budget issues, so they continue with their product evaluation.

Most likely, the decision to buy your product rests with a team of individuals. Since everyone has a unique map of reality, what reality—and whose—will be pervasive within the evaluation group?

TYPES OF BODY LANGUAGE

The ability to recognize and interpret a person's body language can help you validate the quality and truthfulness of the information you are receiving. Let's examine the seven major types of body language we use and observe daily as salespeople.

1. Handshakes
2. Hand movements
3. Breathing
4. Facial expressions
5. Skin color
6. Body posture
7. Speech

It could be argued that a person's handwriting is also a valid form of body language. Since the brain determines the content and form of what is written, handwriting also reflects certain personality tendencies, such as orientation to detail. However, in the world of sales today, handwriting has been almost eliminated by laptops and personal digital assistants. Therefore, it is not a major point of our discussion.

Handshakes

How many times have you participated in a flawed handshake at the beginning of the meeting? Perhaps the other person was more aggressive and you were too limp-wristed? Perhaps one person grabbed the other person's fingers instead of the palm? If you were at fault, this event probably ruined your ability to concentrate for a few moments. Undoubtedly, you planned that when the meeting ended, you were going to correct the earlier mistake with a solid handshake.

You can learn a lot from someone's handshake. Here are some observations. Kinesthetic people tend to shake hands a little longer than Visuals and Auditories. Dominant Kinesthetics will put their other hand on top of the handshake or pat the person on the shoulder or arm. Visuals tend to shake hands with a faster up and down movement. Recessive Kinesthetics tend to not make eye contact when they shake, almost as if they want to end the unpleasant process as soon as possible.

One of the more obvious signs of a person being nervous is the temperature of the skin. Colder hands may indicate nervousness (unless the person has just been outside). We are all familiar with the term "sweaty palms," which indicates a person is in a stressful situation. It is difficult to know what to do after you've shaken someone's wringing-wet hand. Such people know they are nervous, and if they see you wipe your hand off, they will feel even worse. It's human nature to want to make people feel comfortable, not to embarrass them.

Culture plays a role in handshakes. In Japan, the handshake is replaced by a card presentation. A handshake in New York City is different from a handshake in Atlanta. Some people overaccentuate the handshake. They'll lock your hand into their viselike grip or hold your hand too long, as if you were shackled together. They're either insecure or trying to establish an overpowering position. Neither of these actions helps build rapport.

Save an imprint of the handshake from the beginning of the meeting and compare it with the handshake at the end of the meeting. Was it more sensual or colder? Longer or shorter? Was there a change in the amount of direct eye contact? Was there more than one handshake? Did the person actually pat you on the back or touch you in some other way during the handshake? Handshakes provide instant feedback about how a meeting went. Like a kiss with your lover before boarding a plane, the longer and more emotional, the better. From now on, be conscious of handshakes.

Hand Movements

Hand movements will vary based on a person's word catalog. Visuals and Kinesthetics will use hand movements while speaking much more frequently than Auditories. The position of the Visuals' hands will be high in context to their bodies, usually at the chest or above. They will use their hands to point to things. They want to make sure you see whatever it is that is important to them. The fingers of their hands are usually straight or pointed out. They have no problem extending their arms and hands as far as they can because they want you to see the "big picture." They will use their hands as an imaginary marker to help draw a picture of the content they are trying to communicate. Visuals' hand movements will be quicker because they are exploding with thoughts that must be communicated quickly.

Kinesthetics will make "deep" hand gestures while they communicate their feelings. That is, their gestures will be lower on their bodies in accordance with their feelings on a subject. The fingers of their hands will be in a closed or interlocked position. They will be touching and holding their bodies while they speak. They may use their hands to cradle their heads or use their arms to hug their bodies. Their hand movements tend to be slower and more deliberate than Visuals' or Auditories' because formulating feelings takes more time than creating pictures or assembling words.

Auditory people are listening to themselves speak. This alone is a full-time job. Therefore, they will use fewer hand movements. When they do use them, they tend to keep their hands closer to their bodies. Another term for this is "dinosaur hands," since they are being held like the arms of a *Tyrannosaurus rex.* Their hand gestures will tend to be at the middle of the body, lower than Visuals' hand gestures but higher than Kinesthetics'. Their hand movements also tend to keep time with or be at the pace of their voice tempo.

Breathing

You may not have noticed this, but people actually breathe quite differently. Obviously, people breathe at a different pace depending on whether or not they are performing a physical activity. The aspect of breathing that we are interested in, however, is the changes in breathing patterns while customers are in their normal state (when most business meetings take place), and these changes can be quite subtle. If a customer is wearing a suit or jacket or if glancing at the customer's chest would be considered inappropriate, breathing patterns can be observed by watching people's shoulders rise as they inhale and exhale.

Different breathing paces can be observed by watching different areas of the abdomen. Some people breathe fast and some slowly. Some people have a repetitive rhythm to their breathing: deep breath, pause, deep breath, pause. Some people's breaths are quick and shallow. Visuals tend to breathe shallower and higher in the chest, while Kinesthetics breathe deeper and lower in the belly. Auditories' breathing is somewhere in between.

How someone breathes is really not that important. What is important is trying to spot a change in a breathing pattern. A change is a signal that a person's internal communication state has changed and the level of rapport has fluctuated. Meeting new people is stressful and people's breathing will speed up under stress. As they relax, breathing slows. At this point, Heavy Hitters calibrate the pace of the customer's breathing and use it as the baseline to monitor if the respiration is speeding up, slowing down, becoming deeper or shallower, or staying the same. This is valuable information to help identify a customer's state of rapport. People experiencing rapport are relaxed and their breathing reflects this.

Facial Expressions

Regardless of what country you may travel to and what language is spoken, you are still able to communicate with the locals via your universal communication mechanism, otherwise known as your face. Your face is the only part of the body where muscle is directly attached to skin, thereby making possible a wide range of diverse expressions. Since you have been using facial expressions successfully for all of your life, you are already a trained expert.

Our faces represent the emotions we are experiencing. When I am happy, I smile. When I am serious, I may lower my eyebrows. When I am startled, I open my eyes wider. When I am in pain, my entire face tightens. When I am very sad, I cry. We are all familiar with reading these types of highly visible facial expressions. However, in the business world, people rarely express their true emotions outwardly. Facial muscles are used more to inhibit the public display of emotion rather than to show it. Therefore, a salesperson has only small variations of a customer's facial expressions to study.

EXERCISE 8: FACIAL EXPRESSIONS

Let's do a short facial expression exercise. I am going to ask you to think of different emotions and to make the corresponding facial expression. (Don't worry if you are in a public area. Those around you will think you are reading a very interesting book!) While you are making the expressions, pay particular attention to the following: Is your forehead getting smaller or larger? Are the corners of your eyes becoming tight or relaxed? Are your eyebrows rising or lowering? Is your nose moving up or down? Are your nostrils flaring? Are your cheeks rising or lowering? Becoming flat or round? Are your lips, chin, and jaw becoming relaxed or tight? Are your ears and hair moving up and down? Ideally, you want to do this exercise in front of a mirror. Try to hold each expression for five seconds.

Happy	Sad
Frustrated	Hurt
Scared	Laughing
Ecstatic	Peaceful

If you earnestly did this experiment, you may have learned something new. First, you may have become aware of some subtle feature of your face that you hadn't noticed before. We see our faces a lot but usually with only one or two expressions, such as ones we use while shaving, putting on makeup, or smiling for a photo.

Second, as you made each new facial expression, you may have felt a subtle impact on your emotional state since our feelings are "connected" to our faces. With some practice, you will be able to recognize small facial expressions and be able to link the facial expressions back to an individual's communication layers. This is how gamblers tell their opponent is holding four aces.

Fortunately, you have already had a lot of practice recognizing facial expressions. If you are married, you can probably tell the exact emotional state of your spouse with a quick glance. Some people call this intuition. Actually, after numerous interactions, you have categorized every possible combination of facial expressions and have developed a behavioral model. You can also do this with your customers. It's an instantaneous feedback loop to help you understand their reaction to what you are presenting.

Skin Color

To a lesser extent than facial expressions, skin color can also give subtle clues to a person's emotional state. In a tense meeting, for example, you may witness the skin tone of someone who is scared or unnerved turn ashen gray. When successful sales calls conclude, the participants' skin tone may seem warmer. However, this observation may be influenced by your perception of the meeting's results.

Body Posture

A person's body posture is one of the primary communication features of the physical communication layer. Regardless of the activity (sitting, standing, walking, or sleeping), a person's body posture sends a message to the outside world. People are normally in a continual pose, and the manner in which they hold and shape their figures reflects their mental state.

The airport makes a great laboratory to study and interpret body posture. At the check-in lines, study the different ways people stand. Some will stand with a defiant or impatient posture, with arms akimbo (hands on hips and elbows turned outward). Some will slouch in quiet resignation, and others will stand comfortably. Watch people walk. Some people saunter gracefully while others trudge as if they were carrying the weight of the world. Some wander and some are on a march, as if they have to reach the summit of K2 by nightfall.

Airplanes are also good places to reflect on the importance of understanding body language. Once, I boarded a Monday morning flight at 6:45 A.M. from Los Angeles to San Jose. I had planned to work on the plane to prepare for my meetings that day. I boarded early, sat down in my window seat, and started working. The seat next to me was empty at the time. A few minutes later, a business-man approached my row. On this day, I didn't have time for small talk, and I used my body position to communicate I wasn't interested in talking. I did this by "closing" my body posture. I had my arms on the tray table, head down, and my body faced straight ahead. I was intensely focused on my work.

However, it would have been incredibly rude not to acknowl-edge the person who would be sitting beside me for the next hour. As he sat down, I gave him a very quick smile of acknowledgment. It wasn't a warm and friendly "How are you doing today?" smile. Rather, it was an acknowledgment of his presence, an "I come in peace" kind of smile.

He recognized my presence briefly with a very similar greeting. He said nothing and I was relieved. Based on that small physical inter-action, he communicated the following message: "I am a seasoned traveler who also has a lot of work to do and I don't plan on bother-ing you." He unpacked his briefcase and immediately started to work.

Even though we did not exchange a single word during the flight, there was very good rapport between us. We both shared the same benefaction and helped the other accomplish it. It would have been uncomfortable for either of us to explain, "I'm too busy to talk." Even this small exchange would have taken time and energy away from accomplishing our more important tasks. I know he felt the same way that I did. You can have meaningful communication between people solely using body language.

Recently, I had another interesting "conversation" on an airplane. After a long day of meetings, I sat down in my seat on a flight that was barely one-third full. Unlike my closed posture in the previous example, I was sitting normally, as one usually does on an airplane. I had the window seat and a young woman sat down next to me in the middle seat. I greeted her with the customary, "Hello." However, it was an awkward situation since there were so many open seats, and we were going to be crammed together for the next couple of hours.

For the next few minutes, she continually looked at all the open seats. I could almost hear her internal dialogue telling herself that it would be "okay to move." As the departure time approached, her scanning of the open seats became more frequent and urgent.

Finally, she stood up and blurted to me, "You don't stink or anything, but I'm going to move over there." While I did not laugh aloud, she clearly was embarrassed over what she had said. She gave me a facial expression that said, "I don't know where that came from!" and quickly collected her belongings and moved.

What happened? Well, she had just finished an intense internal discussion about whether it would be rude to move. After all, she had rationalized, there were plenty of open seats. However, she didn't want me to interpret her moving as an insult. Most likely, what she said to me were her exact words from her internal dialogue. The pressure mounted for her to make a decision because the plane's door would soon be closed for takeoff. Once that happened, she probably felt she would be "stuck" in this seat for the entire flight. She acted impulsively, making a quick final decision to move. However, I don't believe she intended to offend me. She simply repeated her internal dialogue word for word. Most likely, she was a Kinesthetic. The fact she used a kinesthetic word, "stink," also suggests this.

What can you learn from this story? First, by observing the physical communication layer, you can anticipate someone's future actions. When the young woman was sitting in the plane, she was not relaxed like the rest of the passengers. She was agitated, scanning the open seats. This was incongruent with the natural sitting position on an airplane. Something wasn't right, and I needed to be on guard.

Also, observing the physical communication layer helps to explain verbal communication. Let's assume I had not paid any attention to her movements. She would have blindsided me with her comment. How would I have interpreted it?

BODY LANGUAGE AND GROUP MEETINGS

In sales, we are interested in three main aspects of body language. First, we want to interpret people's state of receptiveness to our ideas. Second, we want to observe body language to help validate our assumptions about people's primary, secondary, and recessive word catalogs. And third, we want to match their body language with the content of their spoken words in order to identify congruencies or potential incongruencies.

The sales world normally uses one of three prevalent meeting positions: when all the participants at a meeting are sitting, when one person is making a classroom-style presentation to a group of people who are sitting, and when two or more people are standing in a conversation. These settings cover the majority of sales situations and are worth studying in more detail.

Group dynamics are very complex. Earlier, we introduced the concept of technical specification language and discussed how technical people's position in their group is determined by the technical content of the words they use. In group meetings, the pecking order is also reflected in where a person sits. Whether at a round table or in a classroom setting, the person with the most influence will choose a dominant place to sit. For example, at a long, boardroom-style table, these people will be found at the center of the table, and a spot will be left for them there even if they are late. If the table is shorter, dominant people will sit at one of the ends, while their subordinates will cluster around them.

At a round table, the dominant position may be the seat facing the door or the one with the best view outside. In a large classroom-style setting, dominant people will sit in the front of the room or in the most visible position. This is the position that provides the best location to see the presentation and to be seen by the audience. Occasionally, dominant people will sit in the very last row so they can be in the position of leaving whenever they please. Regardless of the table type, where a person sits is of primary importance.

Now that you know where influential people will sit, let's examine their posture. Most meetings start with people in a "closed" posture versus an "open" posture. A closed posture is when the body is folded up on itself. Probably the most familiar one is when the arms are crossed on the chest. More subtle closed positions are legs crossed, ankles crossed, hands interlocked on the table, or both hands touching the face. A person in a closed position may also face away from the focus point of the meeting or presenter.

A closed posture does not necessarily indicate a negative attitude. Rather, it is a natural position of skepticism that shifts to an open position as rapport is created. The open position represents the best environment to communicate your message. When people change to an open position, it may be as obvious as their uncrossing their arms and lowering them to the table. More likely, the change will be a lot more subtle. They may relax the tightness of the parts of the body that are folded: arms, hands, legs, ankles, feet, and even lips. They could also move their folded arms from their chest to their waist. Or they could switch position, such as going from legs crossed with the right leg on top to legs crossed with the left leg on top. Watch for these subtle changes and make a mental notation of when they happen. Who was speaking? What was the topic? Was there a variation in facial expression that accompanied the move?

People are opening and closing their positions all the time throughout a meeting. It's important to identify a person's closed and open state and watch for patterns of reoccurrence during the meeting. Heavy Hitters know they need to investigate why they lost a person's open state and will pause to ask the person if she has any questions or try to solicit an opinion on the topic.

Heavy Hitters are constantly surveying all of the meeting participants to see if they are receptive to the presentation. The goal is to uncover any confusion and objections as early as possible. They do not want objections to remain hidden until it is too late to address them successfully. Even if someone else is making the presentation, Hitters do not relax but carefully and continually examine everyone's physical state. Therefore, Heavy Hitters always take a position in a meeting that affords them the best viewpoint to observe all of the meeting participants.

Think about the last time you were in an elevator with a group of strangers. You assumed the natural elevator position where everyone is facing forward toward the door, watching the floor numbers. No one speaks. Everyone is on hold, almost as if in a trance. This is the acceptable body position in an elevator.

Standing conversation also has a natural position. An acceptable distance is kept between the talkers. A comfortable way of presenting the body is found. Usually, it's by mimicking the other person's posture. However, frequently an ongoing negotiation is taking place between the body positions of the people engaged in a conversation. Explaining this negotiation process requires the introduction of three concepts known as pacing, mirroring, and leading.

PACING, MIRRORING, AND LEADING

I drive to the local mountains to go boating during the summer and ski in winter. The trip takes several hours each way. While I am driving, my speed or pace will be determined by several factors besides the speed limit. Usually, I will drive at the pace of the car in front of me, keeping a distance between that car and mine that I feel comfortable with. I will automatically maintain this distance until the pace of the car in front of me becomes too fast or too slow. In either case, this will cause our driving rapport to break.

Sometimes, I will keep pace to the music on the radio and find myself speeding up to the tempo of the song. Suddenly, I'll be jolted into action upon realizing that I am driving faster than the legal limit.

Pacing can be thought of as the natural process of adjusting your tempo to your environment. In both examples, my behavior was being influenced by something else (the car in front of me and the music), and even though I am mindful of how I am driving, I'm not solely concentrating on it. It's as if I have passed the responsibility to my subconscious mind.

On remote roads, cars tend to cluster together instead of being evenly dispersed. It seems that the cars act together as a group and will accelerate or slow down together. I like to drive in these groups because I believe it reduces my odds of getting a traffic ticket. Therefore, when I drive on long stretches of highway, I will adjust my speed to fit into one of these groups of cars. This is "mirroring," which can be thought of as the conscious act of modifying your behavior to fit your surroundings. As opposed to pacing, where your subconscious mind is in control, mirroring requires a physical effort at the direction of the conscious mind.

The car in front of me is also "leading" my behavior. Let's assume I have been mirroring the car in front of me for the last 10 minutes. Suddenly, the driver swerves to the right. I will follow her lead and prepare to swerve to the right, even though I have not actually seen the danger. Leading is the process of influencing another person's action by yours. In this example, if the other driver had been driving erratically as if under the influence of alcohol, I would not have swerved. However, for the past 10 minutes she had demonstrated she was a capable driver. She created a "driver's rapport" so that when she swerved, I followed. Leading requires rapport.

Let's pretend we are driving on a desert highway and see a group of cars in front of us. First, we mirror the speed of the group to stay with them. Once we are part of the pack, we naturally keep the pace to maintain our position. After many miles of driving within the pack, we decide to lead the group by gradually speeding up and taking the pole position. Now all the cars behind us have to mirror our speed.

In terms of the sales call, Heavy Hitters will mirror and pace a customer's speed and tempo to help establish rapport, for example, by mirroring the customer's posture and maintaining the same tempo or pace of breathing. Once rapport is established in conjunction with the dialogue of the meeting, they lead the customer into an even deeper rapport. The customer relaxes, lowers her defensive guard against the salesperson, and an even more meaningful dialogue takes place. The ability to consciously develop a formalized process of pacing, mirroring, and leading and integrating these actions naturally into sales meetings is an extremely powerful sales tool.

Most likely, the Heavy Hitter doesn't have a formalized process to accomplish this. It comes naturally. Salespeople with strong kinesthetic catalogs do this instinctively. However, this process can be learned by anyone with any word catalog.

Heavy Hitters use pacing, mirroring, and leading to gain rapport with their customer. They are constantly monitoring the customer's physical communication—handshakes, hand movements, breathing, facial expressions, and body posture. Hitters know that by changing their style to match the customer's, they will create more effective communication because the customer does not have to expend additional effort to translate the Hitters' message.

Mirroring breathing styles is the first step to helping you create rapport because it makes you recreate the customer's world with your body. If someone breathes slowly, you have no choice but to slow down the pace of your speech and movements along with your breathing. If a person breathes faster than you, your actions will naturally speed up.

Mirroring body posture is accomplished by making a subtle reflection of the customer. The most obvious mirroring is a direct reflection, like the opposite image in a mirror. For example, when someone sits with legs crossed, you sit in the identical position with your legs crossed oppositely. Or you cross your arms tightly to your chest, in the exact opposite position of your counterpart during a conversation while standing.

However, this type of mirroring is too obvious and can potentially be perceived as patronizing. Rather, the mirroring we want to use is much more discreet. Instead of crossing your legs to directly mirror someone, cross your legs at the ankles or even cross your arms. Instead of standing with your arms tightly folded, cross your arms in a looser fold at the waist or stand with your legs crossed.

Let's think about handshakes in the context of mirroring. You start a handshake using a medium grip and instantaneously react to the other person's. If her grip is firmer, you grip harder, and vice versa. The length of the handshake and degree of hand motion you use are also equally matched to the other person's. You have instinctively been doing this mirroring for your entire career.

Assuming you have been successfully mirroring your customer, now it's time to test whether you have rapport by leading. Leading can be thought of as the process of using your actions to guide another person's behavior. Let's assume that you are 15 minutes into a meeting. You have been successfully mirroring the customer's breathing and body positions. You feel you have gained rapport and now want to test if this is true. Slowly, you start varying your breathing, and the other person follows your lead. Slowly, you change your body position, and the other person changes as well. It's just like the example of taking the pole position, leading the cars through the desert.

Through the process of leading, you can determine the level of rapport that exists between you and your customers. If they don't follow you, it doesn't necessarily mean there's a problem. It's normal for people to fall in and out of rapport during meetings. Simply start mirroring again.

Most importantly, through the process of leading, you can influence a person's state to be more open or receptive to your message. Earlier, we discussed how people are opening and closing their body postures throughout meetings. A Hitter's intuition is constantly scanning for closed positions. When it senses someone is closed, it becomes curious and wants to know why. It initiates the investigative process by asking questions or soliciting the opinion of the person in the closed position. The goal of this questioning is to understand what the person's internal dialogue is saying.

Remember, people are always communicating at the physical layer (whether consciously or subconsciously). Even your position while sleeping broadcasts important information about your personality, according to a recent study by the Sleep Assessment and Advisory Service.[2] The study suggests that if you sleep in the fetal position you tend to be sensitive. Sleeping flat on your back with arms at your sides indicates you are reserved, and sleeping flat on your stomach with arms at your head indicates gregariousness. Sleeping on your side reflects an easygoing personality, and sleeping flat on your stomach with arms and legs outstretched like a starfish means you're unassuming.

Observing and understanding the physical layer will enable you to validate whether a person is in an open or closed state. It also works in conjunction with your content-level dialogue to move someone from a closed state to an open state.

MIRRORING AND LEADING CASE STUDY

The best way to understand the concepts of physical communication is to see how these techniques can be applied in a real-world scenario. Let's return to the story of an actual sales meeting recounted at the beginning of Chapter 2 and describe how pacing, mirroring, and leading influenced the meeting results.

The meeting was held in a small rectangular room on the lower floor of an old brick building. The layout of the room was not conducive to a presentation for a group of people. It was narrow and cluttered with obsolete computers. At first, we were unsure which wall would serve as our projector screen.

The sales team consisted of Karl, a local field sales representative, his presales engineer, and me. The customer consisted of the technical team leaders, Mark and Beth, and their manager, Bart. While Karl had had several telephone conversations with Mark about the company's technical environment, this was our first face-to-face meeting. Mark and Beth entered the room first and took their seats. There was small talk before the meeting began among Karl, Mark, and Beth. Mark and Beth seemed at ease.

Bart entered a couple of minutes later. Immediately, Mark and Beth assumed a more formal body posture. Clearly, Bart was in charge. Bart's demeanor also communicated that he was a busy person. He threw himself into the open chair next to Mark and Beth. His posture plainly indicated that his time was valuable and suggested he had better things to do. I assumed from this hurried behavior that this meeting was probably more of an interruption than a scheduled event. While he was physically at the meeting, mentally he was somewhere else. It was obvious that we would have very little time to impress him and get our message across.

The narrowness of the room made conversation with others difficult. From my seat, I couldn't see Bart, nor could he see me. At this point, I announced that I wouldn't be able to view the presentation from my seat and moved to the open chair next to Bart. Karl (the salesperson) was anxious to begin the meeting, but we needed to get some information about Bart in order to try to develop some receptivity to our message.

Just before Karl commenced the meeting, I had a chance to ask, "Bart, how long have you been with the company?" On the surface, this question seems innocent enough, and Bart answered, "Over 20 years. I started out of New Jersey." His answer was very informative from several different aspects. With 20 years of tenure, I surmised, he probably has both political and business savvy. He must know the political structure of the company and must have worked on many different projects. Therefore, he should know how to evaluate vendors, their products, and the process to procure them. This was great content-level information.

When Bart answered the question, his eyes went up and to the right for an instant. As you know from Chapter 4, this is the eye movement of a Visual. Although you cannot make a conclusion about a person's primary catalog from one question, this gave me more information than I previously had. I suspected he was a Visual primary.

When he volunteered his origins, it gave me the opportunity to ask another natural question. "Where did you grow up?" I asked. Once again, on the content level, this seems like a very natural follow-up question. However, it is actually a very complex question because it can be interpreted on several different levels.

His content-level answer was two words, "New Jersey." Again, his eyes momentarily went up and to the right, which provided further evidence that his primary word catalog was visual.

However, the question had another important aspect.

When I asked Bart where he grew up, for a split second he physically had to access his catalog to remember the experience by either recreating a mental picture, a feeling, or a sound about where he grew up. To recreate the experience, he actually had to regress back to when he was growing up (at least for a moment, anyway). Now, I didn't know whether Bart had a pleasant or unpleasant childhood. However, when I asked the question, I knew two responses would happen.

First, through this regression, his current frame of mind would be altered, albeit slightly. If he had a happy childhood, most likely it would affect his current state positively and make him slightly more receptive to our presentation. On the other hand, recalling an unhappy childhood would certainly not help us. Second, by having him regress back to when he was growing up, he would offer additional insights about his word catalog.

His reaction to the question was revealing. He gave only a two-word response; however, he communicated a lot. As he regressed to get his childhood experience, his eyes went up and to the right, where he saw a picture of something (perhaps his family, house, or school). Then, his eyes went down and to the right (the kinesthetic position), where he momentarily experienced a positive feeling. I interpreted it as positive because his facial tone relaxed slightly, and his next two breaths were a little deeper and slower than his previous ones.

Unlike people searching for something specific, like the best day of their life, he also had to interpret what the phrase "grow up" meant. Did it mean where he was born, where he spent his boyhood, or where he spent his years as a teenager? Perhaps he lived in several different places and had to select the best answer. Since his eye movements were very rapid, I had to pay very close attention or I would have missed them.

These two questions were purposely asked to gain rapport. I was trying to get him to slow down and change the way he was thinking prior to our presentation. Also, these two questions had another benefit. Most people enjoy talking about themselves, and I wanted him to know that we were interested in him. We still had a long way to go to gain rapport with him, but at least we were ready to start the meeting.

What if he had responded differently? If he was raised in an unhappy home or suffered some trauma when he was a youth, most likely he would have tensed up even more. At that point, my response would have been to "mirror" his experience. I could have said something like, "I grew up in Los Angeles and hated it." But since his response was positive, I said, "I was in Princeton last Halloween. It was beautiful."

The meeting began with Karl's confirming what he had learned about the customer's environment from his previous phone calls with Mark. Mark answered most of Karl's questions and Bart participated very little. He sat with his arms crossed at his chest, his right leg crossed over the left. He frequently looked up at the ceiling. This would make any salesperson more nervous, and Karl became slightly flustered. I started mirroring Bart's breathing rate and the shallowness of his breaths. I mirrored his closed position, with my hands folded on top of my notebook, my pencil in my right hand, and my legs crossed at the ankles. I also started a VAK count of the meeting's participants. It would later validate my assessment of Bart's catalogs as visual, kinesthetic, and auditory.

After pacing his breathing for a few minutes, I was ready to check to see if we had developed any rapport. To do this, I started leading him by slowing down my breathing. His breathing followed. "Ah, we're making some progress," I said to myself.

The meeting format consisted of Karl presenting the company overview followed by a technical presentation from his presales engineer. I knew the company overview would be challenging, as Karl was an Auditory and he was also relatively new to the company. Because his presales engineer was a Visual, I knew this portion of the presentation would fare better with Bart.

Given this scenario, my internal dialogue told me also to undertake three tasks. First, I would continue to do everything in my power to improve Bart's receptiveness to our presentation. Second, throughout the meeting, I would observe the openings and closings of the posture of each of the meeting participants and further investigate them to find out why they were occurring. And finally, I would serve as Bart's personal interpreter to translate Karl's auditory presentation into Bart's visual world. I would be illustrating Karl's pitch. When Karl made an important comment, I would put it into Bart's language. If Karl said, "Our customers tell us all the time we have great support," I would reiterate his point by saying, "I see reports on all of our support cases, and the average time to fix the problem is two hours."

As the presentation started, Bart's right leg was still crossed over his left leg, and his foot moved every two to three seconds. While mirroring his breathing, I began to tap my pencil in time with his foot movements. After a few minutes of tapping my pencil in rhythm with his foot, once again I took the lead. I slowed down the time between taps. He slowed, too. I stopped, and he stopped.

At this point, I felt sufficient physical rapport had been established. However, Bart still wasn't actively participating in the meeting. It was now time to test the depth of our rapport. I yawned, and he soon followed. I frequently will use a yawn during presentations or meetings as a checkpoint for rapport. If someone yawns when you do, you can assume they are relatively comfortable. A few more minutes of mirroring passed. Then I took my left hand from the table and slowly held it to my left cheek. A couple of moments later, Bart uncrossed his left hand and held it to his ear. We were making great progress. I knew he was listening!

A minute or so later, I uncrossed my legs, leaned forward, and put my arms on the table. A few moments later, Bart uncrossed his legs, leaned forward, and put his arms on the table. From that point on, his participation in the meeting increased. He began asking questions and sharing his opinions. He stayed the entire length of the meeting, which was over an hour and a half.

During this meeting with Bart, my internal dialogue was constantly active. I was listening to the presenter and the other participants and inserting myself in the flow of the conversation. I was identifying the closed and open states of the participants and investigating why. I was planning what I would say next and managing the process of building rapport with Bart. Obviously, I was multitasking many different physical and mental activities. Most importantly, I wasn't solely focused on or exclusively listening to the content of the words being spoken (a frequent mistake of an inexperienced salesperson). I was cognizant of the entire spectrum of communication taking place. A Hitter's internal dialogue is so fully developed that it can do multiple tasks instinctively, intuitively, and naturally. It takes practice, but it can be learned.

You can perform exercises to help build this skill set. At your next meeting, choose one person and spend the entire meeting mirroring and leading the breathing of that person. Similarly, in other meetings, pick a body position, such as a position of a person's hands or feet, and mirror it along with breathing through the entire meeting. Continually add new layers of sophistication to your mirroring and leading. You can even mirror how a person speaks!

Speech

With thousands of different characters, Mandarin Chinese is one of the most difficult languages to learn. Scans taken of the brains of people speaking Mandarin verify that it actually takes more brainpower to speak than English.[3] Unlike English, where words require precise pronunciation, the meaning of a Mandarin word actually depends upon how it is enunciated. While Americans associate the word "Tang" with the famous orange drink that was used in space, in Mandarin it can either mean "sugar," "soup," or "hot" depending on tonal enunciation.

While the pronunciation of our language isn't as dynamic as Mandarin, tone of voice, speed, and volume do convey meaning in subtle ways. In fact, speech is one of the most interesting and revealing aspects of body language. People's primary catalog and the strength of their secondary catalog will greatly affect their manner of speech.

SPEAKING CHARACTERISTICS OF AUDITORIES

Auditories are actually talking to themselves and tend to speak in repetitious patterns. The pattern could be melodic or more like Morse code. The Morse code–type pattern tends to be monotone. Certain words are enunciated in the pattern. In the following examples, all the "dots" are enunciated in a similar way, and all the "dashes" are accented in a different way:

- We are committed to your satisfaction.
  (Dot...dot...dash...dot...dot...dash)

- We guarantee high performance and availability.
  (Dot...dash...dot...dash...dot...dash)

- Some Auditories speak in a monotone voice.
  (Dot...dot...dot...dot...dot...dot...dot)

Other Auditories have speech patterns that are more melodic. Their sentences are more wavelike. Word sizes represent the "crest" of the wave and vary in pitch, tone, or even pronunciation.

- We guarantee high *performance* and availability.

- We are *committed* to your *satisfaction.*

Auditories tend to be very proficient masters of the technical specification language, the nonpersonal, androgynous, technical talk used in the customer's industry. In Chapter 3, we introduced the concept of VAK keywords. These keywords are nouns, adjectives, and verbs that reflect a person's word catalog wiring. Auditories tend to not "leak" or show their word catalogs through the use of VAK keywords as much as Kinesthetics or Visuals. However, when their secondary catalog is kinesthetic, more leakage or VAK keywords will be embedded in their conversations.

Auditories also tend to quote what they have been told by others. They will also quote themselves in their conversations.

Here are more examples of auditory sentence structures:

- "Our meeting went great. Bob told us, 'We did a great job and everyone is excited to work with us.'"

- "The meeting was going really well and then 'Boom, boom, boom,' we were asked some really tough questions."

- "And I started to ask myself, 'Are they still a partner of ours?'"

SPEAKING CHARACTERISTICS OF VISUALS

The speech pattern of a Visual is quite different from that of an Auditory. Strong Visuals are being bombarded with pictures inside their brains. As a result, it is very difficult for them to keep the pace of the words being said synchronized with the pictures being created in their minds. This condition is somewhat analogous to a computer's CPU (central processing unit) having to wait for the mechanical movements of the disk drive to be complete before it can further process any information. As a result, strong Visuals are constantly trying to speed up the mechanical process of speaking. Therefore, they usually talk faster than Auditories or Kinesthetics. Here are examples of sentence structures of strong Visuals:

- "WE ARE COMMITTED TO YOUR SATISFACTION."

- "VISUALSHAVEALOTTOSAYANDASHORTTIME-TOSAYIT."

To Visuals, words are an interruption of the pictures or ideas in their minds. They have to get them out of their internal dialogue as fast as possible because thoughts are constantly getting stacked up. Therefore, they speak with energy and a sense of urgency.

In presentation situations they tend to speak even faster. Their stream of speech may be interrupted only by the necessity to breathe. Have you ever heard someone insert "um" in every other sentence?

Visuals have a tendency to do this more than Auditories or Kines-thetics. These filler words are basically used as a checkpoint to syn-chronize the images in their minds with their spoken dialogue. The um's are also said at the same speed and tone as the other words. Conversely, a Kinesthetics says "um" much slower and in a deeper tone than the other words. Their um's are actually synchronized with their feelings, and this takes more time. You also may notice them looking down when they say "um."

Visuals tend to not only talk faster but also louder. Visuals are painting a picture for their audience. When they are telling their story, they are trying to make the language represent all the detail and complexity of a picture. You've heard the saying "A picture is worth a thousand words." For Visuals, it's true, and they have to commu-nicate all of the thousand words to convey the picture they are see-ing. Therefore, Visuals are the most talkative, too!

Having to always communicate a thousand words at a time cre-ates a lot of energy. When Visuals are making presentations, they will move back and forth across the stage. Auditories will stand in one place or a small space, and Kinesthetics will shift their weight back and forth. Visuals' arm gestures are more exaggerated since they are illustrating a picture with their bodies. They'll outstretch their arms as far as they can horizontally (so that they resemble a cross) to make their point. Kinesthetics are more likely to make the same point by holding their hands vertically (with one hand over the head and one hand at the waist). Auditories hold their hands closer to their bodies and will use arm gestures sparingly.

While making a PowerPoint presentation, Visuals will point at the screen frequently and may use an index finger like a flashlight. Kinesthetics will extend an arm, using the entire hand or palm. Audi-tories will most likely point an arm (in the locked position of a push-up) straight in front of the body or from the shoulder horizontally. You will notice that Visuals' arms are held higher on the body or over the head. Kinesthetics will cradle or hold themselves with their arms and hold them lower, at the waist.

SPEAKING CHARACTERISTICS OF KINESTHETICS

Most people wrongly assume that people with a kinesthetic primary catalog are overly emotional, introverted, or extroverted. This may or may not be the case. Being kinesthetic simply means that they catalog their experiences in terms of feelings. However, people who are strongly kinesthetic will reflect this in their speech patterns, and in turn their personality will be affected.

Kinesthetics tend to speak slower than Auditories and Visuals. Their speech is slower because they are frequently checking their feelings while they speak. Their speech pattern may also be frequently accentuated by their breathing, which is deeper than that of Visuals and Auditories. When speaking to a group, they tend to talk directly to a single person in the audience, while Visuals will constantly scan the audience. When talking about issues, Kinesthetics are more likely to associate a person with the issue or task at hand.

Strong Kinesthetics tend to be more dramatic in their speech patterns and inflections. They commonly insert pauses and voice inflections. Unlike Auditories with their Morse code patterns, Kinesthetics are "feeling" the words they are speaking. As a result, their tone of voice tends to be lower. This is because they are constantly validating and comparing their feelings with what they are hearing and saying.

Here are examples of sentence structures of strong Kinesthetics:

- *"We* are committed to *your* satisfaction!"

- *"I enjoyed* meeting with *you."*

Every communication with Kinesthetics is personal. The emphasis is on the words "we," "your," "I," "enjoyed," and "you" as they directly correlate with the Kinesthetics' feelings. For example, their interpretation of "we" is actually "myself and my company," and their interpretation of "you" is "you and your company." These words represent very personal feelings, so their enunciation is likely to be slower or in a lower tone than the other words in the sentence. Kinesthetics' speech has other patterns. For example, Kinesthetics' voices will tend to rise at the end of sentences or fall and trail off.

CONGRUENCE

How a person speaks is also a good indicator of congruence. When people aren't telling the truth, their tempo speeds up or slows down, their volume gets louder or softer, and their tone is higher or lower than normal. For example, Visuals may slow down their speaking, Kinesthetics may speak faster, and Auditories may change their tone. In addition, people's choice of words will change when they are not telling the truth. People telling the truth will talk in a straightforward manner using ordinary terms. When creating misrepresentations, their word selection is more careful, and they tend to use more sophisticated words. They also speak with precision and are mindful not to repeat the same word twice, unlike natural conversation.

CONCLUSION

Obviously, using all of the different aspects of physical communication (handshakes, hand movements, breathing, facial expressions, skin color, body posture, and speech) is critical to establishing rapport. At this point, it makes sense to summarize what we have learned in order to emphasize the three most important points about developing rapport.

First, you cannot mirror or lead someone effectively until you understand your own wiring. By knowing your word catalog, you will be able to compensate for your weaknesses and take advantage of your natural strengths. You must identify your primary, secondary, and recessive catalogs. You need to determine if you have balanced catalogs, a strong secondary catalog, or a dominant primary catalog.

Second, you must be able to identify the catalogs of the person to whom you are speaking. As we discussed in Chapter 4, you can ask questions that require people to access their long-term memories. Based upon their eye movements, you can determine their word catalog. You can also perform VAK counts to determine their word catalog prioritization. While this is easy to do in meetings with few participants, you need a different model for larger groups. In the final section of the book, we will introduce the concepts of successfully speaking to large groups.

Finally, you are trying to establish rapport through the physical communication layer, and this requires mirroring body postures, breathing, and speech. If you are a Visual talking to a Kinesthetic, slow down and speak in terms of feelings; this will naturally lower your voice tone and decrease your volume. If you are a Kinesthetic talking to a Visual, speed up and speak in terms of pictures; this will naturally raise your voice tone and increase your volume.

If you are talking with people who are wired exactly as you are, you are already mirroring them. Most likely, these are people you naturally communicate with, who are the easiest for you to sell to. However, it takes skill and effort to communicate with someone who has a primary catalog that is the same as your recessive catalog. Ultimately, you want to become a communication chameleon. You want to speak in the customer's language (VAK keywords) and adopt all of the customer's physical communication attributes (body, speech, and breathing).

Certain word catalog combinations communicate better with each other than others. For example, strong Visuals and strong Kinesthetics naturally communicate together better than strong Visuals and strong Auditories. Auditories naturally communicate better with Kinesthetics than with Visuals. Kinesthetics have an intrinsic communication advantage since they are always in touch with their own feelings and are sensitive about the feelings of others. This consideration is incorporated into their communication process.

Auditory salespeople face more of a challenge in presenting thoughts to customers than Visuals or Kinesthetics. If you are an Auditory, you must make a conscious effort to watch the people you are talking to in order to make sure they are grasping what you are saying. To put it another way, your internal dialogue is so developed that it overwhelms your ability to sense how your message is being received. What sounds good to you may not look good to a Visual or feel right to a Kinesthetic. Sometimes, it can be entertaining to watch two strong Auditories hold a conversation. They are so selfishly consumed with their own words that two separate conversations can occur simultaneously. Good advice to Auditories is to stop listening to yourself talk and make sure you are hearing what the customer is saying.

Conversely, Visuals and Kinesthetics should adopt auditory speech characteristics when they are speaking. Just as the chameleon changes colors to match its surroundings, your goal is to change your speaking mannerisms to match the person to whom you are speaking. By mirroring people, we are trying to continue the process of establishing rapport. If people are closed at the beginning of a meeting, we are trying to open them up to our ideas.

When all the observable and distinguishable layers of the human communication model are in agreement, meaning they are all sending the same message, people are unified in their communication and most likely telling the truth. For example, when their words match their physical demeanor and their language usage matches their word catalog, they are being truthful. If one of the layers is incongruent (does not match), you need to investigate further. The incongruence could be as obvious as that of the vice president of marketing candidate who drastically changed the ways she moved her head. Or it could be subtle, such as when she used words that did not match her word catalog wiring, perhaps using an auditory word when a visual one was expected.

Finally, this chapter has reviewed the physical layer of communication. Most likely, you were introduced to new concepts and ideas regarding the expression and the interpretation of the visible attributes of the body. Some aspects of this layer people consciously control and some they cannot. The key point is that the body is another means of communication, even without language.

While we have spent the entire chapter learning how to find the truth about customers, there are three truisms about salespeople I would also like to share with you. While it may seem like an unusual statement, the first truism is not everyone who is in sales should be. In fact, of the thousands of salespeople I have met over the years, I estimate that one in four shouldn't be in the profession. It's not because they lack the necessary personal qualities (the nature of the profession eliminates the unqualified very quickly). Rather, it's the salesperson who is in a continual state of panic and perpetual turmoil that I am referring to. It takes courage, quiet confidence, and competitive aggressiveness to be in sales. Since time is the enemy, why spend the precious days of your life doing something that makes you miserable?

The second truism is about the profound importance of hope. Hope is the belief that our cherished desires, although difficult to attain, will be fulfilled in the future. Salespeople without hope will not weather the trials and heartaches that we face daily. I've met many salespeople who have lost hope—in their company and the products they sell. Although time is the enemy, it's never too late to find your true calling or find sunnier skies at a new company.

The final truism is that Heavy Hitters are in constant search of the truth. They conduct honest internal debates about the likelihood of winning the deal and won't fool themselves with wishful hallucinations. They don't suffer from amnesia when thinking about their past failures. Instead they learn from them.

Some people believe ignorance is bliss and that the future will somehow take care of itself. When 80,000 adults were asked, "If astronomers detect a planet-killing asteroid right before it hits Earth, do you want to know?"[4] Thirty percent answered, "No, I would rather enjoy the last minutes without knowing," while 70 percent answered, "Yes, I would like to be able to prepare for the end." Since the Heavy Hitters I have known are always preparing for the future, they would definitely want to know.

PART TWO

Customer Sales Strategies

HOW SALESPEOPLE spend their time ultimately determines their success. Heavy Hitters have an intense intuition that tells them which customers to pursue and what actions to take. Since having a mentor is the best way to learn how to sell, we want to understand how Hitters work their deals so we can model their behavior. We also want to emulate how they work with their managers and cope with a career that can be both exhilarating and frustrating. In this section we examine Heavy Hitters' strategies for building winning relationships with all of their customers.

CHAPTER **6**

Choosing Your Battles

Since the customer was already using his archrival's product, the Heavy Hitter knew it would take a great deal of effort and a little luck to persuade the company to switch to his solution. In order to win, he dedicated almost all of his sales team's time during the quarter to this one account. If it didn't close, the quarter would be a failure. As the end of the quarter approached, the tension rose. Throughout the last day of the quarter, his manager constantly wanted an update on the account. Everyone's nerves were frayed. Finally, at 5:15 P.M. the fax machine started printing the long-awaited purchase order.

Since the eyes contain more nerve endings than any other part of the body, they are not only the most sensitive but also the most trusted sense. People will say, "I saw it with my own eyes!" and "I'll believe it when I see it!" In reality, our sensory limitations negatively influence our judgments. We think we saw a lightning bolt traveling down toward the ground when it is really retracing its downward pattern and heading up. Not only our eyes but also our ears deceive us by inventing and distorting information and clouding the truth. We hear a siren approaching at a traffic intersection but think it's coming from the opposite direction. When we wash our hands, we think we are feeling water but our skin can only feel the pain, pressure, and temperature that we associate with liquid.

Some people will swear they have seen a flying saucer, when in reality the brain has added visual imagery in its attempt to distinguish an obscure object. The term for this is "pareidolia," and everyone has experienced one. Perhaps the two most common pareidolias are the visualization of the face of the man on the moon and a mirage, the illusion of water in the desert. Pareidolias aren't solely limited to images. When I was a youngster, I remember listening to The Beatles' song "Strawberry Fields" over and over to hear what seemed to be "I buried Paul."

Our senses also tend to taint pure information to favor our belief system. For example, some people will listen acceptingly while a psychic converses with loved ones from beyond the grave. Their desire to believe is reinforced by what they hear. Meanwhile, nonbelievers would consider the same words nonsense.

Salespeople are not immune to similar ambiguities and delusions. Salespeople with "happy ears" tend to believe whatever they are told by the customer. Others view the world through rose-colored glasses and will always interpret information emanating from the customer in a favorable light. This behavior should be expected since the brain produces a chemical (tetrahydrocannabinol) that erases bad memories. Tetrahydrocannabinol or THC is similar to the active ingredient found in cannabis. A recent article published by the American Psychological Association showed that the portion of the brain associated with fear is flooded with THC during periods of trauma.[1]

Ambiguities and delusions are disastrous for salespeople. These conditions cause them to work the wrong deals and make mistakes. However, Heavy Hitters work their deals differently. They have a method and strategy for selecting their battles based upon the individuals they must persuade to buy. To understand their method, the first step is to understand the communication process.

People communicate differently. These differences are directly related to biological factors such as intelligence, personality, and word catalog wiring. Environmental factors including childhood, education, and where they live also play an important role in shaping the ability to communicate. People's surroundings will also greatly impact the demeanor of their speech. If you are in a library, for example, you will soften your voice to a whisper. However, your word selection and volume will be quite different if you are rooting for your favorite team at a football game.

Even though there are over six billion people in the world, no one is quite like you. You have had a completely unique set of experiences in your life. And you have kept a record of your past existence by cataloging pictures, sounds, and feelings. As you make your way through your daily life, you are interacting with the outside world by repeatedly sending and receiving messages. For Heavy Hitters, it's the ability to send meaningful messages and correctly interpret the messages being received that determines their success.

People communicate with a purpose, to achieve a specific benefaction. Benefactions are very personal prioritized needs. For Heavy Hitters the goal is to win the deal at hand. By doing so, they may achieve their benefaction of being the most respected salesperson or buying the new house they desperately want. In order to win the deal, they form an account strategy. The strategy is based upon information they have accumulated about the account, past sales experiences, and knowledge of the product they are selling. They plan a series of tactics that they believe will give them the highest opportunity to win in the shortest time frame and with the least amount of risk. By strategically performing these tasks, Heavy Hitters guide the prospect through the sales cycle.

THE SALES CYCLE

Sales cycle management has two aspects. First is the formalized process that the Heavy Hitters' company has established to win business. Most likely, your company has a defined methodology consisting of a series of steps to gather information about the customer and present information about your solution to the customer.

The second aspect of sales cycle management is the Hitters' personal contribution to the company's formal process—their ability to communicate and create rapport, their perceptiveness, and their past experience working sales cycles. Through repetitive motion, Heavy

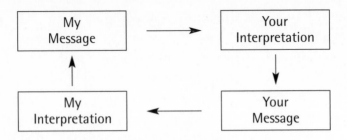

Figure 6.1 Communicating Information

Hitters have developed a reservoir of experiences that they can draw upon to help manage the current deal. They recognize patterns of company and personal behavior and have developed a knowledge base of actions founded on previous similar encounters. Finally, Heavy Hitters know communication and rapport are critical components of every sales cycle. These two elements are prerequisites for a successful sale.

The sales cycle is a formalized information-and-activity exchange. Customers are trying to gather as much information about vendors in order to determine if they are appropriate long-term partners. Meanwhile, Heavy Hitters are trying to gather as much information about the customer in order to determine if they can win the deal. Information is communicated back and forth, and each message that is sent must also be received and interpreted correctly, as shown in Figure 6.1.

However, an obstacle is inherent in this process. Since each message is subject to a person's interpretation, how do you know when your message has been interpreted correctly? Also, how do you know you have interpreted a customer's message correctly?

SEVEN PREMISES OF THE SALES CYCLE

The answers to these questions can be found by applying the seven fundamental premises of sales cycle management. First, all information we give and receive is subject to different interpretation. Second, through continual triangulation, we can ascertain the accuracy of information and determine our position in the account. Third, we need someone inside the customer's organization to help us win by providing reliable information we normally wouldn't have access to. Fourth, we must be flexible. If what we're doing isn't working, we'll change our strategy. Fifth, every deal has a critical moment, or "turning point," where it is won or lost. Sixth, even if we think we have the deal won, we should always be prepared for one last obstacle that must be overcome. Seventh, we'll drop out of accounts where there is no chance of winning and instead go where we are "loved."

Sales Cycle Premise #1

All information communicated between customers and Heavy Hitters (and the sales team) is subject to interpretation and filtering. Here's an example of an e-mail that was sent from Jeff to two managers (Bob and Patti) to update them on the progress of a new salesperson (Mark). The e-mail describes the progress Mark is making with his territory, and it illustrates how the same message can create two entirely different interpretations. Jeff has worked with Bob and Patti for some time and has established rapport with each of them. Patti is an Auditory, Visual, and Kinesthetic. Bob is a Visual, Kinesthetic, and Auditory. As in many of the preceding examples, we are not as interested in the content of Bob and Patti's messages as we are in the message structure.

> TO: Bob, Patti
> FROM: Jeff
>
> I met with Mark this afternoon for his territory review. We had a very long, somewhat pained discussion. He came on board six months ago and has sold very little. When I look at his strategy and examine his activities, they seem to be the same as everyone else's. On the sales calls I have attended, he establishes great relationships with the customers. Overall, I think he has done an admirable job under difficult circumstances. Obviously, I reiterated our company's commitment to him. Let me know your thoughts.

Here's Bob's response to the e-mail. Remember, Bob is a Visual, Kinesthetic, and Auditory.

> TO: Jeff
> FROM: Bob
>
> Thanks for sharing with us the feedback and your thoughts on Mark. It isn't an easy situation. Do you think that it will get better as he establishes his territory?

Here's Patti's response to the same e-mail. Pat is an Auditory, Visual, and Kinesthetic.

> TO: Jeff
> FROM: Patti
>
> 1. What do you think that he will do in sales revenues this quarter?
> 2. Given the circumstances of his territory, what revenue should Mark do for the following two quarters?
> 3. Is his territory really that much worse than other territories?

The same e-mail solicited very different responses. Bob's response showed strong Kinesthetic traits. "Thanks for sharing with us the feedback," "isn't an easy situation," and "get better" all indicate that Bob read and understood this e-mail from the other person's point of view. He projected his concern to the sender of the e-mail (Jeff) as well as the subject of the e-mail (Mark). From his response, you could assume that Bob implicitly agreed with the statements made that Mark is doing an admirable job.

Meanwhile, Patti approached the e-mail differently. We knew ahead of time that Patti was an Auditory. In examining the e-mail, you will notice there are not any auditory keywords in her response. Instead, Patti is asking a series of questions. The questions are in fact the auditory keywords. She basically repeated her internal dialogue as the questions streamed into her consciousness. Most likely, this was the exact order in which she asked the questions of herself.

You will also notice that the point of view of Patti's e-mail is different. It could be inferred that Patti is not necessarily in agreement with Jeff's assessment that Mark "has done an admirable job under difficult circumstances." Her questions, particularly the last one asking if Mark's territory is worse than the others, indicate this, and her response requires further investigation.

People "filter" the information they give and receive all the time. In Patti's case, the process of filtering created a lot more questions. Patti wanted more detailed information as she had several questions she needed answered. In Bob's case, he was more interested in the big picture and the welfare of others. The same e-mail message was interpreted in two distinct ways with two distinct sets of responses. Any information that is presented to the customer is similarly subject to different interpretations. This is the first premise of sales cycle management.

Sales Cycle Premise #2

All information gathered from the customer and presented to the customer must be triangulated to ensure the correct meaning is found. Now that we are aware the information we present and receive isn't 100 percent accurate, how do we validate that the customer received the message we intended? We accomplish this through "triangulation."

In Chapter 3, the concept of the "triangulation diamond" was introduced. The Heavy Hitter is always swinging for a home run, to close the deal. Like a baseball diamond, the triangulation diamond has four bases. On first base, we ask, "Specifically what?" in order to understand the content level of the words being spoken. On second base we ask, "Specifically how?" to help us understand how the customer will take action. On third base, we ask, "Specifically why?" to determine history, perspective, and motivations. We reach home by asking, "Specifically when?" to determine time frames. Finally, the pitcher can throw to any base from the pitcher's mound. We ask, "Specifically who?" of any of the four bases in order to determine who sets the priorities, who makes the decision, or who will carry out the actions.

Triangulation is a repetitive process done over the life of a sales cycle. The Heavy Hitter's most frequent triangulation is with members of the immediate sales team including the manager. Mostly, it occurs directly after a sales call while memories are still fresh. The Heavy Hitter's team members compare notes on their performance and evaluate the probability of winning the deal.

They'll also discuss their "read" of the customer participants from the meeting. Who is for them? Who is against them? And who can be swayed? This is analogous to lawyers during the jury selection process, who try to determine which potential jurors would react most favorably to their client's case. Of equal importance, lawyers want to eliminate those jurors who may be biased against their client. The information gathered from triangulation is continually factored into the strategy.

Many times salespeople are asked underhanded questions by a customer. They are disguised as information gathering but in reality only serve the selfish motivations of the interrogator. Sadly, novice salespeople fall into the trap and try to respond to questions for which there is no correct answer. Anything that is said is used against them.

Whether formally or informally, customers are also doing their own triangulation about the vendor. They'll compare notes with their evaluation team, talk to customer references, and solicit opinions from consultants or industry analysts. They'll create a set of criteria a product must satisfy and guidelines to determine if a vendor will be a good business partner. They will grant a vendor further access based on how it compares against these standards and ranks against other vendors. The better the fit, the longer the time they will naturally be spending on a vendor.

The goal of Hitters' triangulation is to find out the truth about winning an account as early as possible. The sales cycle is a process that occurs over time, and Heavy Hitters are constantly reconfirming information they received earlier to ensure it is still correct. At the beginning of the sales cycle, they'll spend much effort evaluating the product's fit with the customer's need and qualifying the business opportunity. As the sales cycle progresses, Heavy Hitters will keep triangulating to ensure their information is still accurate by validating information they receive from one person with other people. They will also triangulate to determine the personal biases of each individual involved in the selection process. Finding the truth is a time-consuming process, and triangulation is a discipline that requires effort and time.

Sales Cycle Premise #3

You need a coach to win the deal. Heavy Hitters know they need a constant, accurate source of information revealing the internal machinations of the customer's selection process. The term "coach" is the popular name of a person who is the source of this inside information. The ability to locate, develop, and gain a coach is a skill the Heavy Hitter has acquired. Quite often, ordinary salespeople mistake someone for a coach when in fact the person isn't a loyal compatriot.

Several specific conditions must exist in order for a friendly evaluator to be considered a coach. First, coaches must have a personal reason for wanting the Heavy Hitter or his company to win. Second, coaches need to specifically say they want the Heavy Hitter to win and be willing to fight for the Hitter's cause. Finally, the information a coach provides must be accurate.

The ideal coach is the person with the highest authority or influence involved in the selection process. When this person becomes the coach, the Heavy Hitter will enjoy a unique advantage. However, the coach could be anybody inside the customer's company or even outside the company, such as a consultant working on the project.

A coach is the key to successful deal triangulation. Heavy Hitters know that without a coach, they will never truly be able to determine whether they are being told the truth. In Chapter 9, we will review strategies and tactics for finding and developing a coach.

Sales Cycle Premise #4

It is human nature to grow comfortable with our routines and accustomed to our ways. As salespeople, we tend to present our pitch in the same manner time after time, ask the same questions again and again, and rely on familiar tactics. It's only when we lose that we are reminded that every opportunity is unique.

Be flexible. If what you are doing isn't working, do something else! Heavy Hitters are constantly adding customer interactions to their knowledge base of experience. Depending upon the information and circumstances surrounding the account they are trying to close, they select the best course of action from this database by comparing the current deal with past wins and losses.

Throughout the sales cycle, Heavy Hitters are constantly responding and adapting to changing circumstances. If a situation changes, they'll change their strategy, tactics, and behavior. While they are solely responsible for winning the business, they are willing to assimilate advice from others into their strategy. When something isn't working, they'll try something else.

Sales Cycle Premise #5

Every deal has a critical moment or turning point that determines the winner and the losers. In some cases, the turning point is easy to spot. For example, a salesperson may be presenting his solution and encounters a deal-breaking objection that he is unable to overcome. Even though the customer remains cordial for the rest of the meeting, a turning point has occurred and the deal is lost. In most cases, the turning point occurs when the salesperson isn't present. It's in casual hallway conversations or internal e-mails that selection team members share opinions that influence vendors' futures. The only outward sign that a turning point has occurred is the perceptible change in deal momentum as evidenced in Figure 6.2.

You probably noticed the term "buzz kill" on the graph. This represents the person, business reason, political issue, or technical obstacle that causes momentum to turn downward. Ninety-nine out of one hundred times you will not recover from buzz kill. However, some companies won't let salespeople stop working deals. You may

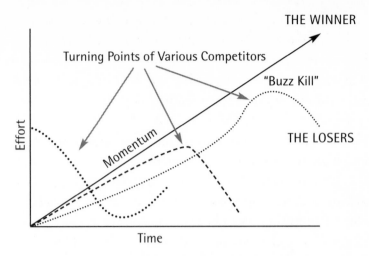

Figure 6.2 Turning Points of Various Competitors

even be familiar with the following drill, which I call the "walk of shame." All the various sales managers meet with the rep and theorize about all the possible ways to win. Then they mandate that the selling continue even though the salesperson knows working on a deal past buzz kill is a waste of time.

Sometimes salespeople will decide on their own to continue the walk of shame. Since they have invested so much time, energy, and emotion into the deal they find it impossible to let it go. This is particularly true for salespeople who have neglected to build up a pipeline of future business opportunities.

Time takes on an additional dimension of meaning during the sales cycle. Usually, we think of time as a continuum. We spend most of our mental energy thinking about the immediate tasks before us. We typically don't consider time to be a finite resource. There's always tomorrow, next week, month, or year. During the sales process, time is not just minutes and days, it is actually a measure of deal momentum. Therefore, forward momentum in a deal represents good or positive time and backward momentum is bad or negative time. Heavy Hitters keep the negative time they spend on deals to a minimum.

Sales Cycle Premise #6

The sixth premise of sales cycle management is that there is always one last obstacle. Even for the vendor who has passed the turning point and won the business, there's always one last impediment to closing the deal.

There might be unknown bureaucratic obstacles in the contractual and procurement processes. Bureaucrats suddenly move into the position of power. They may have felt ignored or left out of the decision process and be ready to exert their authority. As the saying goes, "Hell hath no fury like a bureaucrat scorned." The formal approval process may include members outside the decision process who want to influence the outcome at the last moment. Sometimes, people change their minds in the eleventh hour of the decision-making process. Therefore, the Heavy Hitter continues with caution, remains on guard, expects the unexpected, and never stops triangulating.

Sales Cycle Premise #7

We may admire persistent salespeople and respect the underdog who will fight with passion and battle against the odds. However, sometimes it's impossible to win. Such is the case when your competitor holds such a tight grip on the account there is no way to pry it loose. In some accounts, although they may not say so directly, the customer simply doesn't want to buy from you.

Even facing these circumstances, some salespeople believe the customer is just playing hard to get or treating every vendor in this way (which they aren't). These salespeople mistakenly believe they can turn the situation around by sheer willpower and determination. Recognizing when to abandon an account is as important as knowing what accounts to pursue. Ultimately, you will only win deals where you are given the opportunity to build personal relationships. Therefore, you must spend your time on accounts where you can be "loved." The seventh premise of the sales cycle is to go where you are loved.

I would like to take a moment and explain a curious aspect of human behavior that I have experienced as both a salesperson and professional speaker. I have come to realize that in every audience there are people who simply cannot be sold. Even if you walk on water or levitate an elephant in the air, these people will not follow you. Perhaps it's because of their neurological wiring or maybe the result of some childhood trauma. There's no way to tell where their closed-mindedness came from. Conversely, a similar group of people will fall in love with you, say all the right things, but never buy. They seemed to be enamored with what you have said but don't follow up with any discernable action. Both of these groups are fatal for a salesperson.

Recently, I gave a presentation to a group of executives following the brilliant economist Arthur Laffer, the father of supply-side economics and creator of the "Laffer Curve." The Laffer Curve explains that when tax rates are raised to create more tax revenues, after a certain point the revenues collected actually decrease. Therefore taxes should be fair. In honor of this worthy idea, I would like to present to you the "Martin Curve." (See Figure 6.3.) The Martin Curve

Figure 6.3 The Martin Curve

explains that 10 percent to 15 percent of everyone you try to sell to will not buy, regardless of the effort you put into winning the deal. Also 10 percent to 15 percent will give you all the buying signs and tell you that they love you but never buy anything.

Another interesting interpretation of the premise of going where you are loved relates to cars. I call it, "Chevys versus Mercedes." Not too many years ago, when your car had more than 60,000 miles you started to think that a major breakdown was imminent, and it was time to trade it in. In comparison, automobiles today typically have 50,000- to even 100,000-mile warranties. Two hundred thousand miles is now typically considered the lifespan of a new car because of design, engineering, and electronics improvements.

With this in mind, why will average Americans purchase 10 to 12 cars during their lifetime, one on an average of every three to four years? The answer is psychological obsolescence. In other words, we get tired of our cars long before our cars actually are tired.

All cars perform the same task: They take you from one place to another. However, some people buy Chevys and some Mercedes. There are loyal Chevy owners who buy strictly American cars and Mercedes owners who have never driven anything else. There are also plenty of people who would love to drive a Mercedes but simply can't afford one.

Here's the point of this story. Ignoring your company's marketing claims, perform an honest assessment to determine what you really sell, a Chevy or a Mercedes product. I happen to live in Southern California, where Mercedes are commonplace. What you drive is a very important status symbol, and most Mercedes owners wouldn't even consider a Chevy. Conversely, when I am in Michigan, I rarely see a Mercedes. If you honestly know what type of product you sell you wouldn't waste your time trying to sell it to companies that will never buy—in the same way that you wouldn't open up a Mercedes dealership in Detroit. Finally, you can get an idea if your customer buys Chevys or Mercedes by looking at the key decision maker. What kind of car does he or she drive?

QUALIFYING AN ACCOUNT

Just as seasoned gamblers know which cards to discard and which to keep, Heavy Hitters know when to pursue and when to drop deals. They know their biggest competitor is time. Time is the enemy because time is finite. There are 90 days in a quarter. Hitters know that they can work only a finite number of deals during this time so they must invest time wisely in qualified accounts. Unfortunately, a qualified account can be disqualified at any time during the sales cycle. It takes a lot of flexibility to walk away from an account where there has been a heavy investment of time, energy, and emotions.

Heavy Hitters use a formal and intuitive qualification process for deciding which deals to work intensely and which ones to develop in the background. While the formal qualification process has most likely been supplied to them by their company, they have perfected their own instinctive method of qualification over time.

The formal qualification process involves determining the technical fit of the product to the customer's requirements and the business fit of the product to the customer's needs. This process may range from a checklist of technical questions to an in-depth evaluation of the customer's environment. Depending on the nature of the product, the Hitter may also have to determine whether the product fits the customer's current or planned business processes.

Of all the aspects of deal qualification, ascertaining the technical fit is probably the easiest. The criteria to determine if the account is technically qualified are developed either by product management, by product marketing, or within the sales organization. Through the completion of preimplementation checklists, technical questionnaires, and informal questioning, the sales team determines if the product meets the customer's technical requirements. From the technical perspective, Heavy Hitters position their product differently for each customer based upon each customer's criteria. They decide which features to emphasize and which to deemphasize and how to position their company's story with the customer's technical needs in mind.

Another formal part of qualifying the account is asking basic business qualification questions. The answers to these questions will reflect the company's evaluation and procurement process. Following are typical business qualification questions. These types of questions are second nature to all salespeople.

- How much have you budgeted for your purchase?
- What is the decision process to select a vendor?
- When will a decision be made?
- What are the most important criteria in selecting a vendor?
- What other vendors are you evaluating?
- When will you be implementing the solution?

Heavy Hitters seek to understand what a customer is trying to accomplish from a business and technical perspective. Ideally, they want to actually change the customer's technical requirements to suit their product or, at a minimum, prove to the customer that the product meets a checklist of requirements. The process of qualifying a deal from a technical and business perspective is what most people outside the sales field associate with the term "qualification." When someone from engineering, accounting, or marketing asks if a deal is "qualified," they are referring to these formal processes.

The intuitive process of deal qualification is far more complex. Frequently, nonsalespeople within an organization have a hard time understanding that an entirely intuitive process surrounds the sales cycle. It's understandable since they operate in a more controllable, predictable world, such as accounting or engineering. Accountants know that both sides of a balance sheet must be equal. They work in an analytical world based upon emotionless numbers. They don't necessarily understand why their company's salesperson still may not win the deal if the product technically fits the customer's environment and is priced competitively.

The Hitter's intuitive qualification process is far more important than the formal qualification process. The goal of the intuitive process is the successful search for the truth, and this is not a sequential process like marking items off a checklist. In fact, two competing salespeople could ask the same question and receive identical content-level answers. However, the salesperson with the ability to identify and interpret incongruencies, whether in language usage or physical contradictions of the body, is in a much better position to find the truth and win the deal. The preceding chapter was devoted to finding the truth by spotting these inconsistencies.

The sales cycle has a natural evolution. The first step for customers is to gather information from each vendor. As they gather more information, one vendor begins to look better than the others, its product sounds like it will work better, and they feel this vendor will be a better partner. Naturally, that vendor will enjoy an advantage throughout the remainder of the sales cycle.

However, customers have a dilemma. They still want to collect information from the other vendors to be 100 percent certain they are selecting the right vendor. Or they may want to complete the evaluation process to show others within or outside their organization (management, colleagues, consultants, or government agencies) that their evaluation was thorough and fair. As a result, they offer the other vendors the "customer placebo." In fact, the meaning of the Latin root of placebo is "I shall please." That's exactly what customers do. They'll say anything to please you at the moment, regardless of whether or not it's true.

The customer placebo is present in every sales cycle. One vendor is in a unique position of receiving information from the customer that the others don't receive. As this favored vendor and the customer spend more time together, a higher level of rapport is developed. While this is happening, the customer is presenting misleading information to the other vendors about their position in the deal. Customers give salespeople false buying signs that they are more interested in the product than they actually are. Conversely, they may not share critical information or access to other people in the company as they do with the leading vendor. Unfortunately, the other vendors continue to spend additional resources and time on the account when a decision for one vendor has, for all intents and purposes, been made already.

Heavy Hitters' intuitive process is always triangulating the technical and business qualification questions. When they ask a person a content-level question like "What is your time frame to purchase?" they know they will receive a content-level answer. However, they use their intuition to determine the congruence (or truthfulness) of the person's answer. They will also ask other members of the evaluation team to gather information from their contacts and triangulate each response to form their own opinion. Finally, Heavy Hitters may even triangulate all data points about the account with other people whose judgment they trust, even if they have never met the customer or are completely outside the sales field. They are trying to gather as many opinions as possible to assess their position on the deal, determine their vulnerabilities, and set their course of action.

FIT

Up to this point, we have discussed the qualification of a customer from a business and technical perspective. A third element of fit is called "personal fit." Heavy Hitters are always trying to determine whether they have a personal fit with a customer. From an individual standpoint, they are trying to develop rapport with each member of the selection team evaluating the solution. They know without rapport, they will not win the deal.

They are also trying to develop rapport between the companies, or "company fit." The level of rapport developed between companies will depend upon how the cultures of the two companies match. The higher the level of rapport, the better the odds of winning the deal. However, the personal rapport developed by the Heavy Hitter (and his team) with each member of the evaluation team is more highly valued by both the customer and the Hitter than the rapport between companies.

After Heavy Hitters have determined the level of personal, technical, and business fit with a customer, they make the decision to pursue the deal. Whether formally on paper or mentally, they'll map out their ability to win based upon how they perceive their position in the deal.

SALES CYCLE QUADRANTS

In any account, Heavy Hitters will find themselves in four distinct situations, depending upon the amount of information they have acquired and the level of rapport they have developed. The sales cycle quadrants diagram (Figure 6.4) helps illustrate how Heavy Hitters determine their bearings.

The vertical axis measures the amount of rapport Heavy Hitters enjoy with a customer. For example, a brand-new account would have low or no rapport. A high-rapport account would be one where the Hitter has personal friendships with members of the customer's team. The horizontal axis measures the amount of truthful information being shared by the customer. This is the Hitters' assessment of the quantity and quality of the information they are uncovering. It also includes any unique information from the coach.

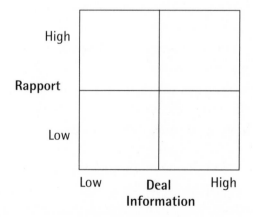

Figure 6.4 Sales Cycle Quadrants Diagram

The sales cycle quadrants correlate to the Hitters' competitiveness in the account. They are in the position of either being blind, competitive, or collaborative. (See Figure 6.5.)

The blind quadrant is where Heavy Hitters have little information about the deal and little rapport has been established. In this unenviable position, they are "blind" about the deal. At the beginning of every new sales cycle, they find themselves in this position. Their immediate goals are to collect information and start the process of developing rapport. As the sales cycle progresses, they know if they are unable to collect pertinent information or develop significant rapport, they should stop working the deal.

The amount of information Heavy Hitters receive from customers will vary. For example, the evaluation criteria could be extremely well documented. A request for proposal (RFP) may be 300 pages long with descriptive narrations about the customers' environment and very detailed questions about the vendor. However, this is only the external aspect of the product selection. The internal political part of the product selection isn't publicly revealed. By establishing rapport, the Heavy Hitter will learn of the inner workings of the customer.

Figure 6.5 Sales Cycle Quadrants—Competitiveness

In the second quadrant, one of the two competitive ones, Hitters have a lot of information but little rapport. They know they must move quickly to establish rapport early in the sales cycle. Without rapport, the likelihood of winning the deal decreases as the sales cycle progresses.

In the third quadrant, Heavy Hitters have established rapport but have a low level of information about the customers' requirements or a high level of uncertainty whether the deal will happen. For example, the Heavy Hitter may have painstakingly developed relationships within the accounts payable group of the finance department of a Fortune 100 company. However, because of the finance department's immensity and bureaucracy, the accounts payable members are unsure of the direction and approval of their project. Therefore, even though rapport is high and the accounts payable group has identified specific business needs, the knowledge of whether there is actually a deal to be closed is low.

Ultimately, Heavy Hitters want to be in the fourth, or collaborative, quadrant. In this quadrant, they have established rapport and are receiving proprietary information that the other vendors aren't. In addition, an interesting paradigm shift occurs in the vendor-customer relationship. The customer begins working with the vendor as a long-term partner while still in the sales cycle. For example, when issues arise about the functionality of the product, the customer works with the vendor to find an acceptable solution. This shift, from being treated like one of the vendors to becoming part of the customer team, is very noticeable. At this point, Heavy Hitters know they have won the deal and update their forecast accordingly.

Hitters move from quadrant to quadrant as the sales cycle progresses. Moving from the blind quadrant to the competitive quadrants marks forward progress in the deal. During the sales cycle, they could also experience setbacks that move them back into being blind. For example, if the coach suddenly leaves the company or is reassigned, the Hitter is blind again.

ENEMIES

While Heavy Hitters know their true enemy is time, they are in daily fights with other enemies who are trying to vanquish them. Heavy Hitters always assume that someone is in the enviable position of being in the collaborative quadrant. Only one vendor can occupy this position. Everyone else is in one of the other quadrants.

Every company and every deal has an archenemy. Most often, it is the same company you compete against in deal after deal. You are probably very familiar with your archenemy and have no trouble identifying it. Most likely, it is the company you hate and fear the most. Your archenemy is also the one competitor who is most often present in the collaborative quadrant.

SALES CYCLES STRATEGIES

An implicit strategy is associated with each quadrant. In each quadrant, the Heavy Hitter executes a strategy that counteracts a competitor or corrects a weakness in the Hitter's current position. The Heavy Hitter will execute one of the following strategies: attack/retreat, seek, sustain, or protect. (See Figure 6.6.)

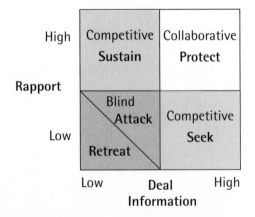

Figure 6.6 Sales Cycle Quadrants—Strategies

Attack/Retreat

If the Heavy Hitter is in the blind quadrant, he will either attack or retreat. The basic premise of the attack strategy is to hurt the competition. The methods are based on the creation of fear, uncertainty, and doubt (FUD). When Hitters are on the attack, they may furnish negative information about their competitors. This information may include bad references, negative press reports and reviews, critical industry analyst comments, and benchmarks showing poor performance.

To motivate a customer to spend additional time with them or to slow the sales process down, Heavy Hitters may attack the competition by drastically cutting the price and offering free services. Or Heavy Hitters can bypass the established evaluation process and present their case directly to the customer's key executives. The attack strategy may even include the conscious decision to do nothing. For example, customers may ask for information, but Heavy Hitters will not provide it until they get the information or commitments they want in return. Doing nothing sometimes frustrates the members of the selection team who are working against the Hitter as it forces them to spend additional time dealing with this disruptive person. Other times, it is exactly what they would like to have happen. They want the Hitter's solution to disappear quietly.

Customers may respond to the attack favorably. They may ask the "attacked" competitor to refute negative claims with direct proof. Thus the level of rapport that the attacked competitor previously enjoyed is reduced. At the very least, the sales cycle will be slowed down. This gives the Heavy Hitter additional time to find and develop a coach.

However, any attack strategy is very risky and will most likely fail. If the results are unsuccessful, the Hitter's own credibility is damaged, and the deal is lost. The Heavy Hitter actually welcomes this result as it makes no sense to work on deals where your involvement is not wanted or appreciated. It is the salesperson with the poor pipeline who continually tries to pry the customer's front door open with his broken foot.

Side by side with the attack strategy is the retreat strategy. After collecting enough information to know they cannot possibly win, Heavy Hitters want out of the deal as soon as possible to continue looking for other accounts.

Seek

Heavy Hitters will employ a seek strategy in the second sales quadrant, where they have a high amount of information but little customer rapport. The seek strategy is very simple: Find a coach. Hitters will introduce themselves and their message to all the relevant people within the account. They will also ask the other members of the team (the presales engineer, consultants, and manager) to assist in the search by infiltrating the account.

Sustain

In the third quadrant, the Hitter's strategy is to sustain rapport with the customer while continuing to gather more information. The "sustain" strategy involves using the coach not only as the on-site eyes and ears of the account (akin to a personal surveillance camera) but also as a go-between to disseminate information. The goal is for the coach to relay propaganda about the Hitter's product and to slander the competitor's. This strategy has a parallel in the presidential election process. Candidates for president will typically use their vice presidential running mates as "attack dogs" against their opponents. By doing this, the presidential candidates maintain their integrity and positive personas. Hitters and presidential candidates want negative information given out, but they can't do it themselves without looking bad.

Protect

Only one vendor at a time can be in the fourth, or collaborative, quadrant. Members of this vendor's team are trying to protect their position from the attack strategies of other vendors. They are trying to fortify their personal relationships to deflect the other seekers. Through the natural strength of this position, they are able to take the high ground over the other vendors by engaging in only positive tactics that emanate integrity or by directly influencing the selection process to favor their solution. They are in harmony with the customer and the customer will actually defend them against others. Once Heavy Hitters are in this quadrant, they obviously want to stay there for the remaining stages of the sales cycle.

Sales Cycle Stages

Heavy Hitters understand that every deal requires an investment of time and resources. The resources are tangible things like people, equipment, and money. Intangible items, including mental energy, credibility, and political capital, are also being expended. All of these items are finite. Through the managed use of these resources, Heavy Hitters gain momentum in a deal. However, as they gain momentum they have to expend more effort and resources. Figure 6.7 illustrates the expenditure of these resources.

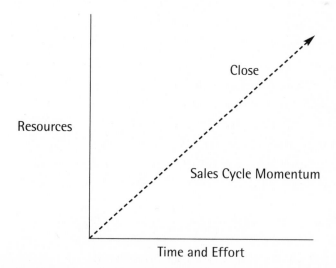

Figure 6.7 Sales Cycle Investments

In reality, the only two positions to be in at the end of the deal are first place, as the winner, or last place, as the first loser. Heavy Hitters would rather finish in last place than end in second place. Salespeople who are proud of a second-place finish are a detriment to their company. The next graph (Figure 6.8) illustrates this point.

You may have noticed that the "momentum" line from the previous graph has been replaced with a "customer placebo" line. The only vendor who experiences momentum is the winner. All other vendors are interpreting the information they are receiving as the truth, when in actuality it is false evidence appearing real (FEAR). Remember the acronym because you will have a lot to FEAR when you are working on a deal using bad information.

Also notice that vendors disappear from the sales cycle at various stages of investment of time and effort. Clearly, last place is better than every place except winning. However, in most sales cycles the investment does not stop suddenly. Rather, a customer is more likely to become unresponsive or make a vendor perform some tasks that

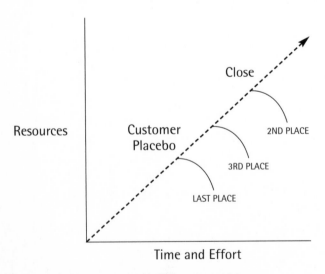

Figure 6.8 Investments by Winners and Losers

it cannot possibly complete. By continuing to jump through a customer's hoops or wasting valuable mental energy and emotions thinking about the deal, the salesperson continues to pour good resources on top of bad. In this situation, the vendor has no hope of protecting its investment to date. It is a sunk cost, and the expenditure of additional time and effort compounds the mistake. The mistake can be magnified even more depending on the sales cycle phase. Learning you are the loser in the eleventh hour of a deal is a frustrating, humbling, and embarrassing event.

SALES CYCLE PHASES

Other distinct phases of the sales cycle are represented by Figure 6.9. The time frame of this entire process is dependent upon the complexity (and associated expense) of the product being sold. For a complex product, the period of time could be as long as a year. For a simple product, it could be as short as one hour.

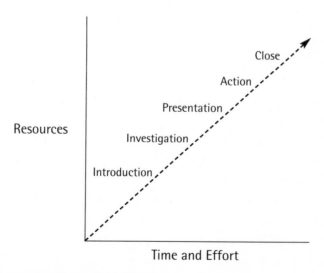

Figure 6.9 Sales Cycle Phases

Every sales cycle starts with an introduction—the action that was responsible for the Heavy Hitter finding the deal. The introduction may be an outbound activity such as a cold call, direct mail, a seminar, or an e-mail. An inbound introduction is when the customer searches out the vendor based upon an industry article, public relations, or word of mouth. Finally, an introduction could be made through a personal relationship such as a customer referral, through a partner referral, or from a consultant. These introductions take advantage of the attachment theory of relationships whereby the Hitter is attached to an existing relationship and bestowed with its same qualities, such as standing, character, and reputation. In other words, assuming the introductory relationship is positive, the Hitter is automatically thought of in the same manner. However, this theory also applies to negative introductory relationships. To Hitters, the source of an introduction is important. They know that relationship-based introductions provide them with the most credibility.

Following the introduction, Heavy Hitters try to gain as much information as possible about the customer's business and technical criteria. They will investigate the customer to determine if their product is a good fit. For a simple product, the investigation could merely be asking a few questions about the customer's environment, such as a copier salesperson asking how many photocopies the customer makes each day. For complex enterprise solutions, the investigation could be a series of on-site meetings to determine the flow of the customer's business operations—its manufacturing and assembly process, for example.

Assuming some level of cursory fit, Heavy Hitters will present their solution in the context of the customer's environment. Depending upon the reception to the solution, Heavy Hitters will introduce a call to action. This may include anything from providing additional documentation to arranging customer site visits for the evaluation of the product. Following the successful completion of the call to action, they are ready to negotiate and close the deal. Once again, the negotiation may include a complex legal process or simply asking for a purchase order.

PRODUCT, FANTASY, AND POLITICS

Three underlying themes are present at each phase of the sales cycle: product, fantasy, and politics. These themes influence the vendor's ultimate selection, and they occur in different amounts and at different stages during the sales cycle. (See Figure 6.10.)

In the early stages of the sales cycle, the customer focus is on the product. The customer wants to understand the underlying technology, feature set, and functionality. As the sales cycle progresses, the fantasy and political themes become more prevalent and important.

All sales involve selling a fantasy. The fantasy is that somehow the product you are selling is going to make the customer's life easier, save the customer money, or enable the customer to make more money. The feature set of your product validates the fantasy elements of your story. The features promote the customer's fantasy. During the sales cycle, you communicate how you can turn your customers' fantasies into a reality, but only when your product is selected.

Evaluation team members also have a personal fantasy. Maybe they want to master new technology to enrich their resumes. Maybe

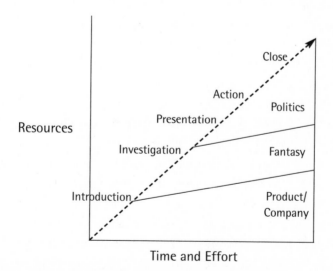

Figure 6.10 Sales Cycle Phases and Underlying Themes

they want to earn bonuses for cutting costs or increasing revenue. Maybe they want to be perceived as heroes within the company or to spend more time at home and less at work. Everyone has a personal fantasy that is associated with the procurement of a product. Whatever the fantasy, it is tied to a very personal benefaction. Heavy Hitters understand and align their strategy with personal fantasies.

Heavy Hitters also understand the political nature of the sales cycle. They know that people will take sides for and against the product. They understand that people within the customer's organization are preoccupied with power or the status quo. As the sales cycle progresses, they know that the decision process will become more political. Ultimately, politics will play a large role in the final decision and only the vendor in the collaborative quadrant will win the political decision.

CONCLUSION

Heavy Hitters work the sales cycle to achieve their personal benefactions associated with closing deals. If you are interested in learning what these benefactions are, take a look at Heavy Hitters' work areas. They may have pictures of sailboats on the wall and dream about being free to sail the world. Pictures of family members may indicate a desire to provide security and a better way of life for them. Sales awards may be prominently displayed as a testament to their sales prowess or indicate their desire for power and prestige. By understanding benefactions you can anticipate the personal and political behavior of both the customer and the Hitter alike.

Any self-respecting book about sales would not be complete without quotations from the ancient Eastern logician Sun Tzu and his famous book, *The Art of War*. Sun Tzu was a Chinese general who lived over 2,500 years ago. Most likely, you have read the book or are familiar with passages from it. Probably the most popular and frequently quoted passage is the following: "If you know the enemy and know yourself, you need not fear the result of a hundred battles. If you know yourself but not the enemy, for every victory gained you will suffer a defeat. If you know neither the enemy nor yourself, you will succumb in every battle."[2]

Some lesser-known Sun Tzu quotes reiterate some of the important concepts presented in this chapter. "Once war is declared, he will not waste precious time . . . but cross the enemy's frontier without delay. The value of time, that is being a little ahead of your opponent, has counted for more than numerical superiority." Time is the ultimate enemy. Heavy Hitters protect their time above all else.

"He who exercises no forethought but makes light of his opponents is sure to be captured by them." Heavy Hitters think about every action strategically. In order to have the best battle plan, they are constantly triangulating information with others.

"The clever combatant will impose his will on the enemy, but does not allow the enemy's will to be imposed on him." Heavy Hitters know once they are in the collaborative quadrant, they have a clear path to win the business.

"He will win who knows when to fight and when not to fight." Heavy Hitters recognize when to attack and when to retreat from a deal.

"Knowledge of the enemy's position can only be obtained from other men. Hence, the use of spies." Heavy Hitters understand they must have a coach to win. They need proprietary information that only a spy can provide. These words are as true today as they were 2,500 years ago.

CHAPTER 7

Building Customer Rapport

As a woman in sales, Tracey faced many obstacles. The market she was selling in was completely dominated by men and all of her colleagues were men. Nevertheless, she was always one of the company's top sales reps and consistently closed the largest deals. Tracey was a person who was able to create "magic" when she was in front of a customer. She could put people at ease while still driving the deal to close. She could ask very tough questions in a very friendly way and persuade people to change their point of view using commonsense arguments. She had a presence that went way beyond her spoken words.

In 2003, Californians witnessed a surreal political event when famous Hollywood action hero Arnold Schwarzenegger was sworn in as governor. Schwarzenegger was chosen during a special election to recall his predecessor, Gray Davis. At the time of the recall election, Davis's approval ratings were the worst of any governor in the 55 years Field polls had been conducted.[1] His political fate was sealed when he announced unpopular tax increases to cover an unexpected $38 billion budget shortfall. The same voters who had reelected him to his second term two years earlier were outraged. As a result of this widespread disapproval and lack of rapport with voters, he became the first governor in state history to be recalled and only the second in the entire United States.

When Schwarzenegger took office, his most daunting task was to get a state budget passed, something that had been nearly impossible to accomplish during the Davis administration. In order to do so, he would have to convince a bitterly divided assembly to vote in unison. How did the former bodybuilder and political novice accomplish it? The headline in my local paper said it all: "Schwarzenegger Won with Soft Sell."[2]

Within the article, several key quotes from assembly members who voted in favor of the budget help explain how Schwarzenegger achieved this minor miracle.[3] According to John Campbell, "He uses more persuasion and strength of character than a hard sell." Todd Spitzer said, "He was amazingly casual. I felt like I was sitting in his house. He has this amazing ability to make people feel at ease." While Schwarzenegger may not be a professional politician, he is a Heavy Hitter when it comes to building rapport.

Heavy Hitters have several unique attributes. They are able to speak in the customer's language, they can decipher their incongruencies in communication, and they have a well-developed model for selecting the deals they pursue. One of the key differences from most salespeople is their ability to create a higher level of rapport with the important members of an evaluation team. In this chapter, we will review how Heavy Hitters determine who can help further their cause and how they build this unique level of rapport. Let's start by examining whom the Heavy Hitters target in their accounts.

Many products require the sales effort to be focused on business line managers, end users, or technologists. Somewhere later in the sales cycle, the purchasing and legal departments will have to bless the selection. At the very least, the selection of the product will have to conform to the standards set previously by the company. For example, most companies have standards regarding which desktop or laptop computers can be purchased.

The sales cycle's complexity is usually in proportion to the scope of the purchase being considered and the size of the company. The decision to buy a new printer for a 20-person advertising firm is very different from the decision by State Farm Insurance to buy printers for all their agents. The sales process will also most likely reflect the complexity of the business and the sophistication of the products the customer produces. For example, the sales process at one of the "Big Three" automakers will reflect the nature and intricacy of the business. However, even a small organization can have a very protracted selection process because the purchase may result in the life or death of the company.

Regardless of the size and complexity of the process, you can classify people within the customer's organization into three basic categories of responsibility: product, management, and executive. Most likely, your solution is targeted at one of these categories. Your initial contact with the account and most frequent interactions with the customer will also be within one of these categories. Let's take a moment to define and understand the nuances of these categories.

PRODUCT CATEGORY

The product category includes those individuals who work hands-on with your product. These people use a vendor's products to create a new product for their company. For example, a computer programmer creates an application (product) by using programming tools provided by a vendor. A telephone operator creates communication (product) by using telephone equipment provided by vendors. A security officer safeguards assets (product) by using surveillance equipment from vendors. People within the product category may have "administrator," "analyst," "technician," "specialist," or "engineer" in their title. Or, their titles will explain exactly what they do, such as "buyer," "mechanic," or "receptionist."

MANAGEMENT CATEGORY

The management category provides direction to each of the various departments of an organization. Departments also may be organized around initiatives or business practices. Typically, people at this level may have "director," "manager," "supervisor," or "leader" somewhere in their titles.

While many different management styles exist, the two fundamental types of department managers are the "domain expert" and the "business expert." Domain expert managers achieved this position by being the most knowledgeable person within their department. For example, a network manager may have been promoted to a management position because of her troubleshooting expertise. The maintenance supervisor may have been the most talented mechanic. The accounts payable manager may have previously been the most knowledgeable clerk. Domain experts are the "alpha," or dominant, resource that all the other members of the group consult with for technical advice.

Meanwhile, business expert managers are responsible for representing their department to the other departments within the company. They rely heavily on the technical opinions of a few key members of their team to make decisions. Typically, they are product category people.

EXECUTIVE CATEGORY

Probably the first instruction all new salespeople are given is to always "call high" when trying to penetrate an account and meet with the most senior executive. However, this is true only if the product you are selling is targeted at the executive category. The only products that will get executive-level attention are those major products that involve major pain for the company (whether in solving or creating a problem), major expenditures, major savings and revenue creation, or major company initiatives. For the sake of simplicity, you can define the term "major" as meaning someone will get fired or promoted over the event. This includes vendors, too!

Companies experience different kinds of pain all the time. There are nuisances that create dull aching pains in every department, such as a temperamental copy machine. There are throbbing pains that may reappear occasionally, like Internet service providers that go down momentarily once or twice every few months. And there are stabbing pains that require immediate attention, for example, when the order-entry system is down and products can't be shipped and employees are sent home. Companies can live with dull aches and prioritize throbbing pains accordingly. It's the stabbing pains that receive immediate attention and dictate budgeting.

In larger companies, the executive level is composed of people who have the word "president" or "chief" in their titles, such as vice president, chief customer care officer, and chief technology officer. In smaller companies, the executive level may also include individuals with "director" or "manager" in their titles.

Each category of responsibility has a different orientation toward the operation of the department. The executive category ensures the company and departments are coordinated with the business strategy and major initiatives. The management category leads ongoing projects, day-to-day operation of the departments, and supervision of the people responsible for "products." Meanwhile, the product category is focused on its microcosm of the department.

GENERALIZATIONS ABOUT WORD CATALOGS AND CATEGORIES

At the beginning of the book, you were introduced to the concept of general words through a discussion about pizza, horoscopes, and fortune cookies. General words require additional words called operators to make them meaningful. In a similar way, "generalizations" require additional investigation and analysis to ensure that they are correct.

Following you will find some generalizations about the most common word catalogs of the people who compose the executive, management, and product categories. These generalizations need to be validated for the particular market space you are selling your products into. No category has an exclusive or definitive word catalog.

Rather, these generalizations are guidelines for you to use to explain your company's story and position your product until you have identified a person's word catalog.

The executive category is most likely to contain individuals with strong visual catalogs. Let's assume you have been working a deal for some time and are in the collaborative quadrant. Your coach has arranged a presentation of your product to the president, whom you have never met. You should present your information assuming that she has a strong visual catalog. As the presentation progresses, you will be able to further qualify the president's wiring and make any appropriate adjustments.

Another strategy is to present all of your ideas and thoughts in neutral wording without any reference to word catalogs. Neutral wording enables listeners to apply the catalog of their choice to gain meaning. Here are some examples of word catalog usage (the first phrase in each pair) and the corresponding neutral wording usage (the second phrase):

- Instead of "I see what you mean," use "I agree with you."

- Instead of "I hear you," use "I understand."

- Instead of "Looks good," use "I think it will work."

- Instead of "I sense you don't like it," use "Do you doubt it will work?"

People naturally gravitate to jobs that suit their word catalog wiring. On average, more Kinesthetics work in people-related positions like nursing, acting, and teaching. Auditories gravitate toward language-based professions and dominate fields that involve writing, talking, and statistics. Visuals work in fields such as advertising, movies, and designing. Here's the main point: If you sell a niche product, the majority of the product category people you interact with will most likely be wired in the same way. For example, you will find an unusually high percentage of people in software programming to be

Auditories. The nature of programming naturally attracts people who have an aptitude for words. Therefore, you should initially mirror the person as an Auditory until you validate his or her exact word catalog wiring.

At the management level, the domain expert manager will have a word catalog that resembles that of the product category people of that industry. This makes sense because they have worked their way up through the ranks. Business expert managers will most likely have visual and kinesthetic wiring. They can see where their team fits into the needs of the company.

All of these generalizations are dependent upon the nature of the market space you sell into. For example, if you are selling a service to the sales and marketing department, that is quite different from selling a product to the engineering department.

EXERCISE 9: GENERALIZATIONS

The preceding generalizations are fairly easy to validate by performing the following exercise:

1. While you are performing the VAK counts on customer calls, add a notation of whether the person is in the product, management, or executive category. When you have collected data during 7 to 10 sales calls, chart the VAK counts for each category.

2. During the next few days, make it a point to spend some time with product, management, and executive category people within your organization. Perform a VAK count for each person you meet and total the VAK counts for each category.

Here's the most important part. You need to identify the category of responsibility your product is targeted to with precision. This is the main group of people you are trying to sell to (executive, management, or product). For your target category, you need to determine if there is a single pervasive word catalog. If there is, you need to take this into account in the development of your sales strategies, messages, customer collateral, and staffing decisions.

During my career, I have sold four basic types of software: enterprise application software, systems software, application development tools, and networking/security software. One of the groups I managed sold products into the security department. The product was specifically targeted at firewall administrators and security analysts, and I was chartered to build the sales team of this start-up business. As I was interviewing, I noticed that I was hiring a large number of auditory salespeople and managers. This began to make me curious.

My previous position involved selling to information technology (IT) management. These people were more likely to have stronger visual and kinesthetic catalogs, so I hired accordingly. However, as I went on more and more of these security product sales calls, I began to realize that the percentage of Auditories within the security industry is very high. Without being conscious of it, my intuition had already begun the process of selecting people that matched the pervasive word catalog of this target audience. In hindsight, it shouldn't have been surprising to find a high number of Auditories in the security area. After all, these product people are responsible for writing and coding the security policies associated with firewalls.

Another interesting characterization of the various people who are involved in the product selection process is displayed in Figure 7.1, which represents four different characteristics that a person can be measured against.

The left axis is the degree to which a person insists that things be done her way. This is called being a "bully." A bully will get her way at any and all costs. Being a bully is not necessarily a negative term, nor does it mean that the person is physically intimidating. It is simply the description of people who will tenaciously fight for their cause. Also, people are more likely to be bullies when they have an elevated status within the evaluation team. The status could be the result of their domain expertise or their title and the authority it commands.

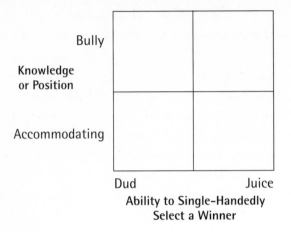

Figure 7.1 Characteristics of Evaluators

At the other end of the spectrum are people who are accommodating. Typically, people with lower-level positions in an organization or low levels of knowledge or experience in a particular area of the company will be more accommodating to decisions being made. They are apathetic to whatever solution is purchased. The degree to which people are bullies or accommodating depends on the effect the purchase decision has on their span of control, position in the company, or ability to perform their job.

On the horizontal axis is the concept of "juice" and the "dud." Simply put, juice is charisma. But even this definition is too simple. Some people are natural-born leaders. They have an aura that can motivate and instill confidence. That's juice. Juice is fairly hard to describe, but you know it when you see it.

Having juice does not mean that these people act like John Wayne, nor are they necessarily the highest-ranking people involved in an evaluation. Instead, they are the ones who always seem to be on the winning side. Only one member of the customer's evaluation team is the bully who has the juice. She imparts her own will on the selection process by single-handedly selecting the vendor and pushing the purchase through the procurement process. She can either finalize the purchase terms or instruct the procurement team on the terms that are considered acceptable.

"Duds" are named after the ineffective firework they represent. Sometimes the fuse of a firework will burn down but nothing will happen. Some fireworks may be very big but produce disappointing results. Duds have a lot of big talk but little action. "Accommodating duds" are people who do not take an active role in the sales process. Even worse are "dud bullies," who try to pretend they have juice but don't. For a salesperson, the realization of this may not come until too late.

For all of the people involved in the sales selection process, Heavy Hitters calculate their amount of juice and their propensity to be a bully. In the following example, John, Jim, Karl, and Rich are plotted according to the Hitter's assessment.

In Figure 7.2, John is a dud bully, Jim is an accommodating dud, and Rich has juice. Hitters naturally gravitate to people with juice. However, a person with juice may be apathetic to the purchase of your product, such as Karl in the diagram. For example, a company's president who has juice probably doesn't care what toner cartridges are purchased for the laser printers. He will be accommodating and support the decision of the people who make that decision. Someone else has the juice for the procurement of toner cartridges. Many people have juice (charisma and authority), but only one person has the juice to single-handedly select the vendor.

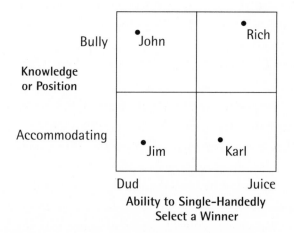

Figure 7.2 Plotting Individual Assessments

Let's assume the same company was making a decision about acquiring another company. In that case, the acquisition review team's decision will surely match the president's preference. She may have imposed her will on the evaluation process through brute force or by finesse. Either way, her preference was "bullied" into the decision. The most powerful position in all of sales is when your coach has juice. If your coach has juice, you win! The next best scenario is when your coach can influence the person with juice.

The bully with the juice has the ability to override the product selection made by other decision makers and even stop the procurement process. At a late stage of a deal, a bureaucrat from purchasing or the legal department might move into the position of the bully with the juice. Sometimes a battle is fought to find out who has more juice, the bureaucrat or the person who previously occupied the bully-with-the-juice position.

Also, if there isn't a bully with the juice in your account, you should be prepared for no decision to be made. Conversely, if a bully with the juice does exist but you aren't able to identify the person, be prepared to lose the deal because you are in a position of extreme risk.

People will argue that some purchases are truly made by committee without a bully with the juice. While a committee does put more "fingerprints of accountability" on the product selection, behind every committee is a bully who has the juice. This person is responsible for the committee's creation or is the person the committee presents his recommendations to.

I want to share with you a memorable, personal story about a bully who definitely had juice.

The local account team had been working with a prestigious financial brokerage firm in New York for five months. During that time, the potential customer had completed a thorough technical product evaluation in its IT lab. The sales team had invested a lot of presales engineering resources in this account. By doing so, the person (product category level) in charge of the technical evaluation had developed into a strong coach. He even approached the sales team to discuss the possibility of joining our company.

Our coach had warned us that the vice president of information services was a micromanager. He personally had to approve all new technology that was brought into "his" organization. Therefore, in order to receive his blessing, a company presentation was scheduled. The sales team can laugh about it now, but the presentation was much more of an interrogation than a business meeting.

From a personal standpoint, the vice president was combative and condescending. For example, as part of the presentation about the company, our sales team explained the patents that we had applied for and been awarded. To this point, he replied, "How do I know that these patents aren't just red herrings [false or nonexistent] to throw off your competition!" The entire meeting felt like we were appearing on *60 Minutes,* being asked by Mike Wallace, "Is it true you beat your wife?" Even though you answer no to the question, you are assumed to be guilty.

Given this set of circumstances, we had limited options to build rapport. First, we maintained our composure and did our best not to take the attack personally. Second, we agreed (profusely at times) with the VP's point of view when it was applicable. And finally, in the most professional, nonpersonal way we could muster, we countered on certain issues by offering other potential solutions. You do not want to directly contradict a bully who has juice.

As we left the meeting, I told the local salesperson that based on the beating we received, I thought it was a long shot the company would move forward with us. However, we had a secret weapon. Our coach would later tell us that our performance was deemed "acceptable" by the vice president. More importantly, our coach continued to lobby on our behalf. Several weeks later, we received our first purchase order from our new customer. It was through the coach's persistent promotion of our solution that we won the deal.

Heavy Hitters understand that they must deal with duds and bullies while they are in hot pursuit of the person who has juice. Heavy Hitters also have their own juice—their ability to create rapport. In order to win the deal, Hitters know how to communicate their message and influence others in the process, building a more intense level of rapport with their customers. The best way to illustrate this is to recount a recent sales presentation and explain the various techniques that helped create rapport.

My company was invited to participate in a seminar with four much larger and more well-known high-technology companies. The seminar's target audience was the product category people within the networking and security area. The audience consisted mainly of network analysts and security administrators. Most likely, the audience members were using one of the other vendors' products, and this was a great opportunity for my company to reach these target customers. However, we knew a lot of information would be covered because all the other vendors would be presenting their products. This created a problem because it would be easy for my company's story to be overpowered by all the other vendors' noise.

Our presentation was third and would last about 30 minutes. The two presentations preceding ours were from one of the largest computer hardware companies and a leading software company. Overall, the audience of about 50 people did not seem engaged. When the presenters asked questions of the audience, there was very little participation. Also, few questions were asked of the vendors following their presentations. A high level of "audience rapport" wasn't established.

I formulated my presentation strategy while watching the tepid reception given to the first two presenters. First, I was going to build a special level of rapport with the audience so that my presentation would have the greatest impact. In one sense, I considered the other presenters as my competitors—not from a product or company point of view but because they were all competing for the audience's mind share and to have their message valued as something important.

Second, I determined that my main benefaction of the meeting was to have the attendees remember who my company was and the problem our technology solved. I specifically wanted to see the audience members sitting "on the edge of their seats" and hear them ask questions at the end of my presentation. Ideally, someone in the audience needed my product today. Regardless, I knew my sales force would be following up personally with every attendee. In anticipation of their calling, I wanted to lay the foundation of credibility by utilizing the attachment theory of relationships, whereby a new relationship inherits positive qualities from a respected preexisting association.

Here are the first few sentences of my presentation. For illustration purposes, I am substituting "ABC Company" for the actual name of my company.

> Hello, I'm Steve Martin with ABC Company. Now, I would like to ask each of you for some help today. During the presentation, when I ask you a question, I would like you to honestly raise your hand. [You'll discover why I used this odd phrase later.]
>
> I know you are familiar with the other companies presenting today. I'd like to know, how many of you are not familiar with ABC Company?
>
> Thank you.
>
> Since you are not familiar with ABC Company, I only want you to remember one thing from today's presentation: ABC Company provides high availability and load balancing software.

Let's analyze this communication event. I opened my presentation with, "Hello, I'm Steve Martin with ABC Company." Behind and to my left was the logo and name of my company projected onto a large screen. Usually, the announcement of my name elicits some soft laughter or at least a smile. With the exception of a handful of people, the audience remained emotionless. My internal dialogue told me it was time to do something drastic to get this audience engaged. It was time to interrupt their pattern of lethargic behavior.

For the past two hours, the audience members had been in the same state of apathetic or weak participation. Frankly, I didn't blame them since the previous presenters were poor speakers. Incidentally, the first presenter to any group greatly influences the demeanor and sets the standard of audience behavior. Unfortunately, the lead-off presentation was flat and unexciting, and as a result, the audience's behavior was similar. This pattern had been established and was now the accepted behavior of the group. To change this, I planned to perform a behavior interruption that would leave the audience members with no choice but to change their demeanor.

"Now, I would like to ask each of you for some help today," I said. The majority of the audience was composed of very technical, product category people. As we generalized earlier, product category people are more likely to be Auditories. Since I have been working with this particular market space for some time, I was fairly certain this was true for most of the attendees.

Asking someone for help is a great tool for Hitters. First, it is a natural human characteristic to want to help others. Within the business environment, the concept of helping others is even more accepted and expected. If you were to make 10 telephone calls to others in your company, the most frequent response following "Hello" would be "How can I help you?"

Asking for help also starts the behavior interruption because people are naturally curious. When I asked "each of you for some help," I knew that all the audience members would become curious and ask themselves, "I wonder what he wants?" In a sense, I was leading the way the audience was thinking by limiting what they could think about. I was getting their attention and forcing them to pay attention to my words.

I followed this statement with "During the presentation, when I ask you a question, I would like you to honestly raise your hand." As I said this, I raised my right hand. Once again, the statement was made in an auditory style. If the audience consisted mostly of visual managers, it would have been more appropriate to say, "Honestly show me your hands." (Again, you'll see why I used this phrase later.)

I also used a different tone in my voice when I said the words "ask" and "honestly." This is known as "marking." I specifically marked those words to call the audience's internal dialogues to attention. Marking has two purposes: It alerts the listener's conscious mind to highlight a specific thought, and it tells the subconscious mind to remember what might otherwise have been ignored. You can use all aspects of body language including hand gestures, facial expressions, posture, and speech to mark words. Words can be marked by varying their pronunciation with inflection, volume, pitch, speed, or accent.

The most common way to mark is to increase the volume. However, decreasing volume, even whispering, is just as effective in business meetings. Even words and phrases can be used to mark other words. If I say, "Listen up!" "Here comes the important part," or "If you're wondering what's next," your awareness and anticipation are heightened.

What does it mean to "honestly raise your hand"? How did you interpret this request? Did I mean for audience members to honestly raise their hands or honestly answer the question? This confusion may have caused a brief internal debate since an attempt had to be made to define what I meant. I actually meant both. Regardless, they still had to pay attention to me and by making this request in a certain way, I was again leading their thought process.

In conjunction with this request, I raised my right hand very slowly in a very specific way. I positioned it very close to my chest, much like the president would do when taking the oath of office. I could have raised my hand as high as possible, but this would be uncomfortable for Auditories. I was trying to engage their internal dialogue by keeping it very busy and attentive to me. By raising my hand slowly, they naturally had to follow it. Again, I was leading their behavior by showing them the "comfortable" or suggested way to raise their hand. If I had been presenting to a predominantly visual group, I would have held my hand higher and moved it faster.

"I know you are familiar with the other companies presenting today," I started. This was a verifiable statement. I was certain that everybody knew the two companies that presented before me. Therefore, as each of the audience members verified this statement with their internal dialogue, it would be true. They had no choice but to agree with my verifiable statement. Verifiable statements help build credibility and extend rapport with the presenter. Now, if I had opened up the presentation by stating that my company had the hottest new technology, there would be no way for the audience members to verify the statement. This unverifiable statement would naturally elicit skepticism and actually hinder creating rapport. Unverifiable statements must be proven true to be accepted.

"I'd like to know, how many of you are not familiar with ABC Company?" I continued. Normally, someone would ask, "How many people are familiar with ABC Company?" I knew my company was much less known than the other, larger companies. Before the seminar started, I even had casual conversations with a few of the attendees and validated they hadn't heard of my company. I marked the word "not" with tone inflection and held my hands chest high, open palmed, to the audience. I asked the question in a negative form and held my palms out to emphasize this. I wanted them to stop and think about the question so I paused momentarily. Their internal dialogue had to repeat the question to themselves to make sure they heard and answered it correctly.

One of my benefactions was to interrupt their noninvolvement in the presentation and get them all to raise their hands, instead of just a few attendees. The response to the question was perfect. With the exception of just a couple of people, all the audience members in the room raised their hands. The manner in which they raised their hands was also important. No one shot a hand in the air like Horshack on *Welcome Back, Kotter*. Rather, they comfortably raised their right hands as I did. "Thank you," I replied. It is very important to show respect and reward the appropriate response.

"Since you are not familiar with ABC Company, I only want you to remember one thing from today's presentation." This sentence has two separate parts that are linked together. The first part of the sentence is another verifiable statement. They had previously raised their hands and acknowledged that they weren't familiar with my company. The second part of the sentence is a direct instruction on what I wanted them to do. Through "linkage," you can tie together two completely different messages. Since the first part is known to be true, the second part will have a higher likelihood of being accepted as the truth.

Let's interrupt this story for a brief experiment. As you finish reading this sentence, you will become aware of your breathing. The first part of the sentence is a verifiable statement. You are reading the words that compose the sentence and, undoubtedly, you will finish reading it. By linking it to the second part of the sentence, you have little choice but to think about your breathing (even if you didn't want to). Because breathing is an automatic process, you may have had to stop reading or breathing for a moment to check how you were breathing. If the sentence had read, "Become aware of your breathing," it wouldn't have had the same impact and effect. Linkage is a very powerful sales tool, and Heavy Hitters continually link true statements to theoretical arguments in order to best argue their case.

As I said, "I only want you to remember one thing from today's presentation," I executed three different types of marking. I inflected my speech by increasing volume and adding urgency to the tone on the words "only" and "one." Physically, I held my right hand up chest high, forming the number one with my hand. Then, I paused for a moment to survey the crowd. I wanted to make sure they were looking at my finger. Everyone I could see was. I also took one step sidewise to the right as I said the word "one." This ensured that they would have to maintain a strong focal point of attention. I watched the audience members' heads move as they followed me.

I continued, "ABC Company provides high availability and load balancing software." Using my speech, I marked "high availability and load balancing." I also changed my hand position from forming the number one to separating my index finger and thumb, as if I was measuring the words "high availability and load balancing." The audience followed the change in hand movement. I was creating an anchor.

As we learned earlier, an anchor is the process of associating a certain feeling or meaning to an object. That morning, the members of the audience were going to hear presentations from four different companies and I wanted to ensure my message wasn't lost. I wanted to ensure it was remembered in their mind's eye.

You may have noticed another aspect of what I said. I purposely created some confusion by intentionally contradicting myself. The meaning of the words I said was detached from the physical message my body was sending. "Detaching" refers to the process of dividing the listener's reality by separating preexisting meanings from the words being spoken. I said the word "one" and formed the number one with my hand. However, I gave the audience two things to remember, "high availability" and "load balancing." A portion of the audience didn't notice I actually said two things. They considered it one statement and I was well on my way to developing rapport with these people. For the portion of the audience that considered these two items, this was not in alignment with their reality. It caused them to do an additional quick internal assessment about what was happening.

Up to that point in the presentation, I had been smoothly leading the audience where I wanted them to go. I had been marking key thoughts and linking messages together. The detaching of information completed the behavior interruption. It was another layer of information that had to be assessed and internalized, causing an additional level of information processing to occur. While this entire series of communication took less than a minute, audience members' state of engagement had changed from apathetic to interested. Their posture even changed and they sat more upright. Their facial expressions changed. It was as if they woke up. Now they were in an appropriate state of receptivity to hear my company's presentation.

Detaching can be an effective tool in situations where you want to change behaviors quickly. For example, when you greet someone, you will typically cheerfully say, "How are you doing?" The automatic response is "Fine" or "Okay." It is the expected and anticipated response attached to that particular question. Let's pretend you respond, "My dog just died." This answer is completely opposite from the expected response. Immediately, the person who asked the question would be detached from being cheerful and become somber or apologetic.

Salespeople are constantly detaching meanings. For example, since almost all customers have dealt with high-pressure salespeople in the past, they have attached a negative meaning to "salespeople" in general. In every sales call, the Heavy Hitter is trying to detach herself from this stereotype through her behavior and actions.

Within my sales organization, I have a favorite phrase that replaces "How are you doing?" I will say in a friendly voice, "Are you helping us?" Basically, I am trying to elicit honest, unedited information from my staff. "Are you helping us?" doesn't have an attached response. If there is good news or bad news, I want to know about it as early as possible. I have found that by changing this small greeting, I can get a very quick, current assessment of someone's recent accomplishments and the important issues they are facing.

STATES OF RAPPORT AND ENGAGEMENT

During the seminar presentation, I was able to change the state of rapport with the audience members in a very short time. I needed their state to change in order to create the best circumstance to have my message accepted and remembered. People experience many different types of states, ranging from fear and hate to love and trust. In the business world, we are typically operating in a very narrow range of states.

"State" also applies to engagement at work. Normal daily business is done in the awake or alert state. You're constantly alert for information, whether it comes from personal conversations, e-mail, or the telephone. And you're performing your duties as a participant of the company. (See Figure 7.3.)

Figure 7.3 States of Consciousness

At the extreme ends of the scale are the avoidance state and the trance state. For example, you will go to a great deal of effort to avoid someone or something that is feared or hated. I dislike going to the dentist. As a result, I try to avoid it as much as possible and procrastinate about scheduling an appointment.

At the other end of the spectrum is being in a "trance." A trance is not necessarily equivalent to being comatose. A trance is entering a state where you are aware of your environment and the stimuli surrounding you but are intently focused on your internal dialogue. For example, my wife and I will read together in bed at night. We are very aware of each other and cognizant of noises coming from other parts of our home. However, since we are concentrating on reading, repeating, and interpreting words, we are very self-centered on our internal dialogues. When I am with my wife, I am very comfortable so it's easy for me to relax and enter a state of trance. Perhaps just by reading these last few sentences you may have felt yourself drifting off a bit.

Heavy Hitters are constantly trying to differentiate themselves from their competitors. While the rest of the competitors are operating in the "normal" range of business rapport, Hitters are trying to change the rules of the game and develop a more intense rapport that is outside the range of normal, where the customer is comfortable and at ease.

The customer has the free will to choose any product he or she pleases. As opposed to the hard sell, rapport is an irresistible force that opens skeptical minds. As Assemblyman Spitzer further commented about his meeting with Governor Schwarzenegger, "He communicated a vision of how this policy would make a difference. I walked out of there feeling like I still had ownership of my decision."[4]

At the seminar, I was trying to achieve an intense state of rapport with the audience members. Since my product can help their businesses succeed, I felt it was important they heard my message. In order to ensure they were listening, I was marking specific words, making verifiable statements, and linking actions I wanted them to perform throughout the entire presentation. As a result, I was heavily exercising their internal dialogues and engaging all of their word catalogs. By doing so, I interrupted their pattern of behavior and was able to lead them to the desired state of business rapport.

You may have been wondering how I knew I had achieved my goal. Through the years, I have developed a model for determining what state an audience is in. During any meeting or presentation, I am constantly sensing each individual's state of rapport. However, this is practical only in groups up to a certain size. With over 50 people at this seminar, this presented a different challenge. In order to validate the group's state of rapport, I had to create an easily observable cue to allow me to make the determination if what I was doing was, in fact, working. By asking the group to raise their hands, I was able to identify a "group pattern." Group patterns are presentation checkpoints used to measure rapport. Since almost all the audience members raised their hands, it was okay to proceed.

Another question you may have is whether I planned the entire introduction. Did I choreograph the physical movements, tone inflections, and the specific questions I asked? The answer is "Not really." It just happened. Through repetitive experience, I have developed the skill to do this. Like learning anything new, I started with small steps, such as marking words verbally and physically. Then I incorporated the concept of linking messages. Finally, I began to tie them together to form behavior interruptions. It takes practice, but it's well worth the effort.

On one of my recent travels I sat next to a regional sales manager who was on his way to corporate headquarters to make a presentation at a management meeting. I couldn't help but notice the first slide of his PowerPoint presentation titled "Year in Review." It consisted of three bullet points: "Sluggish economy still affecting sales," "Marketing efforts not yet taking hold," and "Intense price competition." I started to wonder how his presentation would be received. Would his bosses and peers think of him as a complainer who was making up excuses or would he trigger an honest discussion about what to do under these circumstances? The answer is that his reception would ultimately depend on the level of rapport he has established with the rest of the team.

Rapport also is the answer to problems listed in his three bullet points. In a tough economy, you need customers who will fight on your behalf to secure funds for your products and who will give you an honest answer about whether or not the deal will happen. No company has perfect marketing or perfect products, but customers whom you have rapport with will accept you as you are. Finally, there will always be a cheaper product and the decision not to buy is free. If your customer is your friend, the issue of price becomes secondary.

CONCLUSION

When a doctor gives a patient a sugar pill, the patient feels better because she believes the pill is good for her. We know this as the "placebo effect." As salespeople, we want potential customers to begin feeling better the moment we meet with them and start to explain how we can help solve their problems.

The exact opposite of the placebo effect is called the "tomato effect." It's the mistaken belief that something good is actually bad for you. It's named after an eighteenth-century incident when people became ill after being told that the harmless tomatoes they had eaten were poisonous. As salespeople, we must overcome something similar to the tomato effect with every new customer we meet. Even though we know we have something that will help them, they still think we are trying to harm them.

Not only are customers skeptical, they're nervous. Meeting someone new is a stressful experience, and their internal dialogue is on high alert. One of the biggest challenges salespeople face is establishing a sufficient level of customer rapport to ensure their message is received in an open and honest manner. This is why we must build rapport, to lower customers' defenses and overcome the tomato effect.

Heavy Hitters know that the members of the customer's evaluation team do not share an equal vote or the same level of interest in the decision being made. Some members are apathetic while others are more insistent they get their way. However, one individual has the juice to single-handedly make the decision, and it is this individual whom Hitters strive to build rapport with.

Finally, salespeople are constantly placed into situations where they must differentiate themselves and their product from other attention-getting solutions. In order to stand out and be remembered, they engage listeners' internal dialogue by linking messages together and marking specific words. Like Tracey in the story at the beginning of the chapter, they create "magic" in front of the customer.

To finish the story about the seminar, my presentation was very well received. A short question-and-answer session immediately followed the presentation. Unlike the other presenters, we were asked so many questions that we ran out of time. Perhaps the most interesting event occurred about an hour and a half later.

The final presenter of the day wrapped up the seminar. He thanked everyone for attending and summarized each vendor's presentation. As he summarized my company's product, he did the most complimentary impression. He moved to the exact position on stage where I had spoken earlier, held up his right hand with the index finger and thumb spread, and said, "and the one thing to remember about ABC Company is 'high availability' and 'load balancing' software." I was sitting in the back of the room with my local salesperson. She leaned over to me and said, "He got it!" I winked at her and said, "They all got it!"

CHAPTER **8**

Your Two Most Important Customers: Your Manager and You

> The mood was somber. The vice president of sales had just begun to address the worldwide sales team that had been assembled. The previous quarter had been a disaster. Following 15 straight quarters of unprecedented growth and incredible stock appreciation, the company announced it would miss its revenue targets by over 30 percent. In addition, articles in the press were criticizing the company's aggressive accounting practices and unusual revenue recognition policies. Under these circumstances, the vice president began to speak: "We're just going to have to sell our way out of this thing."

I have a complaint with how the entertainment industry portrays the sales profession. Willy Loman, the main character in Arthur Miller's *Death of a Salesman,* was a cheater who ultimately betrayed his family. The movie *Glengarry Glen Ross* depicts salespeople as a desperate group of life's losers who will resort to anything to make money. In *The Big Kahuna,* Kevin Spacey plays an angst-ridden salesman who regrets wasting his life in sales. In *About Schmidt,* Jack Nicholson plays Warren Schmidt, the main character, who profoundly hates his daughter's fiancé, an underachieving mullet-wearing waterbed salesman. These stereotypes are enough to make parents feel like complete failures if their son or daughter works in sales.

However, those aren't the type of salespeople whom I know. My friends in sales are generally upbeat and have an incredible sense of humor. Since they value relationships, they are loyal friends who always put family first. They're not a group of disillusioned characters; they're entrepreneurs who have the great responsibility and joy of running their own businesses. The best of these businesspeople earn the honor of the title Heavy Hitter.

Salesmanship is not something that can be taught; it must be learned. While you may have been sent to some type of sales training in the past, most likely you learned how to actually sell by trial and error. Or, you may have even watched colleagues to figure out why they are successful. However, where do you learn how to work with your two most important customers: your manager and yourself?

In the previous chapters, we have discussed how to model Heavy Hitters by reviewing how they determine the "wiring" of their customers, how they identify incongruencies to find the truth, and how they select, qualify, and close deals. Because Heavy Hitters are people worthy of imitation, we strive to emulate every behavioral characteristic completely. In this chapter, we continue our modeling exercise by examining how they work with their managers. We want to understand how they manage this all-important relationship.

However, our most important customer is ourself. Sales is a career that can be both exhilarating and frustrating. Where do you learn to cope with the highs and lows in your career? We want to understand who we are and the drives that motivate us to achieve. For newer salespeople, this section will be a form of mentoring, a discussion of how Heavy Hitters view themselves and their career in sales. Experienced salespeople are likely to have a few "aha" moments while reading this chapter when elements of their own behavior and individual sales style are explained.

We'll start by reviewing the strategies Heavy Hitters use to build rapport with their manager. This discussion will include a review of the relevant sales management styles Heavy Hitters encounter. In the second half of this chapter, we will review the complex needs that drive a Hitter's actions. The psychological framework we will use to describe Hitter behavior is based on Abraham Maslow's "hierarchy of needs." Over the years, I have found the theory a useful and intuitively logical frame of reference to explain the complex issues that drive all human behavior. Not surprisingly, once we understand this universal model, we can also apply it directly to customers.

As I was walking the hallway at my office, I overheard a conversation between two managers. One said, "A players hire A players, B players hire B players, and so on." This quote refers to the popular axiom that the best managers will hire the best employees. In sales, this is extraordinarily true. Through the repetitive process of hiring salespeople and observing which ones succeed or fail, A-quality sales managers have developed a keen sense for identifying top sales talent and a methodology for selecting the individual who has the right skills, attitude, and personality. Therefore, they are continually upgrading their sales teams with the "arrival of the fittest."

Conversely, A-quality salespeople recognize their manager will influence their ability to succeed and the atmosphere of their day-to-day environment. Therefore, they want to work for A-quality managers who add value to their sales efforts. This value may range from the managers' charisma to help close business to their proficiency in working on the salesperson's behalf within the company. Ultimately, the success of this relationship is dependent upon the personal "fit" between two people. Heavy Hitters know their sales manager can make their life enjoyable, tolerable, or miserable, and that their mental condition will be determined by this relationship.

UNDERSTANDING YOUR SALES MANAGER

Throughout the course of a career, every salesperson will work with a variety of sales managers. "Sales manager" means the person you directly report to, the individual who gives you guidance and ultimately evaluates your performance. A sales representative in a large company may report to the district manager. Meanwhile, the district manager's sales manager is the regional director, who in turn is led by the vice president of sales. Finally, the vice president reports to the president. Even a president answers to sales managers—the board of directors. Everyone has a sales manager!

Maybe your sales manager was one of the key reasons you joined your company. Perhaps your sales manager was thrust upon you during a reorganization. During my career, I have worked for at least 20 different sales managers. Some were very good and a few were just plain horrible. But I can honestly say I learned as much from the bad ones as from the good ones. It is equally important to understand what you shouldn't model as well as what you should!

A Heavy Hitter knows he can't successfully complete the entire sales cycle alone. He is not Superman. He counts on other people to help him. Just as the Lone Ranger needed Tonto and Batman had Robin, Heavy Hitters need a support team to help them defeat the bad guys, their competitors. The sales manager is a key member of this valiant team.

Rapport was not meant only for the customer. It's just as critical for Heavy Hitters to establish rapport with their sales managers. Heavy Hitters and their managers synergistically "click" together—sharing similar feelings and viewpoints about sales. While this relationship has probably developed naturally over time, here are three steps that anyone can use to build rapport with sales managers.

1. Identify the sales managers' word catalog wiring.

2. Understand their style.

3. Always operate in their world, according to their wiring and style.

The prerequisite to establishing rapport is the identification of the person's primary, secondary, and recessive word catalog. Heavy Hitters have a complete and thorough understanding of their manager's word catalog wiring. And while Heavy Hitters may do this intuitively, it is helpful to use a formal process to ensure accuracy.

Review the last 10 to 20 e-mails your manager sent you and perform a VAK keyword count. In addition, keep a precise VAK count during each of the next three times you speak with your manager (whether in person or over the telephone). The results of the e-mail VAK count should match the VAK counts from your conversations. If not, keep investigating and performing VAK counts until you are 100 percent certain you understand the manager's wiring.

After mapping his wiring, make a conscious commitment to always communicate with him on his terms using his catalogs, regardless of how you are wired. Remember, flexibility is the hallmark of a Hitter. In essence, you are going to treat your manager exactly as if he was your customer—because he is! If he is a Visual and you are an Auditory, adopt a Visual-based catalog when communicating with him. Similarly, if he is a Kinesthetic and you are an Auditory, change to his catalog. Also, adopt his entire spectrum of the human communication model, including the phonetic and physical layers. When I had a manager who had an accent or particular mannerism, I found myself naturally adopting a similar idiosyncrasy. I would even subconsciously adjust my style of dress to resemble his and find myself repeating his clichés.

After you have your manager's wiring identified and internalized, you need to understand his management orientation. Once again, this is analogous to selling to the customer. However, instead of placing him into the product, management, or the executive categories, you will catalog him by his individual sales management style.

SALES MANAGEMENT STYLES

Just as people have different levels of gregariousness, assertiveness, and action-oriented tendencies, sales managers have different sales management styles. Seven management styles are most prevalent. Most likely, your manager will have one dominant style. However, he will probably share a few characteristics from other styles and may even move from style to style depending on the situation. The seven most common sales management styles are the mentor, expressive manager, sergeant, Teflon manager, amateur manager, micromanager, and overconfident manager.

In addition to establishing rapport with their managers, Heavy Hitters also devise a long-term strategy for interrelating with them. With the exception of the amateur manager, the goal of each of these long-term strategies is to create a symbiotic, or mutually advantageous, coexistence between two close associates. The approach Hitters use is based upon the seven different sales management styles and is listed in Figure 8.1.

Before we begin this discussion about styles and strategies, it is important to put the conversation in perspective. Successful navigation through life is based upon a series of continual small adjustments to the circumstances surrounding you. It is not typically done with cataclysmic adjustments. Similarly, these styles and strategies are frameworks to be used while you are accomplishing your normal daily routine in relation to the unique situation surrounding your workplace.

Also, it is human nature to judge others' actions and behaviors using broad generalizations. We typically take a negative position when passing judgments on others as we are comparing them to ourselves and our own idea of perfection. Frequently, people are classified as bad sales managers without any understanding of why they act the way they do. For instance, I remember a group of workers bitterly complaining about the frequent absences and lackadaisical work habits of a particular colleague until they learned he was battling cancer.

Many learned books have been written about sales management philosophies, processes, and how to develop the individual attributes

Management Style	Long-Term Strategy
Mentor	Scholarly Student
Expressive Manager	Empathetic Ego
Sergeant	Straightforward Sincerity
Teflon Manager	Patient Pollyanna
Amateur Manager	Release Relationship
Micromanager	Perfect Performance
Overconfident Manager	Clever Conqueror

Figure 8.1 Sales Management Styles and Strategies

required to achieve success. The intent here is much simpler. You need to study your manager in detail in order to identify and predict his behavior. Based upon the information you gather, you need to create your own plan for working together. This section should cause you to think about your manager in new or different ways. More importantly, by developing and executing a proactive strategy to interrelate with your manager, you gain more control over your environment.

MENTORS

Mentors are charismatic leaders and sales experts who measure their success using three criteria: exceeding revenue goals, creating an environment where the entire team can succeed, and helping all team members realize their individual potential. Mentors are confident in their own abilities and possess the business insight to know what needs to be done and how to do it.

Even though they believe in accountability and a strict code of ethical conduct, they relate well with their team and motivate by positive encouragement rather than fear. They are comfortable with themselves and are able to keep perspective and a sense of resolution during tenuous times.

The mentors' philosophy is an extension of their personality. While their demeanor may range from gruff and cantankerous to friendly and personable, they are well liked and act as a unifying force to their sales team members. Although mentors tend to have a very hands-on management style, they don't meddle in their teams' daily duties. They lead by example.

Mentors' sales intuition has been honed by many years of customer calls; therefore, their judgment is respected and advice highly sought-after. Mentors are highly effective in presentations or one-on-one customer meetings because customers genuinely like them and appreciate their presence. Since mentors usually have strong kinesthetic (or visual) catalogs, they are able to charm customers.

Heavy Hitters want to learn everything they can from mentors, so they adopt a strategy based on being a "scholarly student." They invite their mentors on calls, quiz them about tactics over lunch, or chat with them after hours about their sales experiences. Heavy Hitters have great hope that perhaps one day they will be able to mentor their own sales team.

EXPRESSIVE MANAGERS

Expressive managers are people-oriented with a flair for sharing their emotions and amplifying the emotions of those around them. Most likely, expressive managers have strong kinesthetic word catalogs. They have a natural ability to put people at ease. They are very charming and gregarious individuals who are always ready, willing, and able to discuss personal matters in addition to events at work. They will frequently be seen chatting with coworkers in other departments at the water cooler.

Expressive managers create an environment where a considerable amount of energy is focused on how they are thought of and perceived within the company. They crave attention and tend to be over-dramatic, by either exaggerating their accomplishments or overstating the prevailing circumstances their team is facing. These "sympathy complaints" are subconscious attempts to secure love and affection. Expressive managers are saying, "Pay attention to me!" Because of their need for constant emotional approval, they may become jealous when others receive recognition.

Expressive managers are master motivators of their team, and since people are so comfortable with them, they are very effective on sales calls. Customers perceive them as genuinely nice people who will personally take care of their account. However, their mood swings can be intense, and they have a natural tendency to become bored with mundane tasks because they would rather be working spontaneously based on their emotions. It is their emotions that drive their daily tasks and agenda.

The long-term strategy Heavy Hitters employ to shape their relationships with expressive managers is called "empathetic ego." Empathizing with expressive managers requires sharing their experiences through unselfish listening and continual confirmation that the Heavy Hitter understands the situation or dilemma. Expressive managers experience tremendous highs and lows; participating in the celebration of the good times is just as important as commiserating during the bad.

A key aspect of the strategy involves protecting the expressive managers' ego by supporting their position and validating their worth to others within and outside the sales group. This means only presenting information that supports their beliefs. Obviously this requires knowing where they stand on issues beforehand. One of the biggest insults to any manager, and expressive ones in particular, is being contradicted in public. Conversely, announcing their successes and broadcasting compliments will definitely yield relationship rewards.

SERGEANTS

The sergeant is named after the field sergeant in a military organization. Sergeants develop an intense loyalty to their team, perhaps even greater than their personal loyalty to their company. They are hard workers who are constantly worrying about their "troops." They will even sacrifice their own best interests and tolerate personal hardships if they feel it will benefit their team. Sergeants will usually have strong kinesthetic and visual catalogs.

Sergeants are strong performers on customer sales calls. Since they have participated in so many sales calls, they possess highly developed sales intuitions. As a result, they are excellent mentors to their team. And it is through their direct interaction with their team members that they draw satisfaction from their job.

Sergeants are likable, reliable people who have an intense pride in their work. They have a humble demeanor and will unselfishly pass any praise they receive directly to the team. They wear their emotions on their sleeves, and their team members always know where they stand. While they understand their place in the organization and are confident of their own ability, they still feel somewhat expendable and may suffer from self-doubt. They do not accept criticism easily and will take faultfinding to heart. However, sergeants are typically some of the last people to leave a failing company and may have a history of staying with companies long after the good times have passed.

The strategy for building a successful relationship with a sergeant is based upon "straightforward sincerity." Since sergeants are "tell it like it is" people, Heavy Hitters' communication with them is open, honest, and candid. For example, sergeants want to know the bad news as soon as possible and don't appreciate it being sugarcoated.

Sergeants expect a sincere relationship in terms of words and actions. When they confide in their trusted team, it is imperative the team members maintain confidentiality. Since sergeants defend their team's honor, it is expected they will do the same. As opposed to editing oneself to suit the expressive manager's ego, building rapport with a sergeant involves supporting the person by honoring the friendship. Not surprisingly, Heavy Hitters' maxim for working with sergeants is the same motto used by the Marines: *semper fidelis,* "always faithful."

TEFLON MANAGERS

Teflon managers are pleasant, agreeable, and polite people who have strong visual catalogs. However, unlike sergeants, you may never really get to know Teflon managers, even after working with them for years. They avoid disclosing personal information or give just enough to be thought of as friendly. From this standpoint, some people will consider them superficial. Another characteristic of Teflon managers is their ability to stay above the daily fray of politics. Yet while they seem cooperative, they are usually very stubborn when it comes to their personal agenda.

Regardless of the situation, Teflon managers are even-keeled and rarely frazzled. They always seem to be in control of their emotions and relate to others mainly in an edited, business demeanor. You will not find these people yelling in the office, and they rarely socialize or develop personal friendships with coworkers. They will share their honest feelings only when there is little personal risk and if sharing this information benefits their business position.

Nothing sticks to Teflon managers. Bad news that would devastate sergeants or expressive managers bounces off them. Teflon managers just keep moving forward and never seem to be depressed or give up. They enjoy prestige and title and act the role accordingly.

Working for Teflon managers creates an interesting dichotomy because of their personal nonattachment, comfort with solitude, idealized self-image, and desire to remain safe from criticism. Heavy Hitters employ a "patient Pollyanna" strategy to dovetail with these Teflon manager characteristics. First and foremost, Heavy Hitters will go to great lengths to ensure they do not make their manager look foolish but, instead, wise and proficient at all times. Therefore, Hitters always exude a cheerful, pleasant disposition to communicate everything is okay, even under the most dire circumstances.

To help keep themselves immune to criticism, Heavy Hitters adopt a "politically correct" demeanor, rarely making cynical statements and repressing any open display of anger or disrespect to others. Patience and temperance are virtues Teflon managers appreciate. Perhaps during their upbringing Teflon managers were taught "If you have nothing nice to say, then say nothing at all." Regardless, this becomes the Heavy Hitter's new mantra. A Hitter would definitely not tell long-winded stories about personal problems or detailed accounts of the history of a deal as they would with an expressive manager. Rather, they keep the interactions brief and talk only about the big picture.

Teflon managers expect a high degree of loyalty and perfection from their staff, and Heavy Hitters try to achieve these standards. Most interestingly, no news is considered good news, so Heavy Hitters do not bombard Teflon managers with information. However, Heavy Hitters take advice from Machiavelli's *The Prince,* when he said that it is better to give bad news all at once and leak good news patiently over time.[1]

AMATEUR MANAGERS

Amateur managers are the toughest of all the types to work for. While they may make a great first impression, analogous to a great first date, each subsequent date becomes more painful and frustrating. Amateur managers may have any word catalog, but most likely they have a stronger auditory catalog and weaker kinesthetic catalog.

Amateur managers most likely do not have an extensive background in sales, are very new to sales management, or lack the ability to manage a sales force. Since they lack practical experience, their management style suffers from an identity crisis. As a result, plans continually change and the sales organization suffers from a lack of focus. Their shortage of sales experience also renders their advice on deals unreliable and their participation in sales calls ineffective.

Amateur managers fear being judged negatively by their superiors and peers, as well as their subordinates. As a result, they may perceive the company as unfriendly or hostile. Their fears may also play an interesting part in their decision process. Under stress they become worried and indecisive or they propose so many different solutions that nothing ever happens. Or they may create outlandish plans and elaborate schemes that can't possibly be implemented in the real world. The mood of the sales department changes from moment to moment. Sometimes there is a cheerful permissiveness while other times it is run with ironfisted authority.

Amateur managers may have a misconception of their own strengths and an incorrect perception of how the organization views them. They also have a demonstrated history of broken relationships and a tendency to try to fix business problems by anointing a new "hero of the day." This person is expected to fix the organization's problem and receives great initial support. Soon thereafter, the support wanes and amateur managers start to blame the hero for the department's problems.

The long-term strategy for working with amateur managers is directly opposite from strategies for all of the other management styles. Instead of investing in and building the relationship, you actually search for a way to be released or escape from it. The strategy for liberation from the amateur manager is called "release relationship."

Several different methods can be used to be released from the relationship. Heavy Hitters could ask for a transfer or reassignment, seek a promotion, quit, or be fired. Each of these is perfectly acceptable. "Being fired is acceptable?" you may be asking yourself. Absolutely. Heavy Hitters know time is short and they do not want to waste their lives making incompetent people money. They want to surround themselves with successful people they respect. They have the confidence to stand up for themselves and what they believe in.

Another more daring way to release the relationship is by "firing" the amateur manager. When a disgruntled sales team bands together, unemotionally documents their grievances over time, and presents them logically to the amateur's boss, the wheels of justice will start turning.

Executing the release relationship strategy is postponed in two situations: (1) when the Heavy Hitter's income level is not being affected and the working environment is acceptable and (2) when the Heavy Hitter is able to ignore the manager's authority and become self-governing. However, in both cases, the eventual solution is to end the relationship.

MICROMANAGERS

Micromanagers are the most organized and methodical of all the management types. They have a strong sense of responsibility to their company and they pride themselves on achieving their revenue goals. They tend to be black-and-white, all-or-nothing thinkers who want things done their way. They may have laboriously created methodical processes for every aspect of their job, most likely having used these same processes at previous companies. Their endless stream of formal and informal regulations distracts salespeople from achieving results.

They may be well-known for their temper and are not considered people-oriented. In fact, they dislike human resource issues and are not regarded as great recruiters. They tend to hire people who they know will carry out their instructions to the letter, and even though one of the team members may achieve success, they will criticize that person if it wasn't done their way.

Micromanagers will have a long list of tasks on their whiteboards and keep records of all top accounts there in plain view. Micromanagers are a good fit for a company that needs to bring order to a sales environment that is transitioning from a start-up to a more mature organizational phase. They will usually have strong auditory and visual catalogs.

Heavy Hitters adopt a long-term strategy based upon their concept of the "perfect performance" of an efficient, industrious, and competent salesperson. Working efficiently equals being organized in the mind of a micromanager. Industriousness is akin to a single-minded, business-only attitude toward the job as evidenced by working long hours. Finally, the competent salesperson will complete tasks using the established processes.

To micromanagers, work and play are two entirely different matters. Therefore a sober disposition and attention to daily routines are necessary to function in a micromanager's world. In addition, the constant flow of information is critical to ensure a smoothly functioning world, and Heavy Hitters will overcommunicate by staying in constant touch.

OVERCONFIDENT MANAGERS

Overconfident managers are on the opposite end of the humility spectrum from sergeants. They tend to be self-centered and self-absorbed. While charming and gregarious in public, they rarely have deep relationships in private. When they do take an active interest in developing a relationship, it is because they believe it will benefit their cause—having orchestrated strong relationships with their superiors.

Overconfident managers usually have strong auditory and visual catalogs. They just love to talk about themselves and don't exhibit a great depth of feeling for others. They may boast of past successes and frequently recount stories about these achievements, regardless of whether someone may have heard them before. Not surprisingly, arrogance makes them susceptible to making judgmental mistakes. They also enjoy being the life of the party and know how to make any party an unforgettable event. They are typically flashier dressers and very concerned with their appearance.

They will receive strong reactions when they participate in sales situations. Some customers will absolutely love them while others will have an equally strong, opposite reaction. Similarly, they will not relate equally with all members of the team. Rather, they will have a few favorites who resemble them.

They are not open to feedback and are known to get quite defensive when criticized. They will get the job done their way and succeed at any cost. Although they are not exemplary planners, their sheer drive and tenacity make them well suited for roles where they have to launch a new product line or a new company.

Overconfident managers build a sales team of fighting gladiators who possess extraordinary willpower, mental toughness, animated spirit, and intelligence. To be included in this team, Heavy Hitters adopt the "clever conqueror" long-term strategy.

Since Heavy Hitters regularly sell to people who are better educated and more technically proficient than they are, they know there's a difference between a smart person and a clever person. A smart person knows how something works, while a clever person knows how to get something done. The clever salesperson is skillfully talented and tactically shrewd in finding a way to win.

To be a conqueror, you must attack your enemies, be comfortable fighting for the cause, and not be afraid of rankling people in the process because the end justifies the means. It also means not exposing any weakness, such as fear, self-doubt, sadness, or embarrassment. As Julius Caesar said, *"Veni, vidi, vici"* ("I came, I saw, I conquered").[2] Only the attacker can be victorious; at best, the defender will merely survive.

APPLYING SALES MANAGEMENT STYLES

In order to build rapport, Heavy Hitters understand their manager. They know their manager's primary, secondary, and recessive word catalog and understand his management style. Essentially, Heavy Hitters want to not only mirror the manager's communication but also understand and correctly mirror his behavioral style. To ensure success, they create and execute a long-term strategy based upon the manager's style and designed to create rapport or occasionally intentionally break rapport, as is the case with the amateur manager.

You probably noticed that each word of the long-term strategies' names begins with the same letter (release relationship, empathetic ego, and so on). These are called alliterations. Alliterations are repetitions of the same letter or sound at the beginning of adjacent words. Alliterations help the mind to remember by creating an association or "key" for easier storage. For example, "clever conqueror" is definitely easier to remember than if the strategy had been called "smart warrior."

The vice president of sales who said, "We're just going to have to sell our way out of this thing" at the beginning of this chapter is a classic example of an overconfident manager. He was so full of his past achievements that he was not in touch with his current situation. It's also an example of a manager who destroyed the faith of his sales force. Given the magnitude of the problems facing the sales organization and the growing publicity surrounding the company, the salespeople should have been presented with a plan to reestablish the company's image. When they weren't, the sales team's faith in the company was lost.

The result was predictable: a mass exodus of people from the company. After many years with this company, I also left. Within a few months of the speech, the vice president was out of a job. He was out of touch with his sales force, and understanding the needs of the sales force starts with knowing the individual needs of the Hitter.

SALESPEOPLE THEN AND NOW

When I started my career in the early 1980s, I worked as a programmer in a computer firm. Throughout this company, salespeople were held in low esteem. They were thought of as egotistical, expendable equivocators. While other departments (engineering, IT, and accounting) included many people with advanced degrees, the sales organization didn't have this quantifiable measuring stick of intelligence. Nor were salespeople thought of as being particularly creative, like those in the marketing department. The role of the salesperson was anything but prestigious. Thinking back, I can't remember going to any party and hearing anyone proudly exclaim, "I'm in sales and I'm proud of it!" Rather, people would sheepishly explain they were in sales.

The structure of most sales departments mirrors these perceptions and is based upon a militaristic, centralized chain of command. Today, salespeople should be looked upon in an entirely different light. The impetus for this change should be the realization that some of the most talented leaders in a company are in the sales department. More importantly, salespeople are trusted with the company's most valuable asset—customers! While the job they perform and skill set they possess are quite different from those in any other area of the company, it could be argued their job is the most important one in the company. To validate this statement, you only need to ask any employee being laid off because the company missed its last quarterly revenue goal.

Companies that may have previously considered salespeople a necessary evil should now seek to understand their needs and requirements. Consequently, the structure of today's sales organization should more closely resemble an interactive democracy. While the priority still remains on individual enterprise (the ability to make lots of money), salespeople's right to express their opinion should be emancipated. They are not thoughtless foot soldiers; they are important sources of information about the company's customers.

Sales management philosophy of the past was that behavior was primarily motivated by a compensation plan. And while a compensation plan plays a fundamental role, truly understanding what motivates salespeople is a much more complex issue. In particular, what drives Heavy Hitters to succeed is different from what drives the average salesperson. Probably the best way to describe a Hitter's behavior is to introduce it in the context of Maslow's hierarchy of needs. While the model is not new, it is a concise way to easily explain the actions and attitude of Heavy Hitters. However, it is not solely limited to them. The model applies universally to all people, including customers.

HIERARCHY OF NEEDS

Abraham Maslow is the father of humanistic psychology, who published his theory of a hierarchy of needs in the 1950s.[3] The theory explains that human beings need to satisfy an ever-escalating set of needs, which begin with biological deficiencies, ascend through social requirements, and ultimately culminate in the fulfillment of deeper spiritual needs. Before an individual can climb the ladder to fulfill a sophisticated need, the preceding lower-level need must have been met.

Maslow's theory was revolutionary during its time. His contemporaries focused only on abnormal personalities (Freudians) and animal research (Pavlovian behaviorists), thus reducing the human experience to instinctual impulses or simple mechanical concepts. Until Maslow, little focus had been put on the humanity of humans and their potential for excellence. Maslow felt people were basically trustworthy, self-protecting, and self-governing. It's an optimistic view of the human spirit compared to the pessimistic theories of that time. The basic premise is that humans want growth and love.

Just as we study Heavy Hitters to comprehend how they accomplish their sales achievements, Maslow studied exceptional individuals to try to understand the upper limits of human capability. Through his analysis, he defined four levels of needs: physiological, safety, belonging, and esteem. Only when all of these needs are met can people maximize their potential. Much like the popular army recruiting jingle, "Be all that you can be," Maslow referred to this highest level of achievement as "self-actualization." In order to become self-actualized, all of the preceding needs must be met in Maslow's specific order. Figure 8.2 depicts the hierarchy of needs with the higher-level needs ascending the pyramid.

Salespeople are constantly traversing up and down the pyramid. At the end of closing a record quarter or year, a Hitter will be at the top of the pyramid. However, as the new quarter or year starts, the sales numbers are reset to zero, and he quickly drops to the lowest level of need.

All Hitters have a distinct personality, an individual capability to understand technical concepts, and a certain amount of sales experience. Therefore, they have their own particular, unique needs. Heavy Hitters want managers to recognize their individuality and exhibit a genuine inquisitiveness about what makes them tick. They want their managers to motivate them and to see that their needs are met.

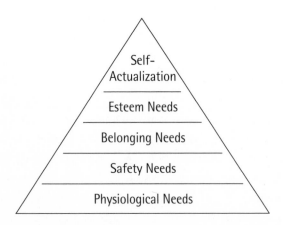

Figure 8.2 Maslow's Hierarchy of Needs
Source: Toward a Psychology of Being, 2nd Edition, Abraham Maslow

Let's assume for a moment that you are Shaquille O'Neal's basketball coach. You would not motivate him by threatening to throw him off the team if he didn't score 40 points in a game. This would not be the best way to get his best effort. More likely, you would motivate him by having him understand that his legacy and reputation are on the line in every game.

Heavy Hitters want a manager who knows where they are on their personal hierarchy of needs. Sometimes, they may simply want to be left alone. At other times, they may want reassurance. If a particular competitor is a problem, they want their manager to help find a way to win the deal and rally other departments to contribute to this cause.

Heavy Hitters need their managers to build a sales infrastructure that satisfies their lower-level needs so that they can get to the top of the pyramid as quickly as possible. As Shaq's coach, you would not spend a great deal of time teaching him how to slam-dunk. He already has this physiological need mastered. Rather, you would make sure that he had the best medical care available to handle his physical needs. You would ensure that the other members of the team were a complementary fit. You would guarantee that the game plan was well thought out and communicated to everyone. Heavy Hitters want managers who create the best opportunities to succeed. Let's take a deeper look at each level of the hierarchy of needs from the Hitters' standpoint.

Physiological Needs of the Hitter

In Maslow's model, physiological needs are the basic needs for food, water, air, sleep, and shelter. Maslow's premise is that we are all consumed with satisfying each of these needs. However, once they are satisfied, we quickly reorient ourselves toward the next set of needs. If I had been wandering the desert for several days, my main goal would be to find water. Once my thirst was quenched, I would focus on food, sleep, sex, and so on.

For Hitters, physiological needs include the stability of their company, the competitiveness of the product, and the soundness of the marketplace. Successful sales without these three physical needs being met is tremendously difficult. After the quarter closes, the Hitters begin again with the most rudimentary need—finding new opportunities. Being part of a stable well-known company with a leading product will naturally help resolve this need. The time frame in which Hitters are able to build their pipeline will be determined by how well their physiological needs are being met.

Even if your company position is stable and you have a product that is competitive, you still have to be selling to a viable target market. Although Heavy Hitters could sell for a great company and have the best possible solution, they may be competing with a new technology paradigm. For example, selling word processor systems when the market has shifted to personal computers or selling videocassette recorders when the market has shifted to DVDs is an ill-fated position to be in.

Safety Needs of the Hitter

Maslow stated that after your physiological needs are met, you will begin the pursuit of safety needs, or needs that establish stability, such as home, family, and religion. Within sales, safety needs include information on how to compete with other vendors. While a company provides theoretical arguments on how to sell its product, it is the sales manager and the Heavy Hitter who convert them into real-world reasons that persuade a customer to buy. The composition of a Hitter's sales territory is also a critical safety need. A depleted, barren sales territory will force a Heavy Hitter back to the physiological need level.

One of the most important security needs is the sales management style and competency of the Hitter's manager. After interviewing hundreds of salespeople, I have found that the overwhelming reason they left a position was not because of the company but because of their sales manager. Conversely, Heavy Hitters will endure great hardships and work tirelessly if they have faith in their manager and company. Heavy Hitters will tolerate an inferior manager as long as their income isn't hindered. They'll start to search for a better environment as soon as the commission checks shrink or the bureaucracy becomes unmanageable.

Belonging Needs of the Hitter

People have a natural disposition to belong to groups. Through our involvement in groups, we are able to share similar interests and values, search for a sense of community, and seek affectionate relationships. Take a moment to think about all the groups you belong to. First are the more obvious ones, such as family, friends, hobby clubs, religious groups, and political parties. You can even be grouped by your membership in frequent-flier programs, the neighborhood you live in, and the college you attended.

Sales is the most group-oriented department within a company, and this is not a coincidence. For example, most Heavy Hitters participated in team sports. In casual surveys I have conducted throughout the years, I have found that 90 percent of Hitters played organized sports in high school, and over 40 percent continued to play in college.

Being in sales takes a single-minded drive to achieve a goal. It requires an intensely competitive personality and the willingness to make a commitment and personal sacrifice to winning. The habit of putting in long hours, whether on a baseball diamond, on a football field, on a tennis court, or in a swimming pool, parallels the habits of successful salespeople.

In addition, salespeople do not expect to win every single deal they go after, and people who played sports know how to lose. They are able to handle emotional disappointments, bounce back from a loss, and get themselves ready for the next game. Also, through sports one learns how to accept criticism and perform under duress or difficult circumstances.

Most importantly, playing sports teaches independent thinking. Wrestlers or fencers are in a one-on-one battle with an opponent. They must take advantage of the opponent's weaknesses while executing countermoves to the opponent's attacks. Meanwhile, a football team does not consist of robots who are preprogrammed before every play. While thinking about their specific assignment, players must react and make instant adjustments to the circumstances in front of them as a play develops. All of these attributes inherent to playing sports are applicable to sales.

Heavy Hitters are comfortable with being part of a team and consider camaraderie a benefit of the job. Consider a typical Hitter based in the New York office of a medium-sized company. He is a member of at least six different groups that can be segmented by geography as well as by function:

1. Local groups—These include his immediate sales team, other reps in his office, and all employees in the office.

2. District groups—These include other Heavy Hitters in the offices that compose the district as well as all the employees in each of the offices.

3. Regional groups—These include other Hitters in the districts that compose the region, as well as all the employees in each of the districts.

4. North American sales groups—These include regional groups that make up the North American sales group.

5. Worldwide sales group—He's a member of the worldwide sales organization.

6. Company—The company itself is a group.

Although Heavy Hitters are competitive individuals by nature, they are also team players who support their colleagues. An anonymous Middle Eastern saying is "Me against my brother, my brother and I against the world." This is analogous and applicable to sales groups. For example, the Eastern region group is competitive with the Western region group. When these groups combine to form the North American sales group, they compete against the European sales group. Together, they form the worldwide sales group, which competes against other vendors.

Groups provide a place where Heavy Hitters can be appreciated and accepted and find a platform to rally around a cause. Groups provide Heavy Hitters with the opportunity to be needed and the opportunity to be acknowledged. However, Heavy Hitters want to be more than just members of a group; they want to be leaders. Which brings us to the next level of Maslow's hierarchy of needs, esteem-based needs.

Esteem Needs of the Hitter

The two main categories of esteem-based needs are the need to be deemed an expert and the need for power or position. The only way for a Heavy Hitter to fulfill these needs is to become a top sales producer. It could be argued that some Hitters are solely focused on money. In fact, one of the reasons for the intense preoccupation on the accumulation of money is that it serves as undisputed validation that the Heavy Hitter is a "sales expert."

Heavy Hitters feel their opinion matters and always want to be heard. They truly believe they are experts in the field of sales and know exactly how it should be done. They seek to achieve the alpha (or dominant) position within their group to ensure they are heard. They desire to see their actions emulated by others, and the only way to achieve the alpha position is by becoming a top salesperson.

For this reason, awards are extremely important to Hitters. Personally, I have experienced more motivation and harder work from my sales team by handing out a $45 trophy than would be achieved by increasing the compensation plan by 100 times that amount. Heavy Hitters enjoy the acclaim and the public identification as a group role model. Thus, when I present an award to a Heavy Hitter, it is always done in full view of the entire group. The leadership position Heavy Hitters seek is not necessarily reflected in their title—it is a position of prominence based upon their knowledge and the recognition that comes along with being thought of as an expert.

The second type of esteem need is power or position. Interestingly, I have noticed two different behaviors once Heavy Hitters have achieved the alpha position. The first behavior involves Heavy Hitters becoming intensely focused on remaining in the alpha position. They will tolerate little, if any, distractions from this goal. The second behavior involves Heavy Hitters exercising their newly found prominence in an attempt to advance their career. They will be frequently involved in conversations regarding strategy, planning, and even the performance of other group members with the sales management. Other departments, such as marketing, accounting, and product management, will solicit their opinions on new programs and policies. The entire company considers the alpha Heavy Hitter a success (at least for this quarter!).

Up to this point, the entire discussion about needs has been focused on achieving the practical interests of Hitters, from the physiological needs of the sales environment to the need for power and position. Maslow described the final step in satisfying personal development as self-actualization, or the desire to be everything that one is capable of being.

Hitter Self-Actualization

For Hitters, achieving self-actualization is directly linked to leaving a legacy that will be remembered within the company. Life is about achieving significance more than success. While success is a fleeting, quarter-by-quarter, year-by-year proposition, a legacy can never be taken away. By achieving this maturity level, Heavy Hitters gain peace of mind.

Several years ago, one of my colleagues, a Hitter *extraordinaire*, closed a $28 million sale. This was quite an accomplishment given that within his company, the average deal size was $200,000. In celebration of this achievement, every employee, from the CEO to the receptionist, received a $1,000 check. Over 1,000 people received this bonus. Clearly, this person left a legacy with everyone in the company.

Over the years, I have informally and formally surveyed various Heavy Hitters. When asked, "What is the most important criterion of job satisfaction?" the most frequently mentioned answers are the same. Here they are listed in order of frequency:

1. Making an impact.
2. Learning new skills (sales and technical).
3. Compensation.
4. The quality of the management team.
5. Career advancement.
6. The quality of the product.
7. The culture of the company.
8. The stability of the company.

These results are interesting. The number one response, "making an impact," can be directly associated with the desire to achieve self-actualization. Heavy Hitters want to be remembered in perpetuity. They want to know they made a difference.

Learning new sales and technical skills is an esteem-based need. This need is associated with mastering particular tasks and becoming an expert. Compensation is both an esteem and a safety need. If salespeople are successful, they are well paid. Their compensation will also greatly influence their status and ranking in their local group. Since safety needs are directly related to the consistency and stability of the environment, their compensation must enable them to have a secure personal life for themselves and their families. Similarly, career advancement can be thought of as an esteem need.

Ultimately, the yardstick by which Heavy Hitters measure their success is revenue. While Heavy Hitters always exceed their overall revenue targets, they are not immune from losing. In fact, they will frequently fail on individual accounts. However, baseball players who safely hit 4 out of 10 times at bat are considered great ball players. People do not measure them as 60 percent failures. Rather, they are called 400 hitters. Heavy Hitters measure their own performance similarly. Most importantly, they know that true self-actualization is having those who know them best—their manager, colleagues, and family—respect them most.

MVP

If you were to ask a Heavy Hitter, "What is the most important sales management quality?" the answer would be, "Being treated as an individual." Every Hitter wants to be treated as an MVP. In sports, MVP stands for "most valuable player." For management, in the context of a Heavy Hitter, MVP has a different meaning: "motivate, value, and praise."

Relationships are not automatic; they require investments in terms of time and energy. Heavy Hitters want their manager to understand how to motivate them since they are different from all the other members of the team. The A-quality manager knows that the different members of a team have different styles and viewpoints and that people should be valued for their diversity. Praise should be showered on all people generously. Great managers implement personal MVP plans for all members of their team based upon their individual selling styles.

INDIVIDUAL SELLING STYLES

When salespeople are asked to describe their own selling style in a single word, they give answers like, "consultative," "strategic," "driven," "tenacious," and even "lucky." However, it's nearly impossible to categorize your selling style in a single word since the way you sell is probably very dynamic. Your style is greatly influenced by the customer, the product you sell, how far away you are from your quota, and how much time you have left to accomplish it. Your selling style at any moment is influenced by your circumstances and a complex combination of your instinctive drives.

While your intuition helps you predict the future, your instincts tell you how to react to the present. You can think of your instincts as innate drives that you naturally use to exert your will. Seven basic instincts, when combined together, determine your selling style and your actions at any particular moment. The seven instincts are dominance, hyperactivity, pride, greed, freedom, transparency, and curiosity.

You can group these sales instincts into two different categories: creative (freedom, transparency, and curiosity) and survival (dominance, hyperactivity, pride, and greed). Whereas the survival instincts are associated with attack and defense, the creative instincts have more to do with achievement and self-worth. Let's review each of these instincts in more detail.

Dominance

The drive to take command of a situation (dominance) is instrumental to a salesperson's success. Some salespeople have such a strong dominance instinct that they think of customers as naturally inferior people who deserve to be taken advantage of. In the world of sales, these salespeople are known as "sharks." Sharks don't build rapport; they only know how to take advantage of people.

Even if you are not a shark, at times everyone must act like one. Just as a doctor must prescribe a painful treatment to heal a patient, in some sales situations you must control the customer for their own good. For example, I remember threatening a team of unsophisticated customers, telling them we would not sell them our solution unless they purchased the associated implementation services. Although they said they would be fine, I knew they didn't have the wherewithal to be successful on their own.

Conversely, a salesperson with a weak dominance instinct is never quite in control of an account, operates under the direction of customers, and is at the mercy of their whims. For every account, there is an equilibrium point of dominance versus submission. It's the point where the customer respects your conviction and is not offended by your persistence. Even though you promote your agenda with determination, you are not considered pushy or overbearing.

Hyperactivity

You can think of hyperactivity as your sales metabolism, the pace at which you work your territory. Some salespeople can't stop moving. They're always talking on the phone, sending e-mail, or making contacts. They're nervous and uncomfortable when events aren't humming along actively. Other salespeople are more deliberate in their moves, and they take longer to complete the same sort of activities. Whether one pace is better than the other depends on the environment. For example, a stockbroker needs to be a hyperactive juggler of multiple transactions whereas a financial planner needs to hold a meeting with retirees at a much slower pace.

Pride

You may not have initially thought of pride as an instinct, but it is. Pride is the measure of self-importance and your opinion of your own worth. Pride is also the midway point between arrogance and empathy. Since arrogant salespeople think they already know all the answers, they are less likely to ask for direction or seek input (from customers and managers alike). In general, arrogance is a very bad attribute for a salesperson. However, there are products that actually require arrogant salespeople. These products are usually targeted at an elitist clientele. Put on an old sweat suit and head to your nearest Italian designer boutique if you would like to experience an arrogant salesperson. In this scenario, arrogance is actually an appropriate sales qualification technique.

On the other end of the spectrum are salespeople who sell mainly through empathy. In other words, they are constantly telling customers they are worried about the deal, their job, or a personal situation. They count on the customers' reassurance and natural desire to help.

The natural ability to elicit empathy is a great attribute for a salesperson to have. Recent neurophysiological research shows that a part of the brain called the anterior insula is activated when we watch others experience painful or unpleasant feelings.[4] It's as if we were experiencing the pain ourselves. When we see emotions on another person's face—if someone is crying for example, our eyes automatically fill with tears, too. Empathy can play a very important role in getting customers to relate to you and moving them to fight for your cause.

Greed

Every now and then my friends and I get together and discuss stock market tips. It's interesting to listen to their investment strategies. Some are more conservative and will bet only on a sure thing. Others are risk takers who make large gambles. The instinct that drives their individual behavior is greed.

We normally associate greed with a miserly scrooge or a corrupt character. While this may be society's definition, in sales the greed instinct takes on an entirely different meaning. You have probably worked with many different types of salespeople, and you may have noticed that some gravitated toward working only "big deals" while others "nickel-and-dime" their way to quota. The greed instinct is actually a key influencer in the way salespeople work their territory.

Some salespeople aren't afraid of bold decisions and the consequences they entail. They are dreamers who envision the day when their ship will finally come in. They are unfulfilled working lots of smaller deals. They want to set their line in the deepest water and catch the biggest fish. Meanwhile, other salespeople are quite happy casting their net closer to shore and snagging as many deals as possible. They are more likely to yield to the opinions of others and play it safe. Ideally, a sales force should include both types of "fishermen."

Freedom

Several years ago, I was able to view the Declaration of Independence on display at the National Archives in Washington, D.C. It was inspiring to read the first few lines of the most important document in American history: "We hold these truths to be self-evident, that all men are created equal, that they are endowed by their Creator with certain unalienable Rights, that among these are Life, Liberty and the Pursuit of Happiness."

We naturally assume that "all men" want the individual freedom to exercise complete self-determination. However, freedom is actually the measurable state of independence versus dependency and conformity. Even though all salespeople think for themselves, their assertiveness varies from individual to individual.

Some salespeople are opinionated trailblazers, while others are more likely to go along with the crowd. The trailblazers tend to be rebellious salespeople who will fight any battle regardless of its impact on them. To maintain their independence, they'll vehemently oppose any new sales-related process or procedure. Passive salespeople distance themselves from any confrontation. They quietly set about fulfilling their duties.

Transparency

Every year, the editors of *Webster's New World College Dictionary* announce the "Word of the Year." In 2003, that word was "transparency." They explained that the word was chosen because they noticed a deeply felt need in our society for transparency. But what exactly is transparency? Simply put, transparency is the ability to be exactly who you are and the propensity to be perfectly frank about it. In other words, what people see in you is exactly what you are.

Some salespeople are completely transparent. They are completely comfortable with themselves, let others see exactly who they are, and tell it like it is. On the other hand, other salespeople tend to display less personality and shield themselves behind a more formal demeanor. More often than not, they keep the conversation at a business level, never discussing the deeper personal and political issues that are present in every account. Most interestingly, both extremes are acting in the way they think salespeople are supposed to act with customers.

Curiosity

The old saying "Curiosity kills" simply does not apply to selling. In fact, it's quite the opposite. Your curiosity can actually save you! I have met many Heavy Hitters through the years and one of the main characteristics they have all shared was natural inquisitiveness. It seemed they were always asking themselves why to satisfy their insatiable desire to know.

Like people in general, salespeople have different levels of inquisitiveness. However, the majority have a healthy curiosity. They have grown accustomed to asking questions since it is ingrained into the sales process. They are also adept at answering questions because of their experiences with both customers and managers.

Sometimes salespeople must exhibit the ultimate form of curiosity, obsession. They'll become obsessed with one deal or a goal to the point where it is always on their minds and nothing else in life seems to matter.

You can achieve success with almost any combination and variation of the seven instincts. In addition, the best sales force is the most diverse one. You don't want everyone cut from the same mold since your customers in Texas, Tokyo, Paris, and Perth are quite different.

For example, I have three very good friends with vastly different selling styles who are equally successful salespeople. Mark has extreme dominance and transparency instincts. He's a verbal warrior who'll say exactly what's on his mind. However, he's not reckless about his words. Rather, he uses them with precision to tunnel to the core of the customer's psyche and reveal the hidden biases and silent objections that are always in the back of someone's mind.

Stuart has a completely different style. He naturally evokes a high degree of empathy from his customers. He also knows that it is one of his strengths so he's very transparent about it. His modus operandi is to continually ask customers for help and constantly seek their reassurance about the deal. As a customer recites the reasons why the deal will happen, he triangulates with other helpers in the account.

The technique has an interesting impact on customers as well. By continually repeating why the deal will happen, they convince themselves to buy!

Todd is an extremely curious person by nature. He reminds me of a plane crash investigator because he continually analyzes small pieces of information in order to construct the entire puzzle. He is driven to know how things work and is not comfortable until all the i's are dotted and the t's are crossed. He's also an extremely independent person who is eager to share his theories about why the plane crashed in the first place. He places himself in the customers' shoes and knows when and why they will buy.

All three of these salespeople are incredibly successful, and that's the point. Your individual style is based upon your personal mixture of these instincts, and someone can be successful with any combination. However, these three salespeople share these qualities: They know their strengths, are true to themselves, and don't try to be someone they aren't.

HOW TO COPE WITH LOSING

When we're closing a deal, life's great! When we're on the losing side of a deal, we're miserable and we sometimes feel like our entire world has fallen apart. Losing is a subject that most salespeople don't like to talk about.

First, the only way to act after you receive the painful news is graciously and professionally. Although you might fantasize about annihilating the decision maker's reputation and career, you must fight the urge for confrontation. I speak from experience on this. On more than one occasion I have thrown a verbal temper tantrum when I lost an important deal. Frankly, it didn't make me feel any better; it only made me feel worse.

By exiting on good terms, there's always a one-in-a-hundred chance that the customer may call you back later when your competitor fails. But the real reason for maintaining your composure is your own mental hygiene. Think of it in these terms: You've invested a great deal of energy into something you wanted badly and were counting on. In spite of your best efforts, you have been told that you weren't good enough. You have just been through a traumatic experience. The first step in dealing with any personal crisis is acknowledging it. By doing so, you will be able to get back to selling sooner. To help you get back into the winning frame of mind as soon as possible, here are four recommendations.

1. Commiserate with colleagues. You will start to feel better by talking with fellow salespeople who have been in your position. Sharing your experience and venting your frustrations will help get you back on your feet. Instead of repressing your pain and doubts, catharsis enables you to let go of your negative thoughts and feelings. As Mark Twain said, "When angry, count four; when very angry, swear."[5]

2. Take a break. After a big loss, we often think it's best to buckle up our feelings and put our nose right back on the grindstone. However, no matter how we act on the outside, we're often depressed, tired, and full of self-pity. Unfortunately, this message will be sent subconsciously to customers. As a sales manager, I learned the best way to rejuvenate the team was to institute mandatory "mental health" days. Typically, it was the first business day after the close of a quarter. Regardless of whether you had a good or bad quarter, you were invited to disappear. As a result, everyone came back refreshed and ready to get back to a winning frame of mind.

3. Re-anchor success. In Chapter 3, we introduced the concepts of "anchors." An anchor is the premeditated association of a specific feeling to an object. After a particularly tough loss, you may have forgotten what it feels like to win. In this situation, go visit some "friendlies." These are customers who have purchased from you, like you, and appreciate your company. By doing so, you re-anchor your mind to success.

4. Keep perspective. I remember being on the road and receiving the bad news that I lost a huge deal to my archrival. On the plane flight from New York back home to California, I sat staring out the window. My mind was filled with destructive thoughts and other self-defeating prophecies. About halfway across the country I made a sudden realization. There wasn't a single person in all the cities we passed over who cared. John McKay, the quick-witted former football coach of USC said it best after a heartbreaking loss, "800 million people in China could give a damn."[6]

After we have missed our number, our first reaction is to think the sun has finally set on our career and our hot streak is over. However, there's always next month, next quarter, and next year.

CONCLUSION

In the movie *Cast Away,* Tom Hanks is marooned on a deserted tropical island. He survives for four years by living "one day at a time." His most difficult challenge is not trying to find food, water, or shelter. It is dealing with loneliness. So he paints a face on a volleyball and names his new friend "Wilson."

Many salespeople work alone in remote offices. They are castaways strewn all over the world. Being part of a team is one of the most important needs of a salesperson. My advice to all remote salespeople is this: Talk to at least one fellow castaway a day. You need to stay connected to your troop and feel you are a necessary part of the cause. Your spirits and frame of mind may depend on this lifeline someday. Of course, the one person you need to talk to all the time is your sales manager.

One of Heavy Hitters' most important relationships is with their sales manager, who creates the environment to succeed, motivates them to achieve, and counsels them with advice. The success of their relationship is dependent upon their rapport, and Heavy Hitters mold themselves to fit with their manager. Heavy Hitters will communicate with their manager using his word catalog and implement a strategy corresponding to his management style.

Conversely, an A-quality manager is aware of the unique needs of Heavy Hitters. The manager will develop the sales plan and environment that enable Hitters to succeed and inspire Hitters to achieve. Your sales organization is composed of a broad collection of individuals. Great sales managers know that the best sales organizations have great instinctual diversity.

To finish this chapter, here's an experience that greatly influenced my own management style. When I was a salesperson, I arranged for the vice president of sales to fly into town to participate in some important sales calls with me. The vice president was my boss's boss's boss, and I had several meetings scheduled that day all across town. I thought it would be a great opportunity to show him examples of our accounts, and hopefully we could close one of them. I also wanted to start a relationship with him, and driving him from meeting to meeting would give us plenty of time to get to know each other.

Well, the day didn't work out as expected. From the moment I picked him up at the airport, he was talking on his cell phone. I interpreted this to mean he had more important people to talk to than me. The only interruptions to his stream of telephone calls were the actual sales calls, and he didn't seem very interested in the customers, either!

Up until that point, I was completely and totally committed to this company. I had prioritized my life around work, and I was working long hours and expending an immense amount of off-hour energy thinking about my job. That day changed me. I would never again be as committed to the company.

This was an important personal lesson. When I am on the road with my salespeople, I rarely take telephone calls. I am completely and totally with them. I want to make sure that we have rapport and that their commitment to the company and the sales organization is complete.

CHAPTER **9**

Finding Your Coach

For the past six months, the salesperson had been working non-stop selling his computer solution to a major retailing chain head-quartered in New Jersey. Within the next couple of weeks, the retailer would make its final application vendor selection and start the negotiation process of what would surely be a multimillion-dollar deal. Although the salesperson felt he had developed strong relationships with key members within the information technology department, he was still nervous, as he had yet to meet the president, who was also the company's founder. This angst continued to build until one day, the salesperson saw the president and drummed up enough nerve to approach him. "Hello, I'm with National Computer Company. We've been working with the Information Tech—" The salesperson was immediately interrupted by the president: "Computers! I hate computers!" With that said, he walked away.

I came across an interesting study in *Psychology Today* magazine, in which men and women were asked to rate themselves and their ideal marriage partner. They were presented 19 different traits ranging from honesty to expected income. Based on the results, the following conclusion was made, "When looking for a mate, people don't just look for a good match; they look for someone better than themselves."[1]

This study validated a personal theory of mine, "The Better Person Syndrome." My theory is that when customers are choosing between two similar products, they will not always buy the better product. Rather, they will buy from the salesperson whom they believe is the better person. So while one salesperson may have the best product and be more proficient in explaining its features and functionality, in the end the customer will buy from the person who best matches the personal attributes that the customer admires.

Throughout this book, the importance of establishing rapport and finding a coach have been reiterated as necessary steps to closing the deal. Coaches are individuals who provide accurate information about the sales cycle and competition to you. Coaches want you to win; they're your friends and allies. They also think of you as a superior person and someone they would like to keep company with.

Think about all the relationships you have in your life—deep, close relationships with friends you have known most of your life, casual relationships with colleagues and coworkers, and new relationships with customers. Regardless of how they were formed, all relationships share similar underlying characteristics. In order to find and recruit a coach, it is first necessary to understand the nature of friendships.

A big difference exists between a friend and an acquaintance. An acquaintance is someone with whom you have a cordial relationship. While the relationship is friendly, the unspoken understanding is that neither person will demand significant time of the other to maintain the relationship. Conversely, a friend is someone who unselfishly invests time to maintain the relationship and derives enjoyment from doing so. An acquaintance is someone you know slightly, a well-wisher with whom you may have pleasant lunches and other social get-togethers. A friend is a trusted sympathizer and, more importantly, an active helper. A friend is someone whom you can call at midnight to help fix your flat tire.

Time is a finite resource. Just as companies protect their time by limiting their number of vendor relationships, people limit the time they spend on relationships. They can have a few deeper relationships or many less time-demanding acquaintances.

A friend of mine has maintained contact with literally everyone he has ever worked with. While he doesn't spend extended periods of time with any one person, he expends considerable energy keeping up with his former coworkers. It's been more than 15 years since I have worked with him, but I know if I wanted to reach someone from that company, he would have current contact information. Another friend maintains a small number of very close friends. These are mostly people he has known since childhood. In total, I estimate they both spend the same amount of time on maintaining their relationships.

A QUALIFIED COACH

Salespeople sometimes believe they have a coach when in reality they don't. Heavy Hitters know they have a coach when the person not only provides them with accurate information but also helps them by fighting for their cause. A true coach will represent and promote the Hitter's solution publicly with the Hitter and, even better, when the Heavy Hitter isn't present.

Unfortunately, two major obstacles stand in the way of establishing a coaching relationship with someone. First, finding a person qualified to be a coach is not easy. Within the customer's organization is a pool of candidates, many of whom may develop into a coach. However, it is difficult and too time-consuming to court everyone. Heavy Hitters have a process for ranking and targeting the strongest candidate. Second, time to build the relationship is limited. While most personal relationships have the luxury of growing naturally over months and years, Heavy Hitters must accelerate this bonding process in a matter of days or weeks.

In order to find a coach, Heavy Hitters will identify all potential candidates. First, they will attempt to develop a relationship with the person who has the most juice and is the biggest bully. For example, let's assume that a Hitter is selling to a selection committee consisting of Jim, Karl, John, and Rich. She prioritizes her recruiting efforts.

Since Rich is a bully with juice, the Hitter knows if she can sway him to become her coach, she has won the deal. In addition, she will vigilantly monitor whether Rich has become a coach for another vendor. In case this happens, she knows the deal is lost and she should stop working on the account. (See Figure 9.1.)

Assuming Rich is not a coach for any specific vendor, Karl is in the next most desirable quadrant because Karl has juice. However, he is apathetic to the decision that is being made. In this situation, the Heavy Hitter has an opportunity to explain the merits of her solution and why Karl should care more about the decision.

Let's assume Karl is the manager in charge of the manufacturing team and Rich, who reports to Karl, is the supervisor in charge of selecting new plant equipment. Assuming Rich isn't any vendor's coach, the Heavy Hitter could meet with Karl to explain how her product's maintenance needs are 30 percent less than the competitor's; therefore the production schedule would incur less scheduled downtime. If Karl is very concerned with downtime, this could cause Karl's demeanor to change from accommodating his team's decision to bullying the decision. Then Karl will become the bully with juice and Rich will be accommodating to his decision.

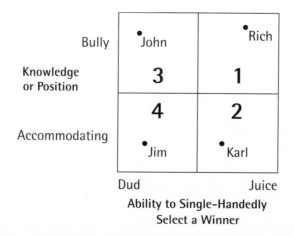

Figure 9.1 Selecting a Coach

As potential coaches, both John and Jim are in less desirable quadrants. However, if the Heavy Hitter determines that neither Rich nor Karl is coaching the competition, they can play an important role in providing another point of reference to triangulate information. However, if either Rich or Karl is coaching the competition, the Heavy Hitter knows she will not win the deal. Just as in poker, a pair of twos cannot beat four aces.

PARTICIPATION PIE

Group dynamics are very complex and often revealing. One way to identify which quadrant a person belongs to is by observing her behavior during presentations and meetings. Earlier, we reviewed how a pecking order is communicated by where people sit during meetings. Whether at a round table or in a classroom setting, the person with the most juice and greatest ability to bully will usually take the dominant seating position.

This dominating behavior is also evidenced in meeting interactions. To explain this, we need to introduce the concept of the "participation pie." The participation pie charts (Figure 9.2) illustrate the amount of time each person interacts in a meeting or presentation.

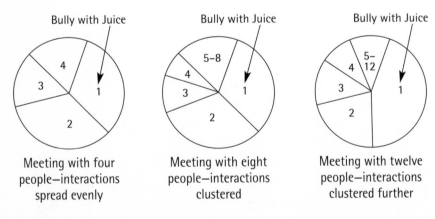

Meeting with four
people—interactions
spread evenly

Meeting with eight
people—interactions
clustered

Meeting with twelve
people—interactions
clustered further

Figure 9.2 Participation Pie Charts

Usually, the person who interacts the most will be the bully who has the most juice. Bullies with juice are in charge and they want everyone to know it. And although dud bullies will be very active participants, the more they participate, the more it becomes obvious that they do not have the stature or expertise they think they do. We have all been in meetings where people like this are contradicted or even publicly chastised by members of their own team. Dud bullies didn't listen to Grandma when she said, "It is better to keep your mouth shut and be suspected of being a fool rather than open it and confirm suspicions."

Another key aspect of the participation pie is how the number of attendees affects the level of participation. In meetings with up to four members, the amount of time each person spends interacting and asking questions is relatively equal. As the group grows to eight people, the interactions become clustered around several people. Usually, these people are in the first or third quadrants. In larger groups, up to 12 people, the majority of interactions are usually among a few individuals. These people are most likely in the first or second quadrants.

Once Heavy Hitters have determined and ranked their potential coaching candidates, how do they actually proceed? The simple answer is, just as they develop a personal friendship, they develop a coach.

FRIENDSHIPS

Who are your friends? Most of my friends are in my same age group. I was introduced to most of them through an activity, whether it was work, school, or a hobby. We share similar backgrounds, live in the same geographic area, and have complementary personalities. Interestingly enough, most of my friends' word catalogs mirror mine. They are wired as I am. Their stronger catalogs are the same as mine. In fact, I cannot think of a single close friend whose primary catalog is the same as my recessive catalog. Maybe opposites don't actually attract.

Also, we share similar values and motivations. We are striving to be successful, we are raising children, and we want meaningful lives. Certainly, we have diverse tastes and interests. However, we have far more in common than we have differences.

My friends' personalities are also similar to mine. The term "personality" refers to all aspects of a person's individuality. While everyone's personality is as distinct as a fingerprint, some traits of behavior can be classified to help understand a person's attitude, habits, and conduct.

Finally, my friends know that I will always act with their best interests in mind. I would help them, just as they would help me, fix that flat tire at midnight.

EXERCISE 10: LONG-TERM RELATIONSHIPS

Take a minute to do the following exercise. On a piece of paper write down the names of your closest friends and how many years you have known them. Then calculate the average time you have known your friends by adding all the years together and dividing by the total number of friends. What was your average? In my case, the average is over 15 years.

Fifteen years is a long time, and that's the point. Friends think in context of long-term relationships just as customers do. The behavior of both parties in a long-term relationship is very different than in a fleeting short-term relationship. Honesty, integrity, and selflessness are the bonds that create long-term relationships with your friends, as well as your customers.

DEVELOPING FRIENDSHIPS

Basically, it is human nature to associate with people similar to oneself. Like animals in the wild, we tend to herd together with our own kind. Most likely, your friends share your interests. You were probably introduced to them through a mutual activity and over time an enduring connection formed.

The process for developing friendships has four major characteristics, and these characteristics can also be utilized to develop a coach. First, two people have an "intersecting activity." Second, a "kinship in communication" is established. Third, they have similar motivations and value systems. Finally, they have agreeable personalities that understand and appreciate each other. Let's examine each of these characteristics further to understand how Heavy Hitters develop a coach.

Intersecting Activities

Going into a first sales call with a new customer, Heavy Hitters don't know who their coach will be. Fortunately, through intersecting activities, circumstances are created that allow people to get to know each other and exchange dialogue. The first intersecting activity is the sales call itself. The customer is interested in the product and the Heavy Hitter is interested in selling it. Since this mutual interest has brought together two people who most likely would not have met otherwise, it is the most important intersecting activity.

Through intersecting activities, people display their personality types, word catalog wiring, and value systems. Since the Heavy Hitter in our example sells high-technology products and the customer is employed in high technology, they probably share many other intersecting activities. They each follow the industry, use the same products (PCs, Windows, and cellular phones, for example), and perform many of the same activities (compose e-mails, write reports, and create spreadsheets). They read the same publications and know many of the same people. Even though they haven't yet met, they have a lot in common!

The Heavy Hitter uses this initial intersecting activity to begin building a personal relationship. For example, I know one salesperson who has developed a unique way to create personal friendships. On a first call, he will describe how his product works technically and answer questions, as you might expect. Because he has a technical background and brings authority to the interchange, his credibility builds. Also, he is a computer game expert and at the end of the call he will always ask if anyone plays computer games. In almost every call, one or more members of the customer's team is just as passionate about games as he is. They'll launch into a discussion about SSX 3, JAK II, or Halo. Immediately, the roles of customer and vendor are changed and he is bonding with the person. This mutual interest sets the stage for developing a personal relationship and ultimately a coach.

You may not be an expert at computer games, but think about all the potential subjects you can discuss:

raising kids	the cost of living	home ownership
cars	computers	dating and marriage
college	food	professional sports
traveling	dieting	music
movies	airplanes	toys
humor	astronomy	clothes
pets	poetry	religion
art	gardening	the economy
antiques	body piercing	billiards
investments	horses	karaoke
books	beer	firearms
television	origami	cigars

The Hitters' strategy is to use the first intersecting activity (the sales call) to find additional personal intersecting activities. By doing so, the Hitter is developing rapport with the *entire* person, not just the *business* person—building a personal friendship.

Kinship in Communication

One of the main objectives of this book is to identify and improve how people communicate. At the content level, the particular words people choose to use are directly related to their activities. For example, people in the high-technology industry use the technical specification language to communicate about computers. "Two phase commit" and "EJB" mean something important to a software programmer. Similarly, the terms "SSX 3" and "Halo" are significant to a computer game expert. They are part of the language of game users. Each intersecting activity topic previously listed also has a unique content language.

In order to have a meaningful conversation about an intersecting activity, you need to understand its language. For example, a conversation about stock investing requires an understanding of terms such as "price earnings ratio," "market cap," and "stock shorting." If you are talking with someone about dieting, being able to discuss the Atkins or Zone diet makes your participation in the conversation credible. Through the use and understanding of these common terms, rapport is established.

We also know that meaning comes not only from what you say but how you say it. Heavy Hitters are continually building rapport by mirroring the word catalog of the people with whom they converse. They know their customer's primary, secondary, and recessive word catalogs. They adjust their vocabulary to resemble, sound like, and feel like the customer's. They coordinate their posture, speech, breathing, and movements, becoming Ginger Rogers to the customer's Fred Astaire. The flow of communication becomes enjoyable, natural, and comfortable—the goal of every Heavy Hitter's customer friendships.

Motivation and Values

Heavy Hitters always delve beneath the surface, the technical and business criteria, to uncover individual motivations. Customers may have their "official" reasons for purchase decisions; however, Heavy Hitters know there is also an "off the record" truth. The final decision is really driven by the desire to achieve a personal benefaction on the part of a few individuals. Therefore, like a psychologist, Heavy Hitters concentrate on eliciting the deep feelings and desires from the patient. In this case, the Hitter is trying to determine the principles, standards, incentives, and priorities of the key decision makers. Always in the back of the Hitter's mind is the question, "What is this person's benefaction?" In other words, what is driving this person's behavior and how will my product help achieve it? And how do the various individual benefactions mesh? Even though a wide range of benefactions is possible, each benefaction is individually personal and self-centered.

Maslow's hierarchy of needs—physiological, safety, belonging, and esteem—applies to the customer as well as the Hitter. Here are two examples of how the customer's behavior is explained using the hierarchy of needs:

Peggy wants to select a product with new, cutting-edge technology. By adding a valuable skill set to her resume, she will be able to command more money in the marketplace.

- Physiological. She wants more money in order to buy a home for her family.
- Safety. By knowing this new technology, she has the security of having a marketable skill.
- Belonging. The industry periodicals and her friends are enamored with this new technology, and she's tired of feeling left out.
- Esteem. There's power in knowledge. Knowing something her colleagues don't puts her in a superior position.

Matt is a project leader who wants to select a particular vendor's product because it is successfully used by so many other local companies.

- Physiological. A successful project is an opportunity to demonstrate his value to the company. He wants to keep his job during these difficult economic times.
- Safety. He's risk averse and feels that by controlling the selection of the technology, the project will be successful.

- Belonging. He can share tips with and leverage the experience of other local users of the product.
- Esteem. If the project is successful, he'll earn the promotion he's always wanted.

Heavy Hitters intuitively map out the needs of every person involved in the selection of their product. They are searching for confidants who have a vested interest in selecting their product because it will help them attain their physiological, safety, belonging, or esteem needs.

Heavy Hitters will frame their conversations and product in terms of fulfilling these needs. In the first example the Hitter's strategy is to reiterate that her product is cutting-edge. She will provide collateral materials such as industry articles, press announcements, and technical documentation that confirm its technological advantage. She will capitalize on belonging needs by introducing Peggy to her other customers and the local user group. She will provide access to the technical individuals within her company to reemphasize the innovation and uniqueness of the technology and accelerate Peggy's learning of it. She wants to help Peggy become knowledgeable and powerful.

In the second example, the Heavy Hitter will try to demonstrate to Matt that her solution is the least risky by providing thorough product demonstrations, an on-site evaluation, and ongoing implementation meetings. Customer references and site visits will also provide independent validation. If Matt feels confident the Heavy Hitter's solution will work, he will support it against solutions he believes are dangerous or unsafe.

While I am not a proponent of requiring salespeople to fill out forms and paperwork, at times you need to map out a complex sales situation. Sometimes, we are so embroiled in an account that we only think of our next action item tactically and forget what is truly driving the people who make the decision. The form shown in Figure 9.3 can help you identify benefactions and ensure that your action items take into account the human nature of each individual in the sales process. The goal of this form is to force the salesperson to think about the deal from a psychological perspective.

Name	Title			
Word Catalog	Primary V	A	K	(CIRCLE ONE IN EACH ROW)
	Secondary V	A	K	
	Recessive V	A	K	

Need	Personal Benefaction	Action
Physiological		
Safety		
Belonging		
Esteem		

Figure 9.3 Customer Benefaction Form

Complete a form for each member of the customer's selection team. Enter the name and title. Then, after you have identified his or her word catalog wiring, circle the corresponding catalog. The remainder of the form is used to plot a course of action based upon the person's physiological, safety, belonging, and esteem needs. Once a form is completed for each person, compare all the team members' forms. Do they share the same wiring? Do they have different benefactions? What sales tactics (or actions) would have the greatest impact? Which ones must be executed first or have a sense of urgency? These forms help discipline busy salespeople to stop and consider the customers' orientation before executing account strategies.

Heavy Hitters always align their strategy with the personal needs of an individual. By doing so, the individual will support them and their product. People who have a vested interest in having the Heavy Hitter win naturally evolve into coaches. But even with a coach firmly ensconced at their side, Hitters are constantly aware of the personal benefactions of each of the individuals involved in the decision and work to solve potential conflicts before they arise.

Agreeable Personalities

Remember the last time you made a very important personal decision? Perhaps it was a major purchase such as a house, a car, or stocks. Maybe it was a personal decision to get married, start a family, or change jobs. Whatever the case, many different factors influenced the decision you made. Ultimately, your decision was based upon logic, feelings, and the characteristics of your personality.

Early in my career, I made the transition from a technical position into sales. My new employer sent me to several well-known sales training programs. Each of these programs taught some form of personality training using a variation of Carl Jung's philosophy of psychological types. Most frequently, it was the Myers-Briggs Type Indicator (MBTI). The MBTI uses four measurements to classify a personality into one of 16 different types.[2] These measurements include your level of extroversion, whether you use intuition or physical observation to make decisions, how much you trust logic versus feelings, and finally, whether you perform detailed analysis or make instantaneous decisions.

Armed with this newly learned information, I eagerly went about trying to apply it to my sales opportunities. However, it didn't match what I was experiencing. I quickly realized that classifying my prospect's personality into one of 16 types didn't help my sales efforts. It seemed to me that the customer's personality was situational. That is, depending on the circumstance the same person acted differently. However, over time I began to realize what was important. I started to identify my prospect's dominant personality traits and link them to the sales cycle experience. Essentially, I created a practical knowledge base of sales cycles that was indexed by the prospect's major personality traits and my success or failure.

PERSONALITY TYPES

During the past 20 years, I estimate that I have met over 20,000 people. While I believe each person has a unique personality, I have found that key personality attributes can be classified, measured, and used to predict behavior during the sales cycle. By building a similar knowledge base, you can determine which strategy will provide the highest probability of winning. Heavy Hitters do this intuitively.

The best formal model for classifying personality types is the five-factor model. This model has five personality factors (or dimensions): negative emotionality, extroversion, openness, agreeableness, and conscientiousness.[3] Each of these factors has six facets, and each facet has a low, medium, and high measurement. The facets describe the major characteristics of the factor.

Each individual's personality is a mixture of all five factors, and obviously many different combinations are possible. Rather than try to classify each personality type, Heavy Hitters have a different strategy. First, they sense the strength of each factor to determine which ones are more prominent. Heavy Hitters know that people with higher measurements of agreeableness, extroversion, and openness are more easily developed into a coach than someone who exhibits low measurements of these factors.

As they are working an account and becoming familiar with the customer, Heavy Hitters are judging certain personality factors based upon the strength of the dominant facets. (Remember, each factor is composed of individual facets.) They are also on the lookout for particular facets that have extreme measurements. For example, if someone has a very low measurement of the activity facet (extroversion factor), a Hitter knows the sales cycle will proceed at a leisurely pace. Therefore, it makes little sense to push the customer to move forward. However, if the customer has a very high activity facet, the Hitter can predict the sales cycle will be swift and vigorous and adjust her strategy and the pace of activity with this in mind. Essentially, the Hitter is mirroring the customer's dominant personality factors and facets and adjusting the strategy in order to be perceived by the customer as a match.

Once a prominent factor and facet are recognized, Heavy Hitters will select their course of action based upon previous experiences with people who had the same attributes. They are always adding to their knowledge base of individual behavior patterns. They continually classify personalities, associate them with the success or failure of the relationship, and link them to the characteristics of the sales cycle. They will draw upon these past personal experiences in order to choose the appropriate behavior and select the optimum strategy to develop a coach. Heavy Hitters are lifelong, full-time, professional students of people.

For each of the five factors, the following examples of sales processes will help you learn specific tactics for selling to a customer with a prominent factor. In these examples, I will also identify the customer's primary word catalog. Identifying their catalogs is important, as people's wiring directly influences their decision-making process.

FACTOR 1—NEGATIVE EMOTIONALITY

People have different tolerances for stress, anger, and worry. At one end of the spectrum is the person who is always experiencing a crisis. At the other end is the calm, collected individual who is unshakable, even under immense pressure. From low to high, the six facets of negative emotionality can be found in Figure 9.4.

If a customer is an even-keeled person with low negative emotionality facets, Heavy Hitters will mirror that behavior during the sales cycle. Heavy Hitters know the sales process will be logical, unhurried, and sedate. They will adjust their style and tactics accordingly.

Kurt had worked in the same local government agency for over 20 years. During this time, he had risen to the position of

Facets	Low	Medium	High
Worry	More calm	Worried/calm	More worried
Anger	Slow to anger	Not too quick to anger	Quick to anger
Discouragement	Seldom sad	Occasionally sad	Often sad
Self-Consciousness	Seldom embarrassed	Sometimes embarrassed	Easily embarrassed
Impulsiveness	Seldom yielding	Sometimes yielding	Often yielding
Vulnerability to Stress	Resists stress	Handles some stress	Is prone to stress

Figure 9.4 Facets of Negative Emotionality

director. The agency was migrating from antiquated mainframe systems to state-of-the-art computers and software. Kurt was in charge of selecting the new technology. Kurt's environment was structured around order and predictability. He had strong auditory and kinesthetic catalogs. Everything, including his appearance, his office, and the process to select the new solution, reflected this.

Susan, the Heavy Hitter, had to make an important decision early in the sales cycle. She had to decide whether to pursue the business. Based on Kurt's personality, she knew that she would not be able to accelerate or change the selection process. Kurt's orientation was long-term, and there would be no quick decisions. The evaluation process would be well thought out and lengthy. The winner would be the last vendor standing, the one who exhibited the attributes necessary to have a long-term partnership with the agency. In essence, the sales cycle was a miniature dry run of the long-term relationship.

To develop Kurt into a coach, the Heavy Hitter's strategy was to prove that she and her company were "like" Kurt. She had to adopt Kurt's calm, unimpulsive traits (not an easy task for a high-energy salesperson). First, she adopted his personal demeanor. Every communication with Kurt was structured and well documented. When meeting with Kurt, she consciously slowed down her speech, breathing, and mannerisms from her normal hyperactive pace.

Part of the Hitter's strategy was also to introduce herself to Kurt's other longtime business partners, the members of Kurt's staff. Through these meetings, she gathered more information about Kurt. She was told about a past incident when a vendor tried unsuccessfully to go around Kurt to sell his solution. She met with other vendors with whom Kurt had existing relationships. From these vendors, she hoped to uncover any potential pre-existing relationships that might work against her. She was also demonstrating to Kurt her desire to enter Kurt's world and his network of relationships.

As the sales cycle progressed, the other vendors' patience and commitment to the opportunity waned. They had miscalculated their ability to shorten or subvert Kurt's process. As this happened, Kurt spent more time with the Heavy Hitter, which gave her the chance to build a personal relationship. The Heavy Hitter learned Kurt rode horses, had served in the military, and, surprisingly, had been married twice. Kurt ultimately became her coach and shepherded the purchase through the bureaucratic sales process of the agency.

While an aggressive, high-energy strategy might be appropriate in certain sales situations, the decision to model Kurt in a complementary reactive manner was an equally effective strategy.

At the other end of the spectrum from Kurt is a person who is impulsive, doesn't handle stress well, and is a constant worrier. He would have a high negative emotionality factor. This type of person is oriented around crises.

Larry was worried. There had been talk about outsourcing his group's application development function. Since he had been with the transportation company for over 13 years, he was also angry with his employer and somewhat discouraged with his current predicament.

One project that he had unsuccessfully tried to get funding for in the past was a new online reporting application to replace paper reports. He had ulterior motives for completing this project. He knew that once the flexibility of online reports was introduced, it would be well received, and perhaps a more positive view of his group's value would be adopted. Also, the reporting system would become irreplaceable, requiring continual enhancements and maintenance from his team. Larry asked all the leading reporting tools vendors to present their technology to his team. Of course, none of the vendors had any background information about Larry's dilemma.

However, the Heavy Hitter had a different strategy for the meeting. Prior to the technology presentation, he met with Larry to further understand his needs. From this meeting, he determined that Larry had three problems. First, there wasn't enough time for his team to learn the new tools and build the application to meet Larry's schedule. Second, Larry was concerned that his team was not technically capable of completing the project. Finally, Larry didn't have a defined budget approved for the purchase! This information makes any salesperson nervous. Was Larry serious about the purchase or just "kicking tires"? Was there even a project?

Then the Heavy Hitter decided to do something to separate himself from the other vendors. While the other vendors would tell Larry how much easier their product was to use, the Heavy Hitter would build a prototype of the reporting system. He wanted to show Larry (a strong Visual) that his project could be completed successfully within Larry's constraints. However, prior to committing the resources to execute this strategy, he completed a background check of Larry. He wanted to know if Larry had juice. By understanding the past projects Larry had successfully managed, he was able to satisfy himself that Larry was not a dud. The Heavy

Hitter decided that the strategy had an acceptable risk and committed the resources to build the prototype.

All the other vendors gave Larry and his team a presentation of their company, their product's feature set, and a short product demonstration. It seemed to Larry that any of the vendor's products would meet his requirements. To add to Larry's confusion, all of the products were priced similarly.

However, the Hitter's presentation was different. He showed the completed prototype application. Following this, he dissected the prototype, displaying the unique features that had made the prototype so easy to create. Larry's team was excited! The Heavy Hitter was invited back the following week to show the application directly to the nontechnical employees who would ultimately use the reports.

Building the prototype had other benefits. In order to create it, the Hitter's technical team met with Larry's team to determine basic functionality. This is a much more desirable intersecting activity (or pretense) for them to build relationships than the duress of a sales presentation.

While the technical relationship was being developed, the relationship between the Heavy Hitter and Larry changed dramatically. Larry asked for a detailed proposal for training his team and a bid to build the entire application. To do this required constant communication between Larry and his team and the Heavy Hitter and his. The other vendors were locked out of the opportunity.

The presentation to the users the following week was a success. They wanted the application—the sooner the better. Money was allocated, terms were finalized, and the project was completed successfully 90 days later. Larry was extremely happy until the next crisis.

Heavy Hitters know there is a path to every piece of business. They understand that they must walk the path in the shoes of their customer.

FACTOR 2—EXTROVERSION

People have different capabilities to build and manage relationships. Extroverts are comfortable with lots of relationships, while introverts tend to be reserved and more comfortable being alone. Obviously, extroverts are one of the most preferred of the five factors to sell to, while introverts are more challenging. Figure 9.5 shows the six facets of extroversion.

An introvert, or a person with a low level of extroversion, is generally thought of as being shy. However, a more appropriate way to think of an introvert is as a person who is predominantly concerned with her own thoughts or internal dialogue. In addition, introverts are usually independent, and this presents an additional challenge for a Hitter.

> Gary is a network engineer for a large bank who works on complex low-level networking issues. He is on call by pager around the clock in case the network goes down. Gary's opinion on net-

Facets	Low	Medium	High
Warmth	Aloof	Attentive	Cordial
Gregariousness	Prefers to be alone	Likes being alone or with others	Prefers company
Assertiveness	Stays in background	Stays in foreground	Is a leader
Activity	Leisurely pace	Average pace	Vigorous pace
Excitement Seeking	Low need for thrills	Occasional need for thrills	Craving for thrills
Positive Emotions	Seldom exuberant	Sometimes exuberant	Usually cheerful

Figure 9.5 Facets of Extroversion

working technology and products is highly valued throughout his department. A new product would not be purchased without his explicit approval. Yet in several meetings with Gary, the Heavy Hitter had been unable to develop any significant relationship with him. It seemed that Gary (a strong Auditory) couldn't relate to salespeople.

But the Heavy Hitter had a secret weapon. She introduced her system engineer to Gary. While the two technicians' relationship started off slowly, it ultimately turned into a friendship. One of the key turning points was when they installed an evaluation copy of the software on Gary's network. Because of the operations environment, this work had to be done at two in the morning and took several hours to complete. Through this early-morning intersecting activity, their relationship became personal—as relationships often do when people are working side by side under difficult or unusual circumstances. Gary recommended the purchase of the Hitter's product.

Although the Heavy Hitter tried, she never developed more than a congenial relationship with Gary. But in the end, she didn't need to as she was able to "draft," or ride the wind of another relationship, to find her coach.

The extrovert, on the other hand, is a friendly, outgoing person who is usually more verbally dominant in social settings. The extrovert enjoys giving as well as receiving attention.

Bob is the director of information technology for a small division of a multibillion-dollar conglomerate. Bob wanted to make his mark, not only within his organization but also within the parent company. Bob's vision was to create the ultimate IT operation. His organization would become the model to be emulated by all the other IT organizations affiliated with the parent company. As a result, he deployed the latest products in his attempt to build his technology "showcase."

Bob was a high-energy person who moved at a fast pace. In order to drive his agenda, he was constantly meeting with his own team, as well as the other departments within the organization. His demeanor was friendly and optimistic. Bob had strong visual and kinesthetic catalogs.

The Heavy Hitter frequently met with Bob. Through these meetings, the Heavy Hitter truly understood the depth of Bob's conviction to accomplish his goal. Bob had a fantasy. The Heavy Hitter determined the best way for Bob to become his coach was to match fantasies. Instead of focusing on product features and functionality as Heavy Hitters may do with an introvert, the sale to Bob would be at a higher, more strategic level. The Heavy Hitter offered Bob a way of achieving his vision.

The Heavy Hitter used his manager extensively during the sales cycle. These customer meetings were more like conversations between friends who daydreamed about their future plans. Bob needed comrades who believed in him and would shower him with support. While this strategy would have little impact on an introvert, Bob viewed the Hitter's company as an integral component for achieving his dream.

FACTOR 3—OPENNESS

Some people are happiest when they are in a familiar environment with defined daily routines. They seek structure and are focused on the task immediately at hand. They would be classified as having a low openness factor. Others seek variety and are open to new experiences. They may dream about the future, seek deeper meanings for their emotions, and be genuinely curious. They would be classified as having a high openness factor. The facets of the openness factor are shown in Figure 9.6.

A person with low openness will concentrate on a vendor's "here and now" characteristics, including vendor stability, technical support, product features, and the quality of the product.

Facets	Low	Medium	High
Fantasy	In the here and now	Occasionally imaginative	A dreamer
Aesthetics	Uninterested in art	Moderate interest in art	Major interest in art
Feelings	Ignores feelings	Accepts feelings	Values all emotions
Actions	Likes familiar	Likes a mixture of new and familiar	Prefers variety
Ideas	Narrow focus	Moderate curiosity	Broad curiosity
Philosophy	Conservative	Moderate	Open to new values

Figure 9.6 Facets of Openness

John was an extremely difficult person to sell to. He was the vice president of information services for an outsourcer of computer applications. John had been a product person who had worked his way up to the executive level. His technical expertise made him even more intimidating to vendors.

He was a realist who based his decisions on facts rather than ideas or emotions. He was a strong Auditory who was only interested in discussing the "here and now." With every topic, he carefully selected his words to reflect their accuracy. Like Joe Friday from the *Dragnet* television show, he wanted nothing but the facts.

With John there wouldn't be any detailed discussions about the company's vision or any deep personal conversations. The topic would always be the product—how it worked, what features it lacked, and details about the underlying technology that most customers would consider minutiae. However, John needed to hear all the particulars.

Developing John into a coach involved several critical steps. First, the Heavy Hitter never went to a meeting with John alone.

She always had her system engineer or other technical team members on hand to help answer John's questions.

Second, the Heavy Hitter and her team gave only definitive, truthful answers to John's questions. They answered his questions with the same precision as they were asked. They wanted to maintain their credibility. They edited their usual extravagant product claims to mirror John's conservative demeanor.

Third, they always worked with John's best interests in mind. They wanted him to know both the features and limitations of their product. It made no sense to sell John a product that didn't meet his requirements. Rather, it was important that his expectations were set correctly during the sales process. They arranged for a detailed on-site technical evaluation of their product and provided technical resources to assist him.

During this evaluation process, an interesting change in John began to occur. He began to openly criticize the other vendor's sales tactics and honesty. Also, he uncovered many flaws in the Heavy Hitter's product. However, instead of criticizing the product and declaring it unsuitable, he worked with the Heavy Hitter's team to find workarounds for these limitations. John was now the Hitter's coach.

Heavy Hitters wear many sales hats. In some situations, they are the customer's friends. In others, they are the promoters of the company's vision. In this situation, the Heavy Hitter became the human dictionary of all the facts about her company's products.

As opposed to John's narrow focus, people with high openness prefer variety and are much more in touch with their own feelings.

Tom was the manager of the information technology department for a small college. Tom was an engaging, interesting person. He was friendly, outgoing, and easy to talk to. He was even a part-time actor and member of the Screen Actors Guild. Since he was a strong Kinesthetic, acting came naturally. Tom's background didn't include any formalized computer training, yet somehow in his past he had become involved with computers.

Tom's world was more political than technical. He spent the majority of his time meeting with the various deans and placating them. His department was staffed with young graduates who didn't have any previous business experience. While Tom did not get deeply involved in the detailed technical issues, he clearly had juice and approved every decision within the department.

When the Heavy Hitter met Tom, his first impression was that Tom was bored and unfulfilled by his job. When he tried to talk about his products, Tom kept changing the subject back to the Hitter by asking personal questions about his family and where he grew up. This was not a typical sales call!

However, what many salespeople would have viewed as small talk was actually a key part of Tom's decision process. Tom was trying to determine if there was a personal fit between him and the Hitter. For Tom, this was an important business prerequisite. The Heavy Hitter mirrored Tom and asked him the same type of personal questions. Tom described his childhood in the Midwest, his affinity for the Chicago Cubs, and his desire to retire in a few years. As a result, a meeting that should have taken 45 minutes lasted over 2 hours.

Many additional meetings would follow where product features and functionality would be discussed in addition to lunches and happy hours where they discussed personal life. But the most important aspect of Tom's sales selection process was already decided; he liked the Hitter, and they became friends.

If you are unsure whether a customer is your friend or a business acquaintance, apply the barbecue test. Would you invite the person to your home on a Sunday afternoon for a barbecue with your family and close friends? If you would and the customer would accept your invitation, then you are most likely friends, or there is enough compatibility for a friendship to develop. The more important question is whether your customers would invite you to their barbecues.

FACTOR 4—AGREEABLENESS

Some people get along better in groups than others. They have a high level of agreeableness. These people take direction and seek the approval of others. Conversely, people with a low level of agreeableness are more independent, interested in their own well-being, and concerned with either acquiring individual power or remaining autonomous. Figure 9.7 presents the six facets of agreeableness.

> Paul was the manager in charge of information systems security in a well-known financial services company. He would be accurately described as someone with a low agreeableness factor. His main responsibility was to ensure customers' data was safe and secure. The position held a lot of responsibility and commanded equal authority. A breach in a customer's data could have significant financial implications. In addition to the legal liability, the unfavorable press would impact the company greatly.
>
> Paul was a tough-minded authoritarian. He didn't meet vendors; rather he verbally abused them in front of his staff! These staged events were designed to showcase his considerable knowledge and the extent of his authority. Paul didn't trust anybody.

Facets	Low	Medium	High
Trust	Skeptical	Cautious	Trusting
Straightforwardness	Guarded	Tactful	Frank
Altruism	Uninvolved	Willing to help others	Eager to help
Compliance	Aggressive	Approachable	Deferential
Modesty	Superior	Equal	Humble
Tender-Mindedness	Hardheaded	Responsive	Easily moved

Figure 9.7 Facets of Agreeableness

He spoke negatively about other divisions of his company and how he would manage them differently. Paul had strong auditory and visual catalogs.

Developing Paul into a coach was critical. He was the bully who had all the juice. If the Heavy Hitter didn't win him over, she wouldn't win the deal. She knew it was pointless to argue with Paul, as there was nothing to be gained by doing so. He would not be swayed by any vendor's logic or reason. Paul marched to his own drumbeat.

Paul would choose the solution he believed was in his own best interest. So what did Paul want? He wanted to be a hero. He wanted to prove he was a smart businessman. He was seeking the recognition he felt he was entitled to. The Heavy Hitter's mission was to ensure that the selection of her product helped Paul achieve his needs.

Paul was considering replacing the company's existing security vendor because of continual product stability problems and the quality of its support. The product was originally purchased before Paul was hired, and the company had spent a significant amount of money purchasing and implementing it. Knowing this, the Heavy Hitter worked with her management to package a very compelling proposal that included a full product trade-in credit and free implementation services. This excited Paul! He would take great pride in boasting to his managers how he not only fixed the problem but essentially got their money back, too.

The Heavy Hitter continually sold to Paul's ego. At every opportunity, she elicited Paul's feedback, not so much for its own merits but rather so Paul could hear himself talk about the Heavy Hitter's solution. She arranged for Paul to meet with others from the Hitter's company—the technical support manager, the product management team, and various members of the executive staff. By doing this, the Hitter's colleagues were subjected to Paul's pontificating, and the Heavy Hitter was freed for other tasks. The Heavy Hitter even arranged for Paul to be invited to join her company's customer advisory committee.

Paul would ultimately become a fantastic coach and an incredible champion. He was sold on the Hitter's company as well as the product. Finally, someone was treating him with the respect he deserved. Later, he even met with the president about the possibility of joining the Hitter's company. Paul wasn't such a tough guy after all.

Heavy Hitters know you must understand your customers' desired benefactions in order to lead them to your solution.

FACTOR 5—CONSCIENTIOUSNESS

Conscientiousness can be defined as a person's degree of diligence and ability to complete tasks. People with a low level of conscientiousness will procrastinate and put in the minimal effort to get the job done. Meanwhile, people with a high level of conscientiousness will go to great lengths to ensure their duties are completed correctly. Figure 9.8 presents the facets of conscientiousness.

Facets	Low	Medium	High
Competence	Unprepared	Prepared	Capable
Order	Unorganized	Half organized	Well organized
Dutifulness	Covers obligations	Is casual about priorities	Has strong conscience
Achievement	Casual about success	Serious about success	Driven to succeed
Self-Discipline	Distractible	Mix of work and play	Focused on work
Deliberation	Spontaneous	Thoughtful	Careful

Figure 9.8 Facets of Conscientiousness

For the past five years, Lou had worked as the system administrator responsible for the database operations at a medium-sized electronics manufacturer. Lou was not the type of person who was intensely focused on his career. He was a happy-go-lucky guy who did the minimum to get by. This also applied to his interest in technology. While he understood concepts, he did not seem particularly interested in mastering the details. Lou would be classified as having low conscientiousness.

Although he was part of the evaluation team, he was not a key influencer of the group. In team meetings, his only contribution was an occasional wisecrack courtesy of his dry sense of humor. In short, Lou was an accommodating dud. In spite of this, the Heavy Hitter made a special effort to get to know Lou.

Acknowledging Lou's traits, the Heavy Hitter arranged unusual activities that were outside the work environment. To become better acquainted, the Heavy Hitter took Lou to lunch at eclectic restaurants, to the local pub, and even miniature cart racing at the nearby mall. The Heavy Hitter was normally an intense person with a very high conscientiousness factor. However, he had to suspend this personality characteristic when he was around Lou. Over time this "odd couple" actually found they enjoyed each other's company.

None of the other vendors paid any attention to Lou, as they considered him trivial to the decision process. In addition, none of the vendors (including the Heavy Hitter) was able to develop a coach out of anyone else on the selection team. Lou was the only coach to be found. For the Hitter, Lou developed into a great source of information about the company's political environment and how the sales process was progressing. While the other vendors were flying blind, the Heavy Hitter knew who was for and against his product and what objections he had to overcome. He knew the prices bid by his competitors. Lou even told the Heavy Hitter he had won the deal before it was publicly announced.

A person with a high level of conscientiousness will most likely be in a leadership position or a key player in the product selection process.

> Mr. Johnson was the chief information officer of a multibillion-dollar publicly held medical device manufacturer. He was the prototypical executive: confident, capable, and successful. However, one huge problem in selling to Mr. Johnson was that it was impossible to meet with him personally. For purchase decisions, he had several trusted lieutenants who did most of the data gathering and analysis.
>
> Mr. Johnson would become involved only very late in the sales cycle, after the preliminary recommendation had been made for his review. Until that time, the Heavy Hitter would have to work within the established process and find a coach elsewhere. In the Hitter's case, she was able to accomplish this with one of Mr. Johnson's direct reports, Michelle, the vice president of applications development. She was much easier to gain access to and meet with.
>
> Michelle made every vendor complete an immense RFP and laborious spreadsheets. Each product feature and operation had to be fully documented. Following the responses, Michelle performed a meticulous hands-on evaluation of each product and painstakingly documented her findings. It was clear that Michelle felt the decision process was a direct reflection of her competency.
>
> It wasn't until Michelle was completely satisfied with the Hitter's product that her demeanor completely changed from cross-examiner to collaborator. Suddenly, Michelle was strategizing with the Hitter about presenting her recommendation to Mr. Johnson. Michelle scheduled the meeting with Mr. Johnson to present her decision and asked the Heavy Hitter to attend. The Hitter knew the deal was won if they made it successfully past this final hurdle.
>
> Michelle planned and rehearsed every detail of the presentation. The Heavy Hitter was fearful that Michelle's decision could be overruled, and Michelle was fearful the Heavy Hitter would

somehow embarrass her. The demeanor of the participants was also rehearsed. Both Hitter and coach had to display confidence and professionalism, along with the etiquette expected when meeting a person of Mr. Johnson's stature.

The Heavy Hitter and her manager arrived early to meet Michelle at Mr. Johnson's office. The Heavy Hitter was nervous, and while the meeting seemed like life or death to her, it was just a small item on Mr. Johnson's daily calendar. They had been allotted 45 minutes of his time. Unfortunately, Mr. Johnson was running late and their meeting would be pushed back a half-hour and shortened to 20 minutes.

Mr. Johnson opened the meeting with an overview of his expectations. He then asked a series of high-level questions about the Heavy Hitter's company, product, competitors, and customers that Michelle and the Hitter answered together. However, rather than the grueling interrogation that had been expected, the Heavy Hitter felt this meeting was more ceremonial. Michelle's attention to detail had already won the deal!

Sometimes not losing the deal is a key part of winning the business. You have to know when to keep your mouth closed. For example, when Democratic presidential nominee Howard Dean bellowed his bizarre screech, his aspirations to work in the Oval Office were over. Dubbed the "I Have a Scream" speech, his red-faced rant was replayed on every television and radio station for days. Overnight, it gained cultlike status on the Internet, and hundreds of remixed songs parodied his "Aaargh." Although he tried to put a positive spin on his outburst, he would never regain the aura of invincibility he had enjoyed just a few days earlier. His biggest enemy was his own mouth.

THE CUSTOMER PUZZLE

There are five different personality factors. Each factor has six facets that are each measured as low, medium, or high. Together, these factors help the Heavy Hitter categorize the individuals she encounters. The Hitter's goal is to build a memory bank of previous experiences with dominant factors and prominent facets. From this storehouse of knowledge, the Heavy Hitter determines the best course of action to win the deal by winning over the decision makers.

Every person involved in the selection process presents the Heavy Hitter with a "customer puzzle." The pieces of the puzzle include finding intersecting activities, determining personal motivations, understanding the customer's dominant personality characteristics, and building a kinship in communication. The glue that holds the puzzle together is sales intuition.

In order to solve the puzzle, the Heavy Hitter must accumulate data. While the information is sometimes obvious, most often it is hard to uncover. Learning how to find and interpret, store, and recall valuable information is a skill that Hitters must develop over time.

In a meeting with two new members of my sales organization, as an exercise about paying attention to details, I asked one to describe the lamp directly behind him without looking at it. He gave an elaborate description of the size of the lamp, the texture and color of the lampshade, and the shape of the base. However, when asked whether the lamp was turned on using a switch on the base, a knob near the bulb, or a chain, he didn't know. He had collected a lot of data but missed one of the most important pieces of information—how to turn the lamp on!

The second salesperson had been intently listening to the discussion. I asked him the same question, "Without looking, describe the lamp behind you." He started to repeat almost word for word what the first salesperson said. I interrupted him: "There are two lamps behind you. How did you know which one I meant?" He had incorrectly assumed that I was asking about the same lamp.

Heavy Hitters always pay attention to the details, never make assumptions about data, and triangulate to ensure the data's correctness. Heavy Hitters are students of people. Being a student means paying attention to the details.

The kinship-in-communication piece of the customer puzzle requires recognizing a person's word catalog and understanding attributes of the customer's personality in order to anticipate their influence on the decision-making process. Some people are impulsive and will make quick decisions based upon their gut feeling. Others will hold long filibusters inside their mind and go back and forth arguing the merits of each solution. Heavy Hitters meld themselves and their account strategy to the customer's personality and individual thought process. Since Visuals, Auditories, and Kinesthetics process information differently, they also approach the decision process distinctively.

For example, choosing a spouse is one of life's most important decisions. A colleague of mine who is a strong Auditory recently told me how he met his wife. They were seated next to each other on a long plane flight. While neither thought the other was particularly interesting, out of boredom they started a conversation. Even though there was not a great deal of physical attraction, by the end of the flight they had exchanged telephone numbers. Since they lived in separate cities, they started talking on the telephone regularly. Through these long conversations they fell in love, and they eventually married.

A close friend of mine with a strong visual orientation has a completely different story about how he met his wife. One night at a party, he saw a beautiful girl walk into the room. He said to himself, "This is exactly who I have been looking for!" He introduced himself to her and even told her that night that he was going to marry her. A year later, he did exactly that.

CONCLUSION

You can think of the customer's personality as being much like the ocean. Without the aid of diving equipment, your view is limited to the surface. Sometimes the surface can be smooth as glass. At other times it's covered with enormous swells with frothy whitecaps. Occasionally, unexpected rogue waves come out of nowhere, wreaking fear and havoc upon ocean travelers. However, underneath the surface is a hidden world of conflicting currents, conspicuous features, and contrasting temperatures that determine what happens on the surface.

The word "ocean" is also a helpful reminder for the five personality factors:

Openness
Conscientiousness
Extroversion
Agreeableness
Negative Emotionality

In essence, we establish relationships with coaches exactly like we establish our personal friendships. We choose our friends based upon common interests and compatible personalities. While we place our friends' interests above our own, we expect them to reciprocate and unselfishly help us in our moment of need. A true friendship is based on honesty and synergy. One party does not dominate or take advantage of the other.

Let's take another look at the story from the beginning of this chapter about the president who hates computers. The salesperson went on to close a multimillion-dollar deal with that company. His coach was the director of information technology, who represented and sold the solution to the president. Neither the salesperson nor any member of his company ever met with the president.

Following the successful implementation six months later, the director of information technology was promoted to vice president. A full year after his first conversation with the president, the salesperson saw him at a trade show and gathered enough nerve to approach him again. He started to introduce himself. "Hello, I'm Steve with National Computer Company—" Once again, the president startled him by interrupting him in midsentence. However, this time he had a much different demeanor. The president shrugged his shoulders and held his hands up. "User-friendly computers!" he said, then turned and walked away. I know that story very well, because I was that salesperson.

PART THREE

The Power of Persuasion

WE TYPICALLY equate persuasion solely with satisfying the analytical mind. However, we are not as objective and analytical as we think, and even the most well thought out decision is ultimately determined by emotional and subconscious influences. Human nature has the final say on every decision customers make. In this section we explain how Heavy Hitters use the power of persuasion to convince the rational and the emotional mind to buy.

CHAPTER 10

The Deeper Meaning of Language

The presentation to the customer's selection team had lasted about an hour and a half. During that time, the salesperson had explained the origins and background of his company. He provided examples of successful customers and spoke of the underlying technology that separated his solution from the competition's. He detailed product features and showed how they would benefit the customer. Finally, he closed the meeting with a discussion about pricing and the resources required for successful implementation.

Although the presentation was filled with facts, figures, and technical information, it was far from boring. The salesperson's presentation style, while professional, was not stuffy or overly rehearsed. He held each person's interest and kept everyone involved by drawing out questions and seeking individual comments. He illustrated the conversation by using descriptive words, animating his speech, and making occasional humorous remarks. The presentation reflected his confidence in the solution and the personal attention he would give the customer following the sale.

After he finished, the selection team members gathered around him as if they were supporters of a political candidate who had just given an electrifying campaign speech. They wanted to spend more time with him and get to know him personally. Most importantly, they would ask him to come back the following week with a price quote and implementation plan.

I recently played golf with a friend of mine who warned me about the hazards before we played each hole. He would tell me about the "water to the left" and the "deep bunker next to the hill on the right." Since I had never played the course, he thought he was being helpful. Unfortunately, I hit the ball everywhere he told me not to. My mind was focused on what not to do instead of what to do. Like my friend, we can sometimes say things and be totally unaware of what we are truly communicating.

The goal of this book is to help you determine the different languages your customers speak and how to structure your message in language that persuades them to buy. This chapter presents the idea that there is a deeper meaning of language, an additional dimension that will ensure your message is accepted, remembered, and acted upon.

You communicate thousands of different messages on any given day. During the average business phone call, you deliver hundreds of unique thoughts. These thoughts are manufactured on the internal assembly line of your mind that starts with a purpose and ends with words being enunciated in the optimum manner. The receiver of your message has to disassemble your package of words to interpret them. Situated below this automatic process is the underlying deeper meaning of language.

Whatever your age and experience in life, you have already mastered how to use language. As a child, you learned the complex process of conveying your thoughts, how to tell the truth, and how to lie. You have become an expert on the nuances of how to say something with maximum impact, and you understand that sometimes what's important isn't necessarily what you say as much as how you say it. You already know how to create a message with a clear and a compelling sense of urgency. Heavy Hitters are no different from the average person in this regard.

However, Heavy Hitters amplify their use of language by adding an additional dimension of meaning and structure within their usual conversations with customers. By doing so, they instill their suggestions into the customer's thought process with what seems like telepathy. The common term for this is "persuasion." Persuasion is not solely a recital of logical arguments or factual information to a customer. Instead, it is the process of projecting your entire set of beliefs and convictions on another human being.

THE FIVE STEPS OF THE DEEPER MEANING OF LANGUAGE

Heavy Hitters employ five steps intuitively to create the deeper meaning of language. By understanding and utilizing these steps you will be able to deliver the same compelling communication.

1. Delivering your message with conviction and congruence.

2. Knowing your listener's benefaction and delivering your message in different languages.

3. Establishing and maintaining a receptive state of uninterrupted rapport with your listener.

4. Guiding your listener's internal dialogue.

5. Delivering your message directly to your listener's subconscious mind using a highly developed form of intuitive persuasion.

At the beginning of the book, I mentioned my interest in hypnosis. I believe the dictionary's definition of hypnosis—"A state like sleep in which the subject acts only on external suggestions"[1]—is actually wrong or at best only half true. In addition, the association of hypnosis with the pocket watch or the staged nightclub spectacle is irrelevant. Rather, hypnosis is about the structure and use of language. You use logical reasoning to talk to the conscious mind. Hypnosis is a label for an additional layer of communication directed at the subconscious mind.

From the perspective of Heavy Hitters, every communication event has the potential to have suggestive hypnotic qualities. If you understand how listeners process language, then you can help manage this process for them. This ensures your message will be successfully received and the action you suggest will be taken. This is a more definitive description of hypnosis. Once you have mastered the following five steps, your ability to communicate will become even more powerful. You will be able to deliver a message that effectively influences your listener with your suggestion.

Step 1. Delivering Your Message with Conviction and Congruence

During recent times, we have had two presidents that were extraordinary Hitters who understood and employed the deeper meaning of language. Presidents Bill Clinton and Ronald Reagan were both prolific speakers with unique talents. In terms of their accomplishments, history will ultimately decide how each of these men is regarded. However, they each enjoyed a unique talent for communication and building rapport.

From a management-style perspective, they both exhibited strong Teflon styles. Both men had juice, and they were both bullies but in very different ways. You could argue that the scandal President Clinton brought upon himself greatly limited his ability to accomplish his agenda. Surely, this was an act of overconfidence. And as with an overconfident sales manager, people either love Bill Clinton or hate him.

As president, he was a master of projecting congruence. Whatever the topic and regardless of who had written the speech, he was able to align his entire body to deliver a spoken message. He had a natural ability to mark words with voice inflections and physical mannerisms, for example, when he clenched his jaw. He seemed to do it consciously to further emphasize his conviction about a topic. Whether he was mad or sad, it became his facial exclamation point.

President Reagan had a natural ability to create rapport with a wide spectrum of people. He was able to obtain support from both major political parties and from people from all walks of life. Although his political enemies may have heartily disagreed with his agenda, they found it hard, if not impossible, to hate him personally. For this reason, he was able to accomplish (bully) more of his agenda.

In 2001, a book of Ronald Reagan's personal writings was published. *Reagan, in His Own Hand* offers some unique insights into the president who was also known as "The Great Communicator." In the book's Foreword, Secretary of State George Shultz recounts the following story about the Geneva Summit in 1985.[2]

> Mikhail Gorbachev suddenly began to harangue us about our Strategic Defense Initiative, our plans for missile defense.
>
> President Reagan exploded. The two leaders went back and forth, interrupting each other and expressing their views with vehemence.
>
> Then Ronald Reagan got the floor. He spoke passionately about how much better the world would be if we were able to defend ourselves from nuclear warheads on ballistic missiles. He was intense as he expressed his abhorrence at having to rely on the ability to "wipe each other out" as the only means of keeping the peace.
>
> The depth of President Reagan's belief was vividly apparent. Ronald Reagan was talking from the inside out. Translation was simultaneous. Gorbachev could connect what Reagan was saying with his facial expressions and body language.
>
> When the president finished, there was total silence.
>
> After what seemed an interminable time, Gorbachev said, "Mr. President, I don't agree with you, but I can see that you really mean what you say."

The congruence and conviction with which President Reagan spoke made an immense impression on Mr. Gorbachev. These two men went on to develop a very personal relationship, and the rapport they built literally changed the world.

Although this meeting didn't result in any breakthrough agreements, George Shultz credited this conversation with establishing the foundation from which many future successful negotiations resulted. And this is an important point to remember. Not every sales call results in a sale. But every sales call is a chance to use rapport to build a relationship.

For example, a Hitter and his system engineer arranged a meeting with a potential customer. Initially, they were very excited about the opportunity. Unfortunately, the company was located in another state, and they would have to spend a full day just traveling there. Once at the meeting, it became apparent that this company was not going to buy their product in the near term. The Heavy Hitter was embarrassed. Both he and the system engineer felt bad that they wasted an entire day.

A couple of months later, the Heavy Hitter received a surprise telephone call. One of the people attending the previous meeting had moved to a new company. His new company was much larger, and he was recommending it purchase the Hitter's product. He specifically mentioned that he was impressed with the Hitter's conviction about his product's capability and belief in his company. Hitters garner many new customers from past sales efforts because customers believe in them. Heavy Hitters internalize their message so their bodies, demeanor, and words exude conviction.

Step 2. Knowing Your Listener's Benefaction and Delivering Your Message in Different Languages

If selling is about speaking the language of a customer, then there are as many varieties of languages as there are customers. By speaking a customer's unique dialect or language, Heavy Hitters are able to create rapport. Let's review the different types of language Heavy Hitters mirror when they speak with a customer.

- Word catalog language. Heavy Hitters consciously use the same word catalog terms as the customer. They paint a picture of their solution to a Visual, tell the product's story to an Auditory, and get a grasp of a Kinesthetic's problem.

- Physical communication language. Hand in hand with the customer's word catalog is the language of the body. Heavy Hitters reflect their customer's dialect using their speech, breathing, hand movements, facial expressions, and body posture.

- Technical specification language. This language is the content-level trade language of the customer. Each industry has its own language and slang with unique terms and nomenclature.

- Intersecting activity language. In order to facilitate the building of a personal relationship, Heavy Hitters are constantly searching for intersecting activities they have in common with customers. Each intersecting activity also has a unique dialect of terminology.

- Orientation language. Heavy Hitters know they need to understand the benefaction of everyone involved in the sale. This includes each decision maker along with recommenders who can influence the selection process. A Hitter finds a way to help them achieve their benefactions through the purchase of his product.

Each customer's language is sophisticated and the dialect unique. In order to truly speak the language of the customer, the Heavy Hitter speaks many different languages that reflect a person's word catalog wiring, body language, jargon of the industry, intersecting activities, and benefaction. Like explorers who are making their first contact with a primitive tribe, Heavy Hitters cautiously study their customers' languages before making any sudden movements. They know any misinterpretation can have catastrophic results.

Step 3. Establishing and Maintaining a Receptive State of Uninterrupted Rapport with Your Listener

In Chapter 7, I recounted the story of the seminar where I performed a behavior interruption to change the audience's demeanor from apathetic and indifferent to engaged and involved. My goal was to create a "receptive state" with each audience member. A receptive state is the positive environment that enables a message to be accepted and remembered.

Creating a receptive state is like hosting a party. Imagine you have invited a group of people together to the intersecting activity of a celebration. Most likely, your guest list includes people who have never met as well as friends. As the host, you want everyone to be comfortable so you make sure the location, facilities, food, beverages, and entertainment are conducive to having a good time. Like a party host, Heavy Hitters are responsible for creating the mental environment (message content) and the communication accommodations (message delivery) for a customer (the guest) during a sales call.

Heavy Hitters consciously create a receptive state at the beginning of every meeting in order to build rapport. As the meeting progresses, they continually monitor the level of rapport of each attendee. The Hitters' goal is to create four different receptive states: personal, technical, business, and political. The first priority is to build a personal receptive state with each individual. To accomplish this, Hitters will try to determine people's unique language, search for intersecting activities they might have in common, and determine the traits of their personalities.

Once personal rapport is established, Heavy Hitters will execute a series of premeditated vignettes to qualify the customer's technical fit. The criteria to determine technical fit have been supplied by their company. However, they do not want to jeopardize the personal rapport they have established. Therefore, they take great care to build a technical receptive state through understanding the customer's problem. They want to ensure they understand the technical problem the customer is trying to solve and compare it against their company's definition of technical fit. Technical problems are quite diverse, depending on the industry. A manufacturer may need more production capacity in its Chicago facility, a telecommunications company may require faster transmission rates for its voice-over-Internet protocol service, and a consumer package goods company may want less expensive, biodegradable product packaging.

The line of questioning the Heavy Hitter uses is not like that of a police officer interrogating the prime suspect in a crime case. Rather, it is interwoven as a natural part of the conversation without much fanfare. These vignettes are designed not only to qualify the technical fit but also to insert logical arguments that the Hitter's solution can solve the customer's technical problem.

As Heavy Hitters demonstrate their primary interest is in the customer's success, they begin to build a business receptive state. At this point, the customer starts to consider the Hitter more than a vendor. He becomes a business consultant who has the expertise to solve the customer's problem.

Finally, the political receptive state is established when the customer uses the Hitter's solution to achieve his personal benefaction based on his physiological, safety, belonging, and esteem needs. Figure 10.1 depicts the ideal progression of rapport and momentum during the sales cycle.

At the bottom of the graph is the concept of time. The amount of time required to create rapport depends on the product you are selling. For example, it may take weeks or months to achieve complete rapport for a Heavy Hitter who is trying to sell a customer millions of dollars of heavy equipment. Conversely, it may take only a few minutes for a less expensive sale like a $300 air compressor.

The Foundation

In order to influence his customer, the Heavy Hitter must lay the foundation of successful communication using the deeper meaning of language. The first three steps of this process—delivering the message

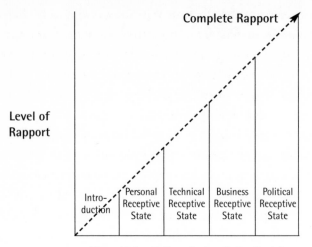

Figure 10.1 Receptive States during the Sales Cycle

with conviction and congruence, speaking in the customer's different languages, and using receptive states to create rapport—must be
completed before proceeding to the hypnotic delivery of the subliminal message. Taking the first three steps alone will help you enjoy
more effective communication with customers and improve the odds
of winning a deal. However, Heavy Hitters want more. They want
their message to be instilled in the customer's thought process as if it
were the customer's own idea. The ability to master the final two
steps of the process ultimately determines the Hitters' persuasiveness.

Step 4. Guiding Your Listener's Internal Dialogue

Your internal dialogue is the never-ending, honest, unedited conversation within your mind that represents your deepest feelings. Basically, you are always talking to yourself. This discussion is the real
you and the summation of your personality. However, we don't usually expose this dialogue to the outside world until we pass it through
our own editing process. The editing process interprets and validates
the information we receive and approves the messages we send. In
essence, we use the editing process to protect ourselves.

However, it is possible to lead or manage another person's editing process. First, you have to establish that you are working in that person's best interest, using the previous steps of the deeper meaning of language. Then you have to be able to guide the person's internal dialogue. To help understand this concept, let's once again examine President Reagan's use of language.

President Reagan was an impressive politician. He utilized his communication talents to win over his customers—the American people, Congress, and foreign leaders. He possessed an extremely balanced communication style that he used effectively to create complete rapport. He spoke with conviction and had a natural command of language that amplified his sincerity. He was also a master at guiding his listeners' internal dialogue.

Before and during his presidency, he wrote over 600 radio addresses by himself, in his own handwriting. They were not the work of a team of speechwriters. The structure and content of these addresses are well worth examining and understanding. "Looking Out the Window" was delivered on January 27, 1978. The text that follows is exactly as he wrote it, with his punctuation and spelling. For the sake of brevity, some cuts have been made. If you can, try to imagine yourself listening to his voice over the radio as you read it.

It's nightfall in a strange town a long way from home. I'm watching the lights come on from my hotel room window on the 35th floor.

I'm afraid you are in for a little bit of philosophizing if you dont mind. Some of these broadcasts have to be put together while I'm out on the road traveling what I call the mashed potato circuit. In a little while I'll be speaking to a group of very nice people in a banquet hall.

Right now however I'm looking down on a busy city at rush hour. The streets below are twin ribbons of sparkling red & white. Tail lights on the cars moving away from my vantage point provide the red and the headlights coming toward me the white.

But I wonder about the people in those cars, who they are, what they do, what are they thinking about as they head for the warmth of home. Come to think of it I've met them—oh—maybe not those particular individuals but I feel I know them.

Someone very wise once wrote that if we were all told one day that the end was coming; that we were living our last day, every road, every street & all the telephone lines would be jammed with people trying to reach someone to whom we wanted simply to say, "I love you."

But doesn't it seem foolish to wait for such a final day and the chance of not getting there in time? And speaking of time I'll have to stop now. OPERATOR I'D LIKE TO MAKE A PHONE CALL—LONG DISTANCE.

This is RR. Thanks for listening.[3]

Here's a paragraph-by-paragraph analysis to help you understand how President Reagan guides the listeners' internal dialogue. I have highlighted the VAK keywords, as well as identified all of the different communication techniques he has interwoven into his message.

It's nightfall in a strange town a long way from home. I'm *watching* the lights come on from my hotel room window on the 35th floor.

The first paragraph of all his radio addresses helps create a personal receptive state for the audience. The words "nightfall," "strange town," "long way from home," provide the mental imagery that enable the listeners to be quickly transported to Reagan's place and mood (in an unfamiliar place a long way from home).

The second sentence is an operator on the first sentence. It further defines where he is physically and forces the listeners to adjust their viewpoint to the 35th floor of a hotel. Both of these sentences are verifiable statements. Most everyone has experienced being a long way from home and feeling homesick. Most everyone has been in a high-rise building. As listeners receive information, they check with their internal dialogue to verify the statement's accuracy. Assuming the listeners have been homesick before, this statement is agreed to and considered truthful. The honesty of the statement is also passed on to the presenter. Verifiable statements enable the presenter to quickly gain credibility and rapport.

> I'm afraid you are in for a little bit of philosophizing if you dont mind. Some of these broadcasts have to be put together while I'm out on the road traveling what I call the mashed potato circuit. In a little while I'll be *speaking* to a group of very nice people in a banquet hall.

Preapologizing is one technique for developing a receptive state with an audience. This is one form of a "softener." A softener eases listeners into the next thought or can be used to set expectations. Usually, these radio addresses discussed the economy or issues of foreign and domestic interest. Here President Reagan is signaling that the intent of this week's message is different. He's adjusting the listeners' frame of mind from being issue based to being more reflective and introspective. Basically, he's telling their internal dialogue to relax a little.

He's on the road, about to give a speech on what he calls "the mashed potato circuit." How do you interpret that statement? Speaking to a group of people in the heartland of America is quite different from speaking to people from the East or West Coast. What would you have inferred if he had called it the "steak and wine circuit"? Perhaps that he considers these dinner speeches less than important and feels he should be performing his "real" job of leading the land. There's an underlying meaning that he is trying to communicate. However, the interpretation of the statement is dependent upon each listener's viewpoint, and there is no right or wrong answer. Regardless of the answer, the listeners' internal dialogue empathizes with the position he is in.

> Right now however I'm *looking* down on a busy city at rush
> hour. The streets below are twin ribbons of *sparkling* red &
> white. Tail lights on the cars moving away from my *vantage*
> point provide the red and the headlights coming toward me
> the white.

The paragraph visually leads the listeners to create more mental
imagery. The words "Right now" grab the listeners' attention. The
listeners' internal dialogue is quickly forced to look down with him
at the street. Then he provides an unusual description of something
seen nightly. This paragraph causes the listeners to create a lot of
mental activity, which in turn forces the listeners' internal dialogue
to become increasingly busy.

The metaphor of the car taillights as twin ribbons is another receptive state development technique using a verifiable statement.
Although you probably have never thought of car lights as "twin ribbons" before, you have seen the taillights of cars as they are lined up
on the highway.

This analogy also draws you closer into Reagan's world. What
was the first thought that came to mind as you read the words
"sparkling" and "ribbons"? Did you associate them with patriotic
events such as "the rockets' red glare" or the ribbons on the Medal of
Honor? Did you link them to something highly valued, such as a
first-place ribbon, or to the sparkle of a diamond or ruby? These
words convey another level of meaning, which is transposed onto the
content of the message. It's up to each individual's internal dialogue
to discern the relevant meaning from all the possibilities.

> But I wonder about the people in those cars, who they are,
> what they do, what are they thinking about as they head for
> the *warmth* of home. Come to think of it I've met them—
> oh—maybe not those particular individuals but I *feel* I know
> them.

When he "wonders" in the first sentence, this causes the listeners' internal dialogue to also wonder. Nearly everyone has driven a

car and can relate to the intersecting activity of driving a car. You've also probably wondered who those people are in the cars next to you on the road. What do they do for a living and where are they going?

Driving is one of the few times during the day that is specifically dedicated to chatting with your internal dialogue. If a listener drives a car home from work, the reaction to this statement may have been, "I do that." If the listener was in his car while hearing this message, he would have definitely said, "Hey, that's me!"

The word "warmth" is a "double entendre." That is, it has two distinct meanings. Remember, this speech was given in January. Did Reagan mean the physical temperature of the home? Or did he mean the atmosphere of emotional affection inside the home? The listeners are left to interpret this sentence, and there isn't a wrong answer.

The final sentence is very important. Here Reagan is sharing his internal dialogue directly with the listeners. If you could view the transcripts of a person's unedited internal dialogue, you would see his "honest" thoughts. In this case we can actually do that as the original writings have been reproduced in the book. Reagan's handwriting shows his exact stream of consciousness, including corrections and amplifications. Therefore, he's speaking with congruence and conviction. He does seem to know the listeners. He's described activities they can relate to. He has been telling their internal dialogue what to think about. He has created a personal receptive state with each individual listener.

> Someone very wise once wrote that if we were all *told* one day that the end was coming; that we were living our last day, every road, every street & all the telephone lines would be *jammed* with people trying to *reach* someone to whom we wanted simply to *say*, "I love you."

Who is this "someone very wise" that he mentions? Depending on the deepness of the receptive state, the listeners may have performed a quick memory search of well-known wise people. Remember, he previously told you to "wonder."

Examine the second sentence again. What's the difference between a road and a street? The listener is forced to make a distinction between the two. Notice how he associates the word "jammed" to road, street, and telephone lines. He is using a single word with two completely different word catalog interpretations. A jammed road is a kinesthetic event. A jammed telephone line is an auditory event. Also, "reaching" someone by road or street is a kinesthetic event; "reaching" someone by telephone is an auditory event. Once again, the listeners have to determine their own meaning from these general words.

> But doesn't it seem foolish to wait for such a final day and the chance of not getting there in time? And *speaking* of time I'll have to stop now. OPERATOR I'D LIKE TO MAKE A PHONE *CALL*—LONG DISTANCE.
> This is RR. Thanks for *listening*.

These two paragraphs are constructed entirely from the perspective of the auditory catalog. By asking a question, he is leading the listeners' internal dialogue and limiting what they can be thinking about. He gives you no choice. You have to answer the question in your mind. His suggestion is that it would be "foolish" not to. In addition, he uses the word "time" in the second sentence as a form of linkage. It links the discussion of your internal dialogue to the action of making a phone call.

The underlying complexity of this message is very sophisticated. Each paragraph is written entirely in one word catalog. He's taking the listeners from catalog to catalog. Here's the pattern:

- Paragraph 1   Visual
- Paragraph 2   Auditory
- Paragraph 3   Visual
- Paragraph 4   Kinesthetic
- Paragraph 5   Auditory

Throughout the example, Reagan has been guiding the listeners' internal dialogue, directing it to create certain images and specific feelings, and telling it to ask certain questions to limit what the listeners can think about. He's using words with multiple meanings and he's speaking with congruence and conviction. He's accomplished the first four steps of the deeper meaning of language and is now ready to move on to the final step.

Step 5. Delivering Your Message Directly to Your Listener's Subconscious Mind Using a Highly Developed Form of Intuitive Persuasion

Like every salesman, President Reagan had a product to sell. As a politician, his product was not only his policies but also, equally important, himself. Each of his radio addresses had a political purpose, and this one was no different. He had a very powerful message that he wanted to deliver that was camouflaged beneath the content of the story. Now I doubt that Ronald Reagan sat down and said, "I'm going to create a message that interweaves all of the listeners' word catalogs and instill subliminal thoughts in their minds." Rather, this message, like all the other ones he wrote, came naturally to him.

Here is the most fascinating part by far. Our subconscious minds are always receiving information that our conscious minds may not even recognize. More importantly, Hitters know that during the course of a normal conversation they can have direct communication with people's subconscious minds that can influence their opinions and points of view. Recently, I had an interesting experience that illustrates the concept of intuitive persuasion and the perceptiveness of the subconscious mind. It happened while I was having surgery for a bothersome knee.

During the previous months, my knee had been a great source of pain and frustration. Instead of my knee healing over time, the discomfort intensified until even walking became a chore. After procrastinating as long as possible, I visited a knee specialist who recommended surgery. Although I dreaded having surgery, I looked forward to being pain free and active again.

While I was being anesthetized for knee surgery, I became quite talkative and animated. While my speech was sober and coherent, my thought process was inebriated. My wife was present, and she would later relish telling me of my somewhat embarrassing behavior.

I have no recollection of anything I said or did. The drugs had disconnected my ability to store any of the events in my short-term or long-term memory. However, my subconscious mind was still alert and gathering information. It was as if I were in a drug-induced state of intuitive persuasion.

I was later told I had a very rational conversation with the doctor in the recovery room where he told me the surgery had gone very well. However, I have absolutely no recollection of this conversation, either. When I awoke a couple of hours later, I sat up and began speaking as if the doctor were still standing at the foot of my bed, although he had left hours earlier. "I'm fixed!" I said aloud.

Although I didn't consciously remember our conversation, I knew the operation had been a success. My subconscious mind had been present to receive my doctor's message on my conscious mind's behalf.

CONCLUSION

The content level of the words you speak is like your own anesthetic that you can learn to use to knock out your customer's conscious mind. It is the customer's conscious mind that is full of objections, doubt, and cynicism. If you can bypass it and speak directly to the subconscious mind, you can send the customer your message without interruption, offer suggestions on how the customer should behave, or explain why he should trust you.

The knockout I am referring to is not the same as that delivered by a boxer who uppercuts an opponent into unconsciousness. Rather, it is using the first four steps of the deeper meaning of language to get past a person's conscious mind. If you speak with conviction and congruence, know your listener's benefaction, deliver your message in "different languages," and establish and maintain a receptive state of rapport to guide the listener's internal dialogue, you will have set the stage to speak directly to your customer's subconscious mind. In the next chapter, we'll unlock the secrets of the final step of the process, intuitive persuasion.

Since we have spent a great deal of this chapter discussing the internal dialogue, it is appropriate to end our conversation with the most important words you say every day, the words you speak to yourself. The source of life's anxieties and problems can be traced to one of three root causes: external circumstances beyond our control, failing relationships between people or groups, and self-produced difficulties we create. How you talk to yourself is the key to dealing with any of these predicaments. If you say to yourself, "It will never work," "I'm going to fail," or "I can't do it," you will most certainly be proven right.

Because the internal voice is inexorably linked to the conscious and subconscious minds, speaking to yourself positively gives you the best chance to succeed. I know I wouldn't want to fly on a plane when the pilot is thinking "We might crash today" or work in an environment where the leaders secretly think "All hope is lost." Therefore, when you are feeling discouraged or depressed, you need to interrupt the negative conversation. Even though you may not feel like it or believe what you're saying, when you repeat positive thoughts your mind-set reflexively improves.

CHAPTER 11

Intuitive Persuasion

The vice president of sales was about to announce the top sales producer for the quarter at the awards ceremony. In the back row, two salespeople were talking to each other.

"Well, it isn't any surprise who gets this award, " said the first salesperson sarcastically.

"Unbelievable. Three quarters in a row," responded the other.

"Yeah, last quarter she closed one big account and this quarter she closes ten small ones," said the envious first salesperson.

"How does she do it?"

"Yeah, how does she do it?"

In Ronald Reagan's message that we reviewed in the last chapter, he created an incredibly deep level of hypnotic, subconscious communication using each of the five steps of the deeper meaning of language. Below (in parentheses following each paraphrased sentence) is his real message to his listeners. This is the encoded message that the listeners' subconscious minds received. It is also a great example of intuitive persuasion.

- In a little while, I'll be speaking to very nice people. *(You are nice people.)*
- Although we haven't met, I feel I know them. *(I know you.)*
- Reach you, to simply say I love you. *(I love you.)*

Why was this message interpreted in this way? On the surface, Reagan constructed a series of everyday thoughts that created the content-level story. He explained the circumstances surrounding his emotional state, talked about the speech he was about to give, and described the sights around him. However, underneath this visible story was an invisible message to his customers, the listeners. The message assured the listeners that Reagan knew them and cared for them. Undoubtedly, it was received by their subconscious minds and influenced those people who heard it.

In every conversation, both conscious and subconscious communication is being transmitted, assessed, and cataloged by each participant. And each layer of the human communication model is capable of sending observable (conscious) and unobservable (subconscious) messages simultaneously. Although each listener can receive only a finite amount of information at any one time, very little of the information that is transmitted across all layers is lost. What isn't consciously received is processed subconsciously.

If you overwhelm the conscious mind's capability to process information, reduce its ability to handle data, or turn it off completely (such as creating a trance state), you will be talking directly to the subconscious mind. Recently, *Scientific American* magazine described this experience in an article on hypnosis: "Over the past few years, researchers have found that hypnotized individuals actively respond to suggestions even though they sometimes perceive the dramatic changes in thought and behavior as happening 'by themselves.' During hypnosis, it is as though the brain temporarily suspends its attempts to authenticate incoming sensory information."[1] Later, we will review different techniques to accomplish this.

However, it is important to recognize that the first step of the process, speaking with conviction and congruence, requires the presenter to be telling the truth. In fact, truth is the key ingredient of the entire process. If your fundamental message is not based upon truth, it will fail. Was Reagan telling the truth or was he just another slick politician manipulating the populace? The answer is that he was emphatically telling the truth. The speech was written in his own handwriting, and by examining it, you can witness his unedited internal dialogue being put onto paper. He was writing down the exact conversation he was having with himself at the time. The subconscious message he delivered was in complete congruence with his actual thoughts. Being a Heavy Hitter requires believing in your company, product, and yourself.

Both the conscious and subconscious dimensions of information are stored together in a person's short- or long-term memory. Once stored, the "complete experience" can be recalled. The complete experience is comprised of all the sights, sounds, and feelings gathered by the word catalogs, along with information that has been collected by the subconscious mind.

For the Hitter, each sales call and every sales cycle results in an incredible amount of data to be stored. Once stored, this information can be accessed during the current sales situation to determine how the Heavy Hitter should behave personally or to select a course of action to win the deal.

INTUITION

This process is called "intuition"—comparing a series of past experiences against current circumstances. You can think of intuition as a highly developed model for making decisions and a powerful heuristic engine that is constantly learning from the past. In other words, you are constantly learning from every decision you make and continually incorporating these new reference points as part of your decision-making process. When you invoke your intuition, you're accessing previous complete experiences in order to gather the widest range of information. Once your conscious and subconscious minds have gathered all the information about a current deal, it can be compared to previous sales cycles you have worked on. This results in the best possible decisions being made.

All salespeople store their conscious experiences. However, Heavy Hitters are able to see a wider spectrum of data, have a keener sense of the situation, and are more in tune with the customer. They have a more fully developed awareness of word catalogs. In addition, they have more effective methodologies to store and retrieve all the visible and invisible layers of the human communication model. Since their intuition is far superior to that of average salespeople, they have a greater proficiency to win business. The formula for intuition can be summarized in the equation in Figure 11.1.

The first half of this equation is the ability to store and retrieve experiences. The second half of the equation is the aptitude to recognize all the available information from an experience using all of the senses. How often have you attended a sales call with a colleague who had a different opinion of the success of the meeting or the quality of the opportunity? Most likely, the difference in "reading" the meeting resulted because one person collected more data than the other and had more experiences to compare it against.

All your life you have used intuition to make important personal and business decisions. Usually, we think of our intuition in a reactive state. You gather information, check with your intuition, then make a decision or take some action. However, another, even more powerful form of intuition is comparable to hypnosis. It's a proactive intuition called "intuitive persuasion."

Intuitive persuasion is a natural extension of intuition with two additional capabilities. The more important capability is that you can deliver your message directly into someone's subconscious mind, as President Reagan did with his radio message. Two key requirements must be in place in order to accomplish this successfully. Listeners have to be in an intense personal receptive state, and their internal dialogue has to be occupied. In other words, personal rapport must be established, and their internal dialogue must be immersed in an all-encompassing activity, even if that activity is resting.

$$\text{Intuition} = \frac{\text{Cataloged experiences}}{\text{(short- and long-term)}} \times \frac{\text{Word catalog}}{\text{awareness}}$$

Figure 11.1 The Formula for Sales Intuition

How many times have you missed your freeway exit while you were driving and woke up afterward? Or have you gone through an intersection and later asked yourself if the light was green? In both cases, you were physically driving your car, but your internal dialogue was very busy talking to itself or someone else, listening to the radio, singing, or daydreaming. Meanwhile, you successfully turned over the driving duties to your subconscious mind. This is an example of your internal dialogue being overloaded and turning inward.

In Ronald Reagan's radio address, he was vigorously exercising all of the listeners' word catalogs. Overwhelming people's word catalogs causes their internal dialogue to start an intense conversation with itself and turn inward. In turning inward, the internal dialogue changes from being externally focused on the outside world to internally focused within the mind. The point of reference of the senses changes from outside the body to the exclusive conversation with oneself. This also happens when people pray, meditate, chant, or engage in activities that require intense concentration, such as painting or drawing.

When the internal dialogue becomes too busy keeping up with the conversation by managing the tasks of creating pictures, sounds, and feelings, it starts to turn inward and turns off the outside world. When bombarded with information, the internal dialogue may even declare itself "lost" and turn inward by having a separate conversation on a completely different topic. Or if a topic of conversation is very meaningful or pertinent to an individual, the internal dialogue discusses how it applies to the individual. I've been a part of many presentations where the customer is too busy implementing the product in her mind to listen to the presentation.

Once turned inward, the internal dialogue is not an active participant, as if the listener's conscious mind has been turned off (or the volume turned way down). Certain bands of information that were previously received consciously are shut down. However, the information is not lost. It is still being received by the person's word catalog, but it is processed and cataloged directly into the subconscious mind. It is at this time that the subconscious mind is open to receiving information and suggestions. For example, this is the precise moment when a hypnotist is able to tell the person who seems asleep (in a deep trance) to raise her arm.

EXERCISE 11: INTERNAL DIALOGUE AWARENESS

Try this exercise to explore how your internal dialogue can turn inward. Start counting backward from one hundred to one. As you are counting, try to sense the specific number where your mind starts to wander. At that point, try to sense when your internal dialogue starts another conversation or begins to turn inward. As it turns inward, you are still aware of your surroundings. However, information is being pushed into the background while you try to focus on the task at hand, counting backward.

Now try a slightly different experiment. Say the alphabet backward. You will notice it is harder to do since there isn't a sequential relationship or pattern among the letters. Therefore, you may have had to first say the alphabet forward in order to reverse it. This creates a more stimulating task for your internal dialogue so it cannot turn inward as quickly. When it does, it is more likely to be from frustration rather than the boredom associated with counting backward.

READING MINDS

The second capability of intuitive persuasion is that it provides Heavy Hitters with the ability to read minds. Of course, no one can truly read minds. Rather, Hitters can predict what will be in the listener's mind based upon the specific words they know they are going to deliver.

For example, if I say, "Don't think about snakes," you have to think about snakes in order to not think about snakes. Therefore, I could have predicted two paragraphs ago that very shortly you would be thinking about snakes since I was guiding your internal dialogue to the idea of snakes.

Whether you thought of rattlesnakes, pythons, or sidewinders, you had to disassemble the sentence in order to interpret it and you had to think about snakes. In addition, most people don't like snakes and by inserting them into the dialogue I am actually breaking rapport. If the subject had been puppies instead of snakes, the effect would have been different.

Intuitive persuasion is an elegant and sophisticated strategy for talking to your customer's subconscious mind. By creating a deep receptive state and guiding the internal dialogue of your customers, you can deliver a message directly to their subconscious minds that will be acted upon. Instead of barraging customers solely with logical arguments, facts, and figures, you are finessing them to believe. While a challenge to execute, once you have mastered intuitive persuasion you will not only enjoy the satisfaction of accomplishment but sell more, too. The equation for intuitive persuasion is illustrated in Figure 11.2.

You'll notice the first half of the equation is the formula for intuition. This part of the equation enables Heavy Hitters to sense all the data emanating from the customer and, by comparing the scenario to past situations, correctly interpret the situation. When intuition is combined with intense rapport and guiding the listener's internal dialogue, Heavy Hitters are capable of an entirely different level of superhuman persuasion.

First, Heavy Hitters create an extraordinarily intense personal receptive state by assuming the customer's word catalog completely. They subtly mirror all aspects of the person's physical communication (breathing, speech, and body movements). They adopt the person's language and word catalog orientation, using their VAK keywords. They will speak the same language and establish a complete kinship in communication.

$$\text{Intuitive persuasion} = (\text{Cataloged experiences} \times \text{Word catalog awareness}) + \text{Personal receptive state creation or rapport} \times \text{Ability to guide listener's internal dialogue})$$

Figure 11.2 The Formula for Intuitive Persuasion

Once intense rapport is established, Hitters add the final ingredient of guiding the listener's internal dialogue—by managing what it can think, keeping it extremely busy, telling it what to do, or even by lulling it into relaxation. Many different techniques can accomplish this, and Ronald Reagan's radio addresses show examples of the most prevalent methods.

TECHNIQUES FOR GUIDING A LISTENER'S DIALOGUE

Next, you will find the title, date, and initial passages of a variety of Reagan's radio addresses along with a brief discussion of the technique being used. Keep in mind that these are small samples of various techniques to occupy the listener's internal dialogue. The techniques can be combined and interwoven into your presentation strategy.

Recessive Catalog Access

Day Care Centers
March 23, 1977

It has been said a baby sitter is a teenager acting like a parent while the parent is out acting like a teenager. Govt. sees it as something much more grandiose.[2]

Here is the technique of recessive word catalog access. Everyone has a primary, secondary, and recessive word catalog. By constructing and communicating your message by speaking with words matching the listener's primary catalog, moving to her secondary catalog, and ending in her recessive catalog, you will have a profound impact on your listener. This technique requires that you understand your customer's word catalog explicitly and are able to establish and maintain intense rapport. If you execute this technique correctly by patiently moving to the recessive catalog in a natural manner, you will ultimately put this person into a hypnotic trance.

The primary catalog is the catalog most frequently used by the conscious mind during daily conversation, while the recessive catalog is the least used and can be thought of as being closer to internal dialogue. Assuming rapport is present, as you access each progressively weaker catalog, the listener's internal dialogue becomes more relaxed. The consciousness of the internal dialogue starts to diminish, and it is lulled into an inward thought process as it disengages from the conversation.

Have you ever had conversations with people who mesmerized you? As they spoke, you could feel yourself slipping away, but you didn't fight it; in fact, it felt good. It wasn't so much the content of their words but their manner of speech that made you feel so relaxed and at ease. It was almost as if your ears were being tickled and your mind was being massaged. If this has ever happened to you, whether in person, over the phone, or even while watching television, most likely the speaker's word catalog was the opposite of yours, and she was naturally accessing your recessive catalog.

In the day-care center example, President Reagan starts with the auditory catalog, moves to the kinesthetic catalog, and ends with the visual catalog. The sentence has a different impact on a listener who is wired with an auditory primary, a kinesthetic secondary, and visual recessive catalog from someone who is wired in the opposite manner. While this sentence alone will not induce a hypnotic trance, by organizing segments of your discussion or structuring sections of your presentation to work from people's primary to recessive catalog, you will be able to speak directly to their subconscious minds.

When speaking to large groups, one way you can determine whether you have group rapport is through "sampling." It's best if you can meet a few members of the audience prior to the presentation to get an idea of their wiring, but it is not necessary. Pick five or six people who occupy easy-to-spot positions in the audience, either in the first couple of rows or at the end of an aisle.

From this sample of the audience, you can judge how your presentation is proceeding and determine what adjustments are needed as you progress. During the presentation, try to keep the majority of the sample members on the "edge of their seats," meaning their internal dialogues are very engaged. Since it is likely there will be a diverse variety of word catalog wiring among the members in the sample, lead several of them into a trance by using the word catalog access technique.

Now most people assume that a speaker is boring if listeners seem to be sleeping when she is talking, and this is true if the speaker didn't intend for them to close their eyes. However, when it is done purposefully, it actually indicates the speaker is in complete control of rapport with the audience.

How do you know when someone is in a trance? It's more comfortable for most people to enter a trance by closing their eyes. So you literally want them to close their eyes or have to fight to keep their eyes open. When they're in the deepest trance, their eyes will slowly move back and forth, and you can watch the impression of the iris as it moves under the eyelid (like rapid eye movement during deep sleep). Other people will enter a trance with their eyes open. Their pupils will dilate and it's almost as if their eyes become vacant.

The recessive catalog access technique is used most frequently because it naturally fits into the flow of a conversation. Let's examine some other ways to guide a listener's internal dialogue.

Contradiction and Confusion

Chile
July 27, 1979

Evidence continues to pile up that for some unexplained reason our diplomats have 20/20 vision with regard to the faults of our friends.[3]

Here the technique is contradiction and confusion. In this example, President Reagan layers different levels of "contradiction." First, there is a contradiction between "evidence piling up" and "for some unexplained reason." Logic dictates that if you have evidence, you should be able to explain what's happening. There shouldn't be an "unexplained reason." The usage of "20/20 vision" also contradicts the rest of the sentence. Normally, you would expect the exact opposite statement, such as "our diplomats are blind with regard to the faults of our friends."

These contradictions cause the listener's internal dialogue to work harder to understand the meaning of what is actually being said. While this internal debate is occurring, the speaker is delivering more words. The resulting backup causes the internal dialogue to become overwhelmed. The internal dialogue may even say, "I give up." Assuming rapport is present, the customer's conscious mind gently slips away, and at this point you can deliver the message you desire.

However, without the credibility of rapport, you've only alienated the listener. Therefore, this technique is risky and works best in certain high-rapport accounts.

Simulation

Olympics
September 19, 1978

A wave is beginning to roll, a worldwide wave and it may just break over the heads of the International Olympic Committee. A great many people dont want the 1980 Olympics held in Moscow.[4]

Here is the technique of simulation. Simulation is structuring language to provoke a particular emotional or physical response. For example, as you read about the wave rolling, you may have naturally increased the pace of your reading and the pitch of your internal voice (like a wave) until it broke in the second sentence. In this way, the structure of the communication simulates the wave.

Here's another example of simulation that illustrates how words can impact the body. You probably have never noticed it, but you breathe in a certain way, and as you breathe, you can feel your chest rising and falling. There's also a certain sensation in your nose when you breathe and you are able to feel the temperature of the air. As you become more aware of your breathing, it's harder to concentrate on other details. Reading this description about breathing may have even stimulated a change in your breathing pattern.

Simulation exercises the senses, engages the personality, and occupies the internal dialogue. Salespeople want the customer to simulate the benefits and feelings of owning their product during the sales cycle. Car salespeople are experts at using simulation. The test drive is a way to get the buyer to simulate the fantasy of owning the car. They want you to enjoy the smoothness of the ride, experience the "new car" aroma, and feel the power of the acceleration. They know a customer who successfully simulates ownership during the test drive is a good prospect for a sale. The same principle applies to Hitters. If they can get the prospect to envision being a happy customer while still in the sales cycle, they are well on the road to winning the deal.

Imagination

Endangered Species
July 6, 1977

How much do you miss Dinosaurs? Would your life be richer if those giant pre-historic flying lizards occasionally settled on your front lawn?[5]

Here the technique is imagination, which entails making the listener form mental images, concepts, situations, and sensations that do not exist or have yet to be experienced. It's a very effective technique to guide the internal dialogue.

The first question in the example causes the listener to create the mental image of a dinosaur. Did you picture a *Tyrannosaurus rex*? a brontosaurus? a velociraptor? The creation of the first image is relatively easy. Just as soon as listeners have created their first image, however, they are forced to make another. The second question requires listeners to create an image of a specific type of "flying lizard" and then place it on their front lawn. This request requires much more effort, as listeners have been directed to create a picture of a creature they probably haven't experienced and combine it with something they see every day. Invoking imagination makes the internal dialogue very busy!

Metaphor

Ocean Mining
October 10, 1978

It may not be the shot heard round the world but the U.S. has finally . . . told the U.N. to stop pushing us around.[6]

Metaphor is the technique here. The "shot heard round the world" is the phrase given to the first musket fire of the Revolutionary War. Metaphors deliver a lot of information quickly as they link to past receptive states. In this example, the skirmish on the Lexington Green was the start of the American fight for independence from an oppressive government. It's a source of national pride and patriotism. Transposing these feelings of independence onto a United Nations that is "pushing" us around is a very powerful transference of meaning.

Split Brain

Seal Hunt
May 15, 1978

It sometimes seems that we can get more emotionally aroused over mistreatment of animals than we can if the victims are human. . . .

A few weeks ago a writer in the *Los Angeles Times* did an article on the 1978 Canadian baby seal hunt. . . . One line in his article was very thought provoking; . . . "If seal pups were as ugly as lobsters, their harvest would go unnoticed."

Accompanying his article was a photo that proved his point. It was a snow white *baby* seal with its black nose &

round eyes looking like something you'd put in the nursery for children to cuddle.[7]

The split brain technique here in essence involves separating the brain by making the listener carry on two concurrent internal conversations. One way to do this is to force the listener to follow separate streams of logic. For example, the first sentence about people becoming "more emotionally aroused over mistreatment of animals" than people is followed by a completely different stream of logic in the next sentence introducing the Canadian baby seal hunt. The listener holds the thought of the first sentence during the second sentence.

Another, more sophisticated example of the split brain technique is to have a factual conversation with the "logical" side of the brain while carrying on another stimulating discussion with the "creative" side of the brain. In the seal hunt example, the first and second sentences start unique streams of logic that are resolved by the side of the brain that solves problems. The third and fifth sentences, which include "ugly as lobsters" and "black nose & round eyes," would be handled by the opposite side of the brain, which is proficient in the arts and drawing.

The split brain technique works well in sales situations since most salespeople are trained, experienced, and comfortable presenting the logical reasons, arguments, and benefits of selecting their product. By adding an artistic dimension of dramatization to the humdrum of a logical dissertation, the entire brain is stimulated and the story is brought to life.

Belief System

Vietnam I
November 30, 1976

Govt. has no greater responsibility than to protect the least among us whereever he may be in the world if his right to life, liberty & the pursuit of happiness is being unjustly denied.[8]

Here the technique applies to belief systems. Over the years, your belief system is formed based on observation, experience, and faith. It may include a spiritual belief in the afterlife, a scientific belief in the big bang theory, or a hope in the Chicago Cubs winning the World Series.

The unique aspect of these philosophical frameworks is that all people consider their own belief system correct. Presenting a message that is in alignment with the listener's belief system adds credibility to a message. Natural defenses of skepticism are lowered since the message is concealed within the Trojan Horse of an existing belief system.

Broadcast-Unicast Messages

The Hope of Mankind
September 21, 1976

> In a dinner at Mt. Vernon back in revolutionary times, Layfayette . . . *turned to his* host . . . *and said* "Gen. . . . Americans even in war & desperate times have a superb spirit. You are happy & you are confident. Why is it?" Wash. answered "There is freedom, there is space for a man to be alone & think & there are friends who owe each other nothing but affection."[9]

This story is an example of the broadcast-unicast technique. Underneath the surface, these anecdotes, parables, and stories have layers of interpretations that convey moral and spiritual lessons.

From the preceding story, you could infer many different meanings. To a historian, it is an account of an intriguing conversation between two great statesmen. To a patriot, it is a story about the importance of freedom. To the insecure, it is a message to be confident. It's also about the importance of friendship, gratefulness, and the American spirit. From a single story, listeners derive their own personal meaning. Their internal dialogue turns inward because it believes the story is intended solely for them.

CONCLUSION

Whether they realize it or not, all salespeople are natural hypnotists who use the power of suggestion to persuade customers to buy. However, unlike professional practitioners of medical or therapeutic hypnosis, they do not place customers into a stuporous trance or deep sleep while the suggestions are instilled. Rather, they use sales hypnosis during the course of normal conversation by speaking with customers in their own terms and at all levels of their individual personality and needs.

Heavy Hitters use hypnosis to disarm customers' conscious defenses. Like therapeutic hypnotists who want to solve their clients' problems, they start by establishing relationships based upon mutual trust and rapport. Both Heavy Hitters and professional hypnotists adapt their use of language to provide individualized treatment, and they both guide their clients through the process of finding the correct solution. Finally, they both use the power of words to implant posthypnotic suggestions in order to create profound changes in attitudes and actions.

The customer's conscious mind acts like an emotion-suppressing system. It is full of doubt, cynicism, and distrust. It is the cautious skeptic that is continually protecting the buyer from making bad choices or forming ill-advised relationships. Therefore, even truthful, helpful information that is presented in the customer's best interest tends to be discounted or ignored.

Fortunately for Hitters, the conscious and subconscious minds can operate together or independently. Intuitive persuasion is a communication strategy for managing a customer's internal dialogue in order to talk directly to one's subconscious mind.

Since the subconscious mind has access to more information, it has ultimate approval in the decision-making process. As Dr. Milton Erickson wrote, "Your conscious mind is very intelligent, but your unconscious mind is a lot smarter."[10]

Dr. Erickson also believed that hypnosis does not really exist. Since hypnosis is nothing more than communication, his assessment is correct. Rather, hypnosis and intuitive persuasion are models for describing how thoughts can be structured and words communicated to produce desired responses. While hypnosis doesn't exist, the words spoken and their impact are quite real.

Over the years, I have conducted training classes with my sales teams about intuitive persuasion. During one of these sessions, I used the recessive catalog technique to place a cynical salesperson into a trance. While everyone else was unaware of any difference in my presentation style, the salesperson was fighting hard to keep his eyes open. After a few more minutes, he slipped into a deep trance. At that point, I interrupted his slumber and asked him to describe his experience to the surprised audience. He explained that although he could hear my words and understand their meaning, something else made him feel very comfortable and relaxed. He enjoyed it and didn't want it to end.

Whereupon I remarked, "I hope all of our sales calls are as satisfying."

CHAPTER **12**

Metaphors for the Mind

To ensure the product worked as advertised, the prospective customer insisted the salesperson take him to visit a customer installation. When the site visit started, the atmosphere between the prospect and the salesperson was tense and the conversation centered upon the business of the day. The customer had a long list of questions to ask and detailed notes on everything he wanted to see. By noon, they had toured the manufacturing and warehouse facilities. Over lunch, the conversation loosened up noticeably. In the afternoon, the prospect peppered key executives with questions about the performance of the salesperson's product and company. By the end of the day, he was volunteering secrets about the competitor's product and proposal. The site visit told a more convincing story than all the previous sales calls between the customer and the salesperson combined.

Flight 683 was on final approach from New York to Chicago O'Hare airport. Without warning, the uneventful flight turned into a horrifying experience. A wind shear violently shook the plane and then the microburst pushed it toward the ground. The pilots instinctively applied full power to the engines, and their high-pitched screams drowned out all other sounds. Inside the passenger cabin there wasn't any outward panic; the wide-eyed passengers sat in silent shock. Although no one made a sound, the furtive glances between passengers said it all: "Climb! Climb! Climb!" Slowly but surely, the plane started to climb. Shortly thereafter, the pilots banked into a violent right turn and the passengers felt like they were on a roller coaster. Thirty minutes later the plane landed safely at Grand Rapids, Michigan.

Three weeks after that flight I received the following letter.

Dear Mr. Martin,

I understand you were a passenger on flight 683 to Chicago. I would like to apologize for any inconvenience and problems you may have experienced because of the diversion. We realize how frustrating it can be when your travel plans are altered for any reason.

We're working to prevent flight diversions and keep you on time but, while the safety and well-being of our passengers are our first priority, we also want you to count on Transglobal airlines when irregularities occur. Thank you for your business, Mr. Martin. As one of our valued customers, we look forward to the continued privilege of serving you in the future.

Sincerely,
John A. Smith
Senior Vice President
Transglobal Airlines

At first, I thought the letter was a nice gesture. However, as the letter sat on my desk the following day, it started to bother me. First, the "irregularity" they referred to was my near-death experience. I honestly thought I was going to die, and they had the nerve to send a form letter with an embossed signature? Also, couldn't they have at least included some free drink coupons as part of their apology? Most importantly, their letter reminded me of the nightmare when I had just about put it out of my mind. Just when I had become comfortable flying again, I now dreaded getting back on another plane and flew with white knuckles for weeks.

The story about Flight 683 is called a metaphor. Metaphors are stories, parables, and analogies that communicate ideas by using examples that listeners can relate to and identify with. Metaphors range from entertaining, lighthearted tales to profound stories that touch the listener's psyche. The fourth-century Greek grammarian Diomedes defined metaphors as "The transferring of things and words from their proper signification to an improper similitude for the sake of beauty, necessity, polish, or emphasis."[1] In particular, metaphors add an element of beauty to the way you present your story to customers as to why they should buy your product.

The story about Flight 683 has several possible interpretations. If you are a frequent flier, the story may have caused you to relive your own horror story. It also shows how sometimes even the best of intentions can be harmful and how businesses edit their communications to such an extent that they lose credibility and customer rapport.

A metaphor is a single story that conveys different lessons and multiple meanings. Metaphors are also a special intuitive persuasion technique that can be used to help people bring about change. In this chapter, we will examine the power of metaphors and explain how they can be used to influence beliefs, opinions, and attitudes.

GETTING PEOPLE TO CHANGE

How do you get people to change? Let's take cigarette smokers as an example. Here are just a few reasons why someone should stop smoking. First, it has been medically proven that smoking causes cancer and 450,000 Americans die each year as a result of smoking.[2] That's more than all the deaths from car accidents, AIDS, suicides, homicides, fires, and drugs combined. Cigarette smoke contains 4,000 different chemicals, and it is estimated that smokers shorten their lives by 5 minutes with every cigarette.[3] Smokers are prone to throat ailments and chronic coughing. Their breath, hair, clothes, cars, and homes stink. Their teeth and fingers turn brown. Smoking is also expensive and the average smoker will spend $3,200 on cigarettes this year.[4] Finally, nonsmokers tend to look down on those who smoke.

Even with all of these proven reasons to stop, people continue to smoke. Ask them why and they'll say, "I enjoy it," "I like the taste," "I can't quit," "I know it's bad for me," or "It's none of your business!" Why don't they stop? Obviously, the nicotine in cigarettes is addictive, but many people have been able to kick the habit. Perhaps the 2002 Nobel Prize winner Daniel Kahneman may have unknowingly found the answer.[5]

The standard model for decision making is that everyone is rational, self-interested, and calculating. Kahneman has suggested that psychological motives truly determine people's decision-making behavior. In other words, the final say on every decision we make is human nature, not logic. Perhaps the real reason people smoke is very simple: It's easier to smoke than it is to stop. The immediate drive to avoid the discomfort of nicotine withdrawal far outweighs any logical reason to quit.

Customers act in a very similar manner. Inertia and the drive to "do nothing" far outweigh the logical reasons you espouse for buying your product. You can recite a litany of reasons and a laundry list of benefits, and the customer still won't buy your product. You need to package these ideas in a format that leaves an impression and creates a call to action, that customers understand, and that convinces them both mentally and emotionally to proceed. Metaphors are linguistic wrappers you can use to change customer passivity into energy and action.

A ROLE MODEL FOR STUDYING METAPHORS

In our discussion about intuitive persuasion, we used language samples from Ronald Reagan. Our interest was not in his political ideology. Rather, we studied his writings to understand the persuasiveness of the "Great Communicator." In this chapter, we will be quoting from another very well-known Heavy Hitter, Jesus Christ, to understand the concept of metaphors. Similarly, we are not interested in the ideology of his words. While thousands of books have been written from a theological perspective about Christ, from a sales perspective his words provide powerful lessons that apply specifically to communication.

Jesus taught almost exclusively with metaphors. In fact, when he was asked why he told so many stories he said, "That's why I tell stories: to create readiness, to nudge people toward receptive insight. In their present state they can stare till doomsday and not see it, listen till they're blue in the face and not get it."[6]

The Bible is composed of 66 different books written by over 40 different authors ("Bible" comes from the Latin word for books). The metaphors Jesus used are found in the New Testament. While Jesus used his stories to explain spiritual theology and moral lessons, for the purpose of our study we are more interested in how something was said and why it was said, rather than what was actually said. Our intent is to understand the purpose, content, and structure of metaphors to help us learn to become more persuasive.

METAPHORS FOR WINNING OVER HEARTS AND MINDS

Pretend for a moment that you are in Jesus's position and have a plan to completely change the world. You would soon realize that you are armed only with the clothes on your back and the words that you speak. Therefore, how would you fight the military might of Rome and the power of the local religious system dominated by the Pharisees and Sadducees?

Even though Jesus was only an army of one, his strategy was to win the war by winning over the hearts and minds of the people. Jesus's weaponry was radically different. He wasn't armed like a Roman soldier. His weapon of choice was metaphors.

Have you ever been in the position where you had to speak to a skeptical and hostile crowd? This reminds me of the normal sales calls we make every day. Your job is to persuade a group of complete strangers to think in an entirely new way, and you are asking them to do something on your behalf.

What do you say and how would you say it? Do you pronounce your purpose, blurt out your mission, and demand that listeners believe? Do you try to build a business case and convince them with logic? Or, do you try to establish rapport with the audience members and then lead them into receiving your ideas? Metaphors enable you to explain your ideas and build rapport with customers in a non-threatening, relationship-building manner.

All salespeople continually offer their own testimony about themselves and their product to build rapport with nonbelievers. Building rapport requires giving product information and proof of the product's benefits in terms the customer understands and believes.

Think about your most recent customer for a moment, or better yet, remember the last time you were the customer contemplating a major purchase. Since you didn't want to make the wrong purchase decision, you were probably apprehensive, anxious, and maybe even afraid. You might have become confused and perplexed by all the different choices. When you spoke to your salesperson, you may have pretended to know more than you actually do or even acted belligerently as a defensive mechanism. You probably misled the various salespeople you met. You may have told them you would come back soon and buy, when in reality, you were only comparison shopping. It is under these circumstances that salespeople must create rapport with the customer.

THE SALESPERSON AS A METAPHOR

You are a walking metaphor. The way you dress, present yourself, and represent your product provides important symbolism to the customer. Your customer has standards and certain expectations about the way you will act, look, and speak. These standards vary greatly among customers, companies, industries, and places. Selling drilling equipment in Texas is different from selling computer chips in Silicon Valley or hotel supplies in Hawaii. Each requires a salesperson to use a different presence and demeanor to build credibility and gain rapport.

These qualities will greatly influence the customer's decision. For example, would you hire a personal trainer who was extremely out of shape? An interior designer who dressed sloppily or out of style? Would you visit a dentist who had terrible teeth and who used dilapidated equipment? Physical presence projects an important message to the customer.

Therefore, it makes sense to dress like your customers and express yourself in the manner they are comfortable with. Frankly, I am not a proponent of salespeople wearing suits. Unless it is the norm and custom that your buyers have come to expect, wearing a suit impedes the process of building rapport. Worse yet, it associates you with your competition and the stigma of being a salesperson. The suit continually pronounces your selfish intention, "I am here to sell you something."

On the other hand, no one wants to associate with a vagabond who looks like he slept in his clothes. Find a point between the two extremes, where the clothes you wear communicate your professionalism without alienating the customer. The way you dress should show that your first concern is the customer's success, not your own self-interests. That's why I frown on fancy clothes, elaborate hairdos, and expensive jewelry such as cuff links and watches. Unless your customers wear them, leave them at home. Remember, a salesperson's dress and demeanor and how he or she treats the customer serve as a metaphor for their future relationship.

All salespeople are friendly, helpful, and attentive during the sales cycle because they know the customer is constantly evaluating them. It's after the sale is made and the commission paid when true service begins. A salesperson's humility is in fact a metaphor for service and selflessness. The ostentatious salesperson that is full of bravado will alienate far more customers than he or she wins over. The customer doesn't expect to see him once the deal closes. Meanwhile, the unpretentious salesperson naturally builds rapport. People expect he'll stay around after the deal closes.

People naturally want to be around positive people. In Chapter 9, we discussed the Better Person Syndrome and how customers want to surround themselves with people who have the qualities they admire. Conversely, salespeople who constantly criticize the competition are unlikely to win over customers. Think about yourself for a moment; do you like to be around people who are negative and demeaning?

TYPES OF METAPHORS

Using the language of metaphors facilitates the learning process by enabling the customer to understand new concepts using terms he or she already understands. They connect the presenter's message to the recipient's personal experience and collective knowledge. Metaphors are more than simple anecdotes or interesting fairy tales. They quickly communicate complex ideas to the conscious mind. More importantly, metaphors are language structures with multiple layers of interpretation. While they talk to the conscious mind, they also communicate with the subconscious mind. Therefore, they are valuable tools that can be used to change a person's habits, disposition, and beliefs.

The three different types of metaphors are educational, personal, and action-based. Educational and personal metaphors are based upon the telling of stories or parables. The PowerPoint presentation your company provides you to present your solution is an example of an educational metaphor. The personal stories you tell about how one of your customers is successfully using your product is an example of a personal metaphor.

Action-based metaphors use physical movement or action to communicate additional meaning and highlight important concepts. A product demonstration is actually an action-based metaphor for how the customer can use your product. Site visits and reference calls are action-based metaphors intended to get the customer to simulate product ownership. Finally, educational, personal, and action-based metaphors can be layered together in any combination.

Educational metaphors help explain new concepts using common terms or everyday situations. Surely Jesus's audience would be familiar with the fig tree and grapes in the following metaphor.

A good tree can't produce bad fruit, and a bad tree can't produce good fruit. A tree is identified by the kind of fruit it produces. Figs never grow on thorn bushes or grapes on bramble bushes. A good person produces good deeds from a good heart, and an evil person produces evil deeds from an evil heart. Whatever is in your heart determines what you say.[7]

We've all seen trees and tasted grapes. They are tangible items that can be seen and touched. However, what's in the heart cannot be seen and is only revealed by the words we speak. This metaphor explains how real and important our words are by comparing them to concrete objects.

Another level of subconscious communication occurs in this metaphor. Grapes and figs were delicacies of the time. They were expensive and highly sought after. Obviously, you eat grapes and figs using your mouth. The underlying message is to have good things not only go in but also come out of your mouth.

Personal metaphors force listeners to transpose the message onto themselves. If you have children, you might have interpreted the part about "a good tree can't produce bad fruit and a bad tree can't produce good fruit" in reference to your children. It may have caused you to pause and think about the role model you provide them.

If you recently said something mean-spirited to someone else, the metaphor may have caused you to consider whether or not you are a good or bad person. While Jesus could have said, "Say nice things to people," talking in terms of a good and evil heart is far more impactful. And it is the personal interpretation of metaphors that makes them so compelling.

METAPHOR STRUCTURE

Salespeople unknowingly use metaphors to explain the features of their products and how they operate. Usually, they consist of short clichés intended to make comparisons such as, "It turns on a dime," "runs seven by twenty-four," and "has all the bells and whistles." However, Heavy Hitters understand that customer success stories (a specific type of sales metaphor) play a very important role in influencing prospects to buy.

The power of customer success metaphors lies in their individual interpretation. Remember, while the conscious mind is listening to the content of the surface-level story, the subconscious mind is deciphering its own message. On the surface, explaining how a customer is successfully using a product is a story the conscious mind will follow logically. Underneath this story, another message can be sent to the customer's subconscious mind that it is in his or her personal interest to select your product.

The average person will hear only seven and a half minutes of a one-hour presentation and remember only half of the words he or she hears.[8] In essence, we don't listen and reject far more words than we actually hear. Therefore, a metaphor's structure is critical. An effective method of structuring customer success stories is by breaking them into four parts: history and situation, options, evaluation process, and decision reason and results. Below, you will find an example of each part and ideally what message should be sent to the conscious mind and the connection to the subconscious.

1. Part 1 describes the history and situation:

- Conscious message. Describe the business problem or condition the customer was trying to solve or improve and the situation that created it.

- Subconscious connection. Specifically identify the people involved in the selection process, including their names, titles, and backgrounds. These are people the customer can identify with.

- Example. "I would like to take a moment to tell you about one of our most difficult customers, ABC Company. Their requirements were so complex they were unsure that any off-the-shelf product would work for them. Frankly, we had never seen a business that processed so many transactions. Their project leader, Bob Smith, was also one of the most meticulous and demanding customers I have ever met."

2. Part 2 presents the options:

- Conscious message. Describe the different products or methods that could have solved the problem or improved the customer's situation.

- Subconscious connection. Explain the impact of these circumstances in terms of the decision maker's job, career, or emotional state of being.

- Example. "Bob decided to bring in the top two products, ours and XYZ's, for intensive evaluations even though he honestly believed that neither product would handle their requirements."

3. Part 3 delineates the evaluation process:

- Conscious message. Outline the process the customer undertook to determine the best solution.

- Subconscious connection. Describe the personality, preferences, and motivations of the evaluation team members.

- Example. "Bob tested every aspect of the solutions: installation, ease of use, performance, and technical support. One month into the pilot test, Bob stopped testing XYZ's product because it just wouldn't scale. He spent another two months verifying every feature of our product. He wanted to make sure everything worked precisely as advertised."

4. Part 4 describes the decision reason and results:

- Conscious message. Describe the final selection and its impact on the decision makers or company.
- Subconscious connection. Translate the outcome into personal terms.

- Example. "When Bob was completely sure of his decision, he made the recommendation to his management team to purchase our solution. Today, Bob is one of our happiest customers and their project has been a complete success. I would be delighted to introduce you to him."

When salespeople meet with a customer, they know they must establish trust and demonstrate competence in order to reduce the personal angst of customers during the selection process. Customer success stories are valuable tools for proving the salesperson and his company are the authority on solving the customer's problem. An authority is someone who has the ability to gain the trust and willing obedience of others.

METAPHORS CONNECT WITH THE SENSES

For a metaphor to have maximum impact, it must connect with the customer's senses. The book of Luke recounts Jesus's preaching to a large crowd along the Sea of Galilee. He opened his sermon with several simple statements (called the Beatitudes[9]) that help illustrate the importance of connecting with the listener by invoking the senses. Let's compare the sensory-based message of the Beatitudes with a generic translation of the same passage. Which one has a greater impact?

The Beatitudes	Generic Message
God blesses you who are hungry For you will be satisfied	God thinks about the unsatisfied.
God blesses those who weep now For a time will come when you will laugh with joy	If you're sad, there are favorable times ahead.
God blesses you who are hated and excluded And cursed because you are identified with me	God appreciates those who experience troubles on my account.

Obviously, the language of the Beatitudes is far more powerful, meaningful, and more memorable. Everyone has experienced hunger, has wept, laughed, and been hated. The language delivers sensory information that requires the mind's interpretation and engagement. You relate to the words. Unfortunately, most customer communication in today's business world is more likely to use generic language than to engage the senses. In fact, we usually exclude any reference to the senses. I jokingly tell people that most business communications are in fact senseless.

The other interesting aspect of the Beatitudes is that the passage is written entirely from the orientation of a Kinesthetic. The key identifier words are "hungry," "weep," "laugh," "joy," "hated," "excluded," and "cursed." While some of these words are associated with physical senses, such as "laughing" and "crying," others are related to the feelings inside oneself, such as being excluded or hated.

Since the Beatitudes are a message of comfort and hope, it's appropriate that they would be delivered from the standpoint of a Kinesthetic. If someone was in pain you wouldn't say, "Sounds like you're in distress" or "It looks like you are tormented." Rather, you would empathize with him, share in his suffering, and say, "I feel for you." Remember, while the kinesthetic word catalog is primarily concerned with the physical senses of taste, touch, and smell, it also includes the experience of internal feelings as well. If someone were to say, "I haven't been myself lately and I'm not sure why," even though there aren't any words that reflect the senses, the statement reveals the person's internal state of body and is therefore kinesthetic.

Finally, a word's interpretation is influenced by its surrounding words and their word catalog orientation. For instance, being "cursed" is both an auditory experience (someone yelling at you) and a feeling (being mad, sad, or dejected after you've been cursed at). Since it is surrounded by the kinesthetic words, it is interpreted from the standpoint of feelings versus sounds.

THE COWCATCHER AND THE HOOK

Most people associate the term "cowcatcher" with the metal grill on the front of a locomotive. However, cowcatcher has an entirely different meaning in the entertainment industry. It's a show's opening moments in which the performers try to grab your attention and cause you to stop and look. The best metaphors start with a great cowcatcher.

The following verse has an interesting cowcatcher: "Consider the lilies, how they grow; they neither toil nor spin; but I tell you, even Solomon in all his glory did not clothe himself like one of these."[10] Upon hearing "Consider the lilies," a Visual might create a mental image of beautiful lilies on a hillside field. A Kinesthetic might associate the words with a cheerful feeling of springtime, the pleasant smell of flowers, or even the warmth of a sunny day. Meanwhile, an Auditory might ask himself the questions, "What about lilies? Why are they important?" Obviously, this simple statement evokes a complex word catalog reaction and makes you stop and think.

The hook is the catchy part of the metaphor that delivers the punch. It's usually found at the end of the metaphor. For example, the hook here is when King Solomon, the richest and most powerful person in the land, is described as being unable to clothe himself as beautifully as a lily.

Notice how the cowcatcher and the hook work together synergistically in the following verse: "It is easier for a camel to go through the eye of a needle than for a rich person to enter the Kingdom of Heaven."[11] Great metaphors have an interesting cowcatcher and a provocative hook.

METAPHORS ARE INTERPRETED INDIVIDUALLY

What sorrows await you who are rich, for you have only your happiness now. What sorrows await you who are satisfied and prosperous now, for a time of awful hunger is before you.

What sorrows await you who laugh carelessly, for your laughing will turn into mourning and sorrow.[12]

How did you interpret the passage? People who consider themselves poor may transpose the warnings onto a wealthy person they know and rationalize that it is better to be spiritually rich than materially prosperous. Conversely, wealthy people may have felt a twinge of incrimination and performed a quick examination of their self-worth instead of their net worth.

The broadcast-unicast qualities of metaphors make them ideal for presentations to large groups since everyone walks away with a personal message. As discussed in the last chapter, a broadcast-unicast message is a single story from which different listeners derive their own meaning.

METAPHORS TUNNEL TO THE TRUTH

We are all familiar with the tunnels that take us through mountains, under rivers, and beneath cities. Tunnels provide a quicker way of getting from one place to another. Language also has its own form of tunneling that conveys purpose in the quickest period of time. Language tunneling compresses the message into its most succinct meaning.

"Can all the worries add a single moment to your life?"[13] is a profound question that Jesus asked his listeners. While Jesus could have lectured about the mental anxiety worry causes, its unhealthy effects on the body, and its negative impacts on the quality of life, instead he tunneled to the core of the matter.

Another type of tunneling comes from the field of quantum mechanics (the study of molecular motion and energy). Quantum tunneling theorizes that certain types of particles have the ability to pass through seemingly impenetrable barriers. Since it happens at light speed, this tunneling gives the impression that the particle is in two places at the same time.

Similarly, language tunneling can cause the mind to be in two places at one time as when Jesus said, "Love your neighbor as yourself."[14] Normally, we view the world solely from our point of view and in terms of our own needs. In fact, this is how many salespeople typically think about their jobs: "It's all about me." In this passage, Jesus instructs the listeners to change their orientation. As a result, their thoughts and feelings represent two different standpoints simultaneously. They become aware of the needs, wants, and desires of others in addition to their own.

HOW METAPHORS WORK: STREAMS OF INFORMATION

It's natural to assume that the brain only processes one piece of information at a time since our internal voice is a single-threaded conversation. However, nothing could be further from the truth. Each of your senses is sending a constant stream of information to the brain. You can't slow down your vision, turn off your sense of touch, and silence your hearing. You can't force your lungs to quit breathing or your heart to stop pumping. It's also impossible to disconnect your internal voice from your conscious and subconscious minds. Fortunately, our brains are designed to receive all of these "channels of information" simultaneously.

While the brain processes these information sources continuously, it does so at different priorities and speed. Although these information streams seem to be instantaneous, they aren't. Your brain actually receives information in bursts and chunks, but since the process is happening so fast, there aren't any discernable separations or interruptions. An analogy of how this works can be found when you download a large file, such as a movie or song over the Internet. A large file is actually split into smaller sections from the source, sent across the network, and reassembled upon receipt. Yet this happens so quickly and seamlessly that it seems to be one contiguous file.

Recent medical proof supporting this theory is based upon the ongoing study of an autistic boy named Tito Mukhopadhyay.[15] Autism is a neurological disorder that afflicts children in the first few years of life and impedes the development of their communication skills. In severe cases, autistic people withdraw completely into themselves and are unable to communicate or interrelate with the outside world.

Although Tito cannot communicate verbally, through the persistence of his mother he has learned how to talk using a computer. He has become famous not only for the beautiful poetry he writes but also for the descriptions he has provided neuroscientists about the inner workings of his mind. Tito describes a world where pieces of sensory information barrage his mind at different velocities. In order to derive meaning, he must mentally put the puzzle pieces together. By studying the brain functionality that Tito is missing, entirely new paradigms about the brain's operation are being considered.

The brain receives and interprets four basic categories or streams of information. However, not all streams of information are treated the same. Some streams can be interrupted by urgent incoming information. In terms of the file over the Internet example, you can stop the download by clicking on the Cancel button and do something more important. Following are the four streams of information listed in order of the priority by which they are serviced by the brain.

Automatic Physical Functions

Breathing, heartbeat, and circulation are the highest priority and serviced at the fastest rate. These systems usually operate at a constant speed except when the brain tells them to speed up or slow down. Think of these systems as powerful lights that are on 24 hours a day.

The Senses

Sight, sound, touch, taste, and smell are always on and always sending information to the brain. The senses are like radio stations constantly broadcasting signals regardless of whether the listener's radio is on or off.

Internal Voice, Emotions, and the Conscious Mind

Operating slower and more deliberately are the internal voice, emotions (happiness, guilt, doubt, and so on), and the conscious mind. Unlike the other channels, they have maximum speeds at which they can process information, much like water flowing through a pipe cannot exceed a certain pressure.

Subconscious Mind

The subconscious mind is a vast reservoir that the various pipes (internal voice, emotions, and conscious mind) flow into. The subconscious mind is the aggregator and archive of all the streams of information. It's the final storage place for experiences, and because of its size and immensity, it moves slower.

Everyone's past includes lapses in judgment and skeletons that we hope remain hidden in our closets. While our decisions and actions may have seemed right at the moment, later on we experienced guilt, remorse, or embarrassment over our misdeeds. Poor decision making is partially a result of the differences in the timing of the information. Although the subconscious mind may process information at a slower speed, its verdict provides the final word. That's why high-pressure salespeople demand on-the-spot yes or no decisions from customers. They want to avoid the subconscious mind.

REACHING THE SUBCONSCIOUS

Effective metaphors create a lot of mental activity as the conscious mind tries to sort out and understand information sent from the various channels. However, upon initial hearing you should not expect an immediate or profound change. Rather, the power of metaphors is how they percolate in the subconscious.

You may recall from Chapter 3 that you can use body language and speech to highlight or mark spoken words so they are remembered by the subconscious mind. You can mark terms by saying them differently from the other parts of the sentence. You can lower or raise your voice, change the pitch or inflection, or accentuate them with more passion. You can point at the audience, raise your hands above your head, shrug your shoulders, move to the right or left, or make other body movements to distinguish certain ideas.

Regardless of how you mark them, the channel of information associated with the senses and internal voice hears the words in real time and processes the information in the conscious mind immediately. However, the subconscious mind recognizes the chunks of data that were marked (intended for it). In one sense, two differently structured messages can be sent with the same words—one for the conscious mind and another for the subconscious mind.

One of the main responsibilities of the subconscious mind is protection. Much like a guardian angel, it's on the lookout for perilous situations and possible circumstances that might endanger the person physically and mentally. To perform this task, it assumes a third-person observation role and acts as a separate entity even though it resides deep inside the individual. Metaphors provide both a content-level message for the conscious mind and an invisible suggestion for the subconscious mind.

EXPLAINING METAPHORS

At the beginning of the chapter we reviewed the three different types of metaphors: educational, personal, and action-based. The purpose of each of these metaphors is to teach, tell, and enlighten the listener, with the ultimate goal of changing his or her behavior. While educational metaphors appeal to the conscious intellect, personal and action-based metaphors can be tailored to the subconscious mind. Also, all three types can be connected, interwoven, and mixed together in any combination.

The proof of a metaphor's success is evidenced by a change in the listener's internal voice. The transformation can range from a subtle readjustment over time to an instantaneous epiphany. Ideally, the metaphor will cause the mind to immediately recognize the importance of the information, accept the message, and start the process of change. Depending on the metaphor's relevance to the individual, the internal voice might change radically and say with conviction, "I will stop doing this!" or "I will start doing that!" In other cases, the message must permeate and grow throughout the subconscious mind and the results are less perceptible. For example, the tone of the internal voice may change from negative and depressed and become more optimistic and resolute.

In the book of Luke, Jesus told more than 25 metaphors. Some were explicit while others were more subtle. When a large crowd had gathered on the water's edge of the Sea of Galilee to hear Jesus speak, he stepped into a fishing boat and asked its owner (Simon) to push offshore so he could be better heard and seen. After he finished speaking, he told Simon, "Now go to deeper water, let down your nets, and you will catch many fish."[16] They caught so many fish the boat almost sank under the weight. In one sense, there were two great catches from the boat that day: fish from the lake and people on the shore. Simon went on to become one of Jesus's disciples. "From now on, you will be fishing for men and women,"[17] Jesus said.

While his followers probably asked Jesus often about the meaning of his stories, he rarely explained them. In fact, he explained only one in the entire book of Luke. This illustrates an important point. Ultimately, it's up to each listener to discern personal meaning from a metaphor. Therefore it's more effective to leave its purpose unexplained and have the listeners sort it out on their own. However, Jesus did explain the following educational metaphor privately to his disciples to prepare them for their future ministry.

> One day Jesus told this story to a large crowd that had gathered from many towns to hear him: "A farmer went out to plant some seed. As he scattered it across his field, some seeds fell on a footpath, where it was stepped on, and the birds came and ate it. Other seed fell on shallow soil with underlying rock. This seed began to grow, but soon withered and

died for lack of moisture. Other seed fell among thorns that shot up and choked out the tender blades. Still other seed fell on fertile soil. This seed grew and produced a crop one hundred times as much as had been planted." [18]

After the crowds had left, the disciples asked Jesus to explain the story.

This is the meaning of the story: The seed is God's message. The seed that fell on the hard path represents those who hear the message, but then the Devil comes and steals it away and prevents them from believing and being saved. The rocky soil represents those who hear the message with joy. But like young plants in such soil, their roots don't go very deep. They believe for a while, but wilt when the hot winds of testing blow. The thorny ground represents those who hear and accept the message, but all too quickly the message is crowded out by the cares and riches and pleasures of life. And so they never grow into maturity. But the good soil represents honest, good hearted people who hear God's message, cling to it, and steadily produce a huge harvest. [19]

Depending on your orientation, this story is both a personal and educational metaphor. From the personal standpoint, you might have thought about the different types of customers you must deal with or associated yourself with one of the types of soil. As Jesus explained the story to the disciples, it also provided a practical lesson about the different reactions to expect from people. This was important information for them to know as they went out on their missions.

METAPHORS HELP SALESPEOPLE MAKE SUGGESTIONS

Salespeople are always asking customers for help, making either direct requests or indirect suggestions. Although each type of request has an appropriate time and place, you run the risk of alienating customers when you ask for support or a favor point-blank—for example, "Will you help me win this deal?" Metaphors are an effective means of acquiring customer assistance with suggestions.

Two types of suggestions can be found in metaphors, foreground and background. Foreground suggestions are explicit, but they deflect the source of the request from the demander. For example, let's pretend I am a passenger in your car and I feel you are going too fast. A direct request would be "Slow down!" A metaphor with a foreground suggestion could be "You know the speed limit is 45 mph and police ticket a lot of speeders here." A metaphor with a background suggestion is "A speeder was in a horrible accident last week in this exact spot." While the background suggestion is more subtle in its delivery, it triggers a more profound reaction.

In a sales situation, a foreground suggestion might be *"Consumer Reports* gave our product the highest rating and recommended it as the best buy." An example of a background suggestion is "One of my customers tried the other company's product and recently switched to ours."

EXERCISE 12: METAPHORS

I would like to finish this chapter with an exercise about the usage, interpretation, and structure of metaphors. The metaphors we will study are my personal favorites. While the topics are quite diverse and at first glance some of these stories may not seem like they relate to sales, they reemphasize principles about becoming a Heavy Hitter.

As you read each metaphor, ask yourself the following questions:

- What is your initial interpretation of the metaphor?
- What is the metaphor's purpose?
- How many different interpretations can you think of that relate to the metaphor?

Following each metaphor is a commentary where the key points and themes are reviewed. However, it is very important that you do not read these comments until you have thought about each of the questions. Otherwise, the exercise will be far less effective.

Finally, there's a natural tendency to want to read faster as you approach the end of a book. Fight the urge to do so. Slow down and take the time to finish this final exercise, and you may find it to be the most important part of the entire book.

The Camera

When I was a guest lecturer at Stanford University, I used an interesting background suggestion. After I had been speaking for a few minutes, I couldn't help but notice a student in the middle of the class. He was continually fidgeting, yawning, and impatiently looking around the room as if he had a more important place to be. At an opportune moment, I asked if anyone in the class had a question and looked directly at him (my first suggestion) for an answer.

On cue, he pronounced to the class what was troubling him. He disagreed completely with one of my earlier statements that decision making is based ultimately on human nature, not logic. The manner in which he spoke was confrontational, and I could sense this made the entire class uncomfortable.

I asked him to tell me what was the last major purchase he made, and he replied, "Digital camera." Then I asked how he made the decision on which model to purchase and if he researched *Consumer Reports* or studied any web sites.

He answered, "No."

Whereupon I asked, "So, which one of your friends owns the camera you bought?"

He was stunned, but to his credit he answered truthfully that he bought the same camera as his best friend.

Looking away from him, I said my second suggestion, "People want to be liked and being part of a group is a very important reason to buy." For the rest of the class he was an ideal student.

This metaphor conveys three major themes. First, salespeople must continually overcome objections, and in every sales presentation there are conscientious objectors. Are you able to recognize them? How do you deal with these people? Do you ignore them and hope they'll go away? Or do you try to address the objection and uncover biases as early as possible?

Second, in every deal you must take calculated risks in order to get past the turning point. This interaction was the most important moment of my two-hour presentation. I took a big chance when I singled this person out and let him air his thoughts. Most likely, other students shared the same concerns, so why not get them out in the open? However, if I wasn't able to address his objections, I would definitely have experienced buzz kill. That's why you must prepare yourself for objections far in advance of a meeting.

Finally, there's another entirely different purpose to this story. We live in very cynical times and we've become a nation of skeptics. I have no doubt that some people will read this entire book and while they may enjoy it, they won't put the principles into practice for a variety of reasons. Perhaps they have been in sales for many years and don't see the need to change. Maybe they're unsure of whether the techniques really work. Others might think they are too difficult to put in practice. Whatever the impediment may be, there's also a message in this metaphor here for them.

If sales is your chosen profession, you must treat it like a profession and continually improve your skills. For example, my dentist continually takes classes on the technological advances and latest techniques in dentistry. Although my children's teachers have taught for years, they are always attending workshops to improve their teaching abilities. My insurance agent keeps abreast of the latest developments in his field. Even my gardener invests in new equipment to make himself more productive. Why is it some salespeople don't feel the need to learn something new about their profession? Conversely, Heavy Hitters are ideal students who know they must never stop learning to stay on top.

A Tale of Two E-Mails

I received distinctly different e-mails from the vice presidents of sales at two well-known companies. Coincidentally, the e-mails were sent within a few minutes of each other. The first e-mail was negative and condescending. The vice president itemized all the reasons he disliked my book. The form of his e-mail was regimented and each point was outlined, like in a legal document. The second e-mail was positive and complimentary. The vice president told me that he thought my book was refreshing. The language in his e-mail was free-flowing, like natural conversation.

I was left wondering why they both took the time to write me, so I sent each a reply. While the first vice president never responded, the second vice president and I traded several e-mails. Eventually, I trained his sales force and we stay in touch to this day.

This metaphor touches on many significant topics. Let's review a few of the more important ones.

- *Know your target market.* In the book's introduction, I discussed how some people think of sales entirely as a process. This first vice president falls into this category and I knew it the moment I saw the structure of his e-mail. He'll never understand or believe in the product since he doesn't fit the customer profile. Meanwhile, the second vice president manages by the principles of *Heavy Hitter Selling*. He's a natural fit to my product.

- *Don't take criticism personally.* Rejection is a fact of life for everyone in sales, including Heavy Hitters. While the first e-mail could have made me think of myself as a failure, it piqued my curiosity instead.

- *Everyone wants to be heard.* It's human nature for people to express themselves, and one of the most important possessions we own is our opinion.

- *Surround yourself with positive influences.* This metaphor begs for the following question to be asked: "Which vice president would you rather work for?" Perhaps you work in an unsupportive, negative sales environment. My advice? Get out!

Selling Past the Close

A vice president of sales told me the following story.

> His company had invested nearly half a million dollars trying to convince one of the world's largest auto manufacturers to use its services. After more than a year of persistent work, his company had finally earned the right to meet with the bully with the juice, the executive vice president, who was also one of the most powerful people in the entire company.
>
> Only three people attended this all-important meeting: the salesperson, the vice president of sales, and the bully with the juice. They were sitting casually around a table and the salesperson was about three-quarters of the way through his Power-Point presentation when the bully with the juice reached over, closed the laptop, and asked for advice on how they should get started with the project. The surprised salesperson stopped momentarily, opened the laptop, and said that he had a few more slides to present.

I think every sales manager has witnessed defeat snatched from the jaws of victory. You have the deal won and someone on your team (salesperson, technical engineer, or high-ranking executive) inadvertently talks the customer out of doing business.

Why do people feel compelled to talk all the time when sometimes silence is golden? In comparison to what the customer has to say, your words are really unimportant. Remember, listen more than you talk.

Why Sales and Marketing Are Always at Odds

I consult with a lot of companies that are struggling with sales and I have found that they all share something in common. Their sales and marketing efforts are at odds. Sometimes, they are even at war. The marketing team lectures the sales department, saying that if only sales would take their advice, its problems would be solved. Meanwhile, the sales department always says it needs something else from marketing. It is clamoring for a silver bullet that will convince the most ardent skeptic to buy.

The root cause of this situation is that sales and marketing have different viewpoints. To the marketing department, selling is a series of steps that you guide a prospect through. These steps are based on the logic of purchasing the product, and the marketing team's job is to provide the tools to move the prospect to the next step. Meanwhile, salespeople must work with the unpredictable part of the process: people. Their job is to formulate an account strategy based upon the people whom they are trying to sell to. They need intuition—what to do and say in a particular competitive situation. Figure 12.1 illustrates this dilemma.

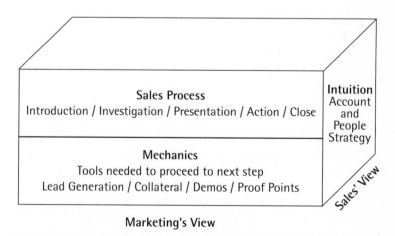

Figure 12.1 The Different Viewpoints of Sales

As a result, friction between the two areas develops. Salespeople feel they must translate theoretical arguments into a practical message while the marketing team believes the salespeople themselves are the problem. The solution to this problem is to define the intuition that sales needs. The first step is to understand the people involved in the sale: the different types of customer personalities, selfish interests that motivate the purchase, and languages the customers speak. Next, identify the circumstances of the sale: the competition, the players (e.g., the bully with the juice), and the deal position (competitive, collaborative, or blind). Finally, a feedback loop for collecting win-loss information should be put into place.

True win-loss analysis is very important and unfortunately, it's a lost art. Most companies never take the time to understand why they won a deal. They examine losses only. And they usually conduct the examination in one of two ways. In the blame game, the account team and various key departmental executives get together to hammer home their own personal agenda using the loss as a lightning rod. The sales team argues it needs a product enhancement or new marketing program while someone else may argue that sales is inept.

In the cumulative dogpile, the salesperson is put under a microscope and every account move is analyzed and criticized by management. It's painful to witness and even worse to be the subject of one of these inquisitions. After the fog of war has lifted, it's easy for the generals back at the corporate office to second-guess the battlefield actions and take potshots at their soldiers. Unfortunately, the cumulative dogpile and blame game impede the flow of critical information and dissuade the truth from being communicated.

A lot of information is in this metaphor, and that's the main point. Metaphors don't have to be obtuse analogies. They can be used to explain very complex problems. For example, the conflict between sales and marketing is a pink elephant at many companies. No one wants to talk about it until the problem becomes so obvious that it must be discussed. This metaphor presents a very different view of why this conflict exists and offers a solution to fix the problem.

Notice the sensory structure of the metaphor. In the first paragraph, marketing "lectures" sales and sales "says" they need something else. Even though they're talking, they're not communicating. Next, an illustration is used to show the problem in a way everyone can understand. The two groups look at the problem from different points of view. Finally, a solution is presented about how to gather the information needed to fix the problem. The solution uses two more metaphors: the blame game and the cumulative dogpile.

Something else is going on here. This story is also about power and control. When marketing tries to dictate sales strategy without listening to sales, the two will be at odds. When sales management doesn't listen to salespeople, the truth is lost.

Finally, this metaphor includes the concept of the "battlefield of sales." Ultimately, sales is a very personal battle between salespeople who fight one another in hand-to-hand combat. In the trenches, every move the salesperson makes is a matter of life or death. The best generals understand the intensity of the fight, share the same sense of urgency as the soldiers in the field, and visit the front lines often.

Shameless Self-Promotion

A weekly newspaper published in my hometown covers local news. It's a small newspaper with only one regular columnist, who writes about high-society happenings. The columnist writes about the exclusive parties she's attended, lavish dinners at friends' houses, and glamorous fund-raising socials. She also always includes a flattering photo of herself among the pictures of the event of the week. However, the most fascinating part is that she writes the column under a pen name and puts her real name in the picture's caption. I guess she thinks nobody notices. Since she is widely recognized in the community, I assume she thinks she's popular when in reality, she's probably one of the most unpopular people in town.

What does this metaphor have to do with sales? Plenty. Replace the columnist with a pushy salesperson, one who is always exaggerating product claims to customers. Or substitute a boastful salesperson who is constantly politicking with his manager in order to get ahead. You could tell both of these salespeople they need to change but they probably won't. It's only when people are able to see themselves as they really are that change occurs, and that's the purpose of this metaphor. Perhaps you know someone whom you should share this story with.

Your Career in Sales

My father-in-law has worked for the same company for over 25 years. This is not uncommon for a person in the aerospace industry. Conversely, of the thousands of salespeople I have met, I can't recall any who have spent their entire careers selling for the same company. In the high-tech industry where I have spent my career, it's almost the exact opposite. Companies, products, and technologies change so often that an old-timer is someone who has been with a company for a few years. Since the average tenures of vice presidents are now less than 18 months, they vanish so quickly you would think they are an endangered species. Perhaps the industry you work in is similar.

Figure 12.2 is a graph that reflects a normal sales career, with each line representing a different job.

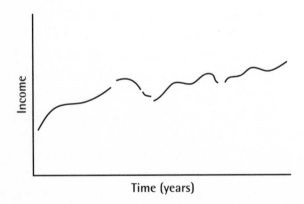

Figure 12.2 A Typical Career in Sales

During the course of a typical career in sales, it is completely normal to change jobs once every few years.

People are always questioning the decisions of others. Maybe someone you know wonders why you are in sales. Perhaps he or she can't understand why you aren't in a more predictable or recognized vocation. You may even start to wonder yourself, since everyone experiences self-doubt from time to time. The purpose of this metaphor is to provide you with reassurance.

One of the many qualities metaphors have is that they can be used to comfort people. For example, when my son didn't make the team, I told him my own story about the time I was cut. He knew that I understood exactly what he was going through and that he was not alone. We ended up laughing together about our misfortunes.

The most significant part of this metaphor is the lines on the graph of a typical career in sales. Did you glance over them or stop and study them in detail? Did you notice the short one or how the income of the longer ones went up and down? Sometimes we just want to know we're normal like everyone else.

The Cat and the Fire

Every year there are wildfires in the hills and mountains of Southern California. Driven by the hot, dry Santa Ana winds, a fire was fast approaching the mountain community of Crystal Lake on September 1, 2002. When 60-year-old Sigrid Thompson called 911, she was sure she would perish in the flames. Sheriff Deputies Paul Archambault and John Rose raced up the burning mountain after receiving the call from dispatchers who considered her "distraught" and "suicidal."[20]

The flames and smoke were so intense that the deputies had to walk the final eighth of a mile to her cabin. As they moved closer, they heard a gunshot. When they finally entered the house, they found Sigrid had just shot her dog and was holding the gun to her own head. When she wouldn't answer the officer's repeated commands to drop the weapon, Deputy Rose asked her what she planned on doing with her cat. She looked at him and said, "The cat?" At which point the officers were able to wrestle the gun away and lead her to safety. Sigrid doesn't own any cats.

Sometimes you must use whatever means are available to interrupt customers' destructive thoughts and stop them from purchasing a competitor's product for their own good.

Salespeople are used to hammering home their key differentiators, such as product facts and features. Usually, we're so eager to talk about them with the customer that we forget we need to be entertaining as well. To truly separate ourselves from the competition, we need to grab the customer's attention and hold it until the end. "The Cat and the Fire" is a provocative title that sparks curiosity. As you continued to read, you learned that Sigrid shot her dog and you might have wondered how the story was going to end. The ending of the story is quite a surprise, too. Finally, the moral of the story is given, which explains its relevance to sales. Great metaphors keep your attention from start to finish.

Debt of Gratitude

I have been kicked out of only two accounts in my entire career. In the first one, the key decision maker had used my archrival's product for years at his previous company. I knew I was destined to lose and kept pressing him for the truth until he hated me. In the other account, the customer treated me like his personal slave until I finally rebelled. Both times, the customer called my manager and told him I should be fired. Fortunately, these two customers came along early in my sales career, and I owe them both a debt of gratitude.

This metaphor about turning bad into good has a great cowcatcher in the first sentence. As you read it, did you wonder who the customers were and if I was fired? Or did it make you think about the tough customers you have had to deal with? It's hard to forget customers who told you to get lost, and nearly impossible to forget the ones who threatened your livelihood.

The other interesting aspect of the metaphor is the hook in the final sentence. But what does it really say? The actual interpretation is completely left up to you. Whereas the metaphor about the cat and the fire spells out the meaning, sometimes it's best to leave the conclusion open-ended.

Kobe Beef

The chairman of a company asked his president to meet with me, and a dinner was arranged at a posh Beverly Hills restaurant. Immediately after opening the menu, I knew I wanted the Kobe beef. I had never had it before and was excited I would finally get a chance to try this legendary delicacy from Kobe, Japan.

However the table conversation was completely unappealing. The president would only talk about the topic she knew best—herself. I got the feeling she wasn't sure why she was there in the first place, as she wasn't interested in anything I had to say. In fact, I was only able to squeeze in a few sentences during the first hour of conversation. She talked about her career, her doctorate, and all of her past successes. Her boasting was interrupted only when she spoke on her cell phone (three times).

Now I have humbled myself many times with difficult customers in order to win their business. However, this person was never going to buy anything I had to sell, and I had had enough. As my sizzling main course was set upon the table, I told her that she needed to learn some business etiquette and that I was going to excuse myself. She was shocked and upset. But I was not going to experience something special with someone who wasn't special. I am sure there will be a better time to try Kobe beef.

The obvious message here is not to be a self-centered egomaniac. However, this metaphor has a greater purpose. It works hand in hand with the previous metaphor to show why I am grateful to those two customers. It's an example of how you can link metaphors together during your sales presentation to create greater meaning.

Let's think about these two metaphors in the context of one another. The first is about learning from failure and the second is about being true to yourself, in other words, applying what you have learned. The Kobe beef represents a deal we are pursuing. Even though we are competitive salespeople who badly want to win every deal, at times you must force yourself to walk away. Do you know when to walk away from a deal?

Recent Study

A recent study found that hypertensive men who drink moderately and have one to two drinks a day have a 44 percent lower risk of dying from a heart attack than nondrinkers with high blood pressure.[21] Of course, Heavy Hitters have known this for years.

When people laugh, at some level they agree with you. Humor helps build rapport and reminds us not to take ourselves too seriously.

The Ringman

BRIAN: I have a question and would appreciate your input. How do you create a sense of urgency with a customer who is not moving ahead?

STEVE: This probably isn't the answer you would like to hear, but you can't do it. Arguing your business case, product benefits, and ROI to an unreceptive customer is almost always a waste of time. You need someone inside the company who will fight on your behalf. You work with this person like a boxer and his trainer. The trainer prepares the boxer for his prizefight by teaching him how to attack and defend himself from his opponent. During the actual fight, the boxer will come back to his corner bruised and battered. The trainer's job is to make him feel like a world champion again so he can get back into the ring.

Heavy Hitters know they must have a coach to win the deal. Coaches are more than acquaintances; they are loyal friends who will fight for you on your behalf. They defend you when you are not around, promote your cause within the organization, and whole-heartedly believe in you.

Another key point of this metaphor relates to fielding questions. The most critical moments of a sales call are when customers ask tough questions. An extremely effective way to answer them is by using metaphors. However, you must prepare the metaphors in advance and have one ready for the most frequently asked questions. For example, when I was asked this question, I knew ahead of time exactly what I'd say. I wasn't fumbling for the answer or redirecting my response to another topic. I was prepared with an answer and spoke with conviction and authority. And as you may recall, how you say something is just as important as what you say.

Spanish Proverb

There's an old Spanish proverb that says, "He who wants to grow rich in a year will be hanged in a month."

Think about your sales career over the long term. Also, sometimes the best metaphor is the shortest one.

Everyone Is Lonely

Counter to common sense, psychologists believe the loneliest time of life is not retirement age but between the ages of 18 and 25. It turns out the age group you naturally associate with schoolmates, friends, and parties actually has one of the highest suicide rates.[22] This raises an interesting point. Regardless of how many people surround someone, how much fortune, fame, and power you think a person has, everyone is lonely in his or her own way. Loneliness isn't only about being alone. It is when you feel disconnected, isolated, alienated, unwanted, inadequate, self-conscious, and unloved.

Keep this idea in mind. The next customer you meet needs a friend.

This metaphor shows an example of an effective "buildup." The buildup is how the metaphor reaches its climax or hook. The premise of this metaphor is that everyone is lonely. However, probably not everyone would agree with this statement. Therefore, information has to be presented in a manner that convinces people to believe.

First, there is a thought-provoking statement about what psychologists (experts on human nature) believe followed by factual information about suicide rates. Then the metaphor focuses on thoughts that the reader must interpret personally. When you read the sentence about fame and fortune, you might have thought about particular movie or rock stars whose self-destructive habits led to their ruination. The thoughts turn even more personal as loneliness is divided into seven different characteristics that everyone has privately experienced. By the time you reach the final sentence, the original premise that everyone is lonely has been proven to be true.

This metaphor serves another purpose beyond the example of how to structure arguments. Working in sales is long hours of drudgery punctuated by moments of fear and excitement. Perhaps the most intense moment is when you meet with the president, vice president, or other bully with the juice who controls the fate of your deal. Remember, it's lonely at the top and *everyone* needs a friend.

ROI versus ROH

Recently, I participated in a panel discussion about sales strategies. The audience was composed of salespeople and their managers. One of the other panelists was the top executive at a Fortune 500 company, and he represented the customer's point of view.

He made three important statements when it was his turn to speak. First, he said that his entire organization was designed to protect him: "Don't bother trying to cold-call my office. Work with my people." Second, he said he doesn't believe vendors' ROI arguments: "Everyone's got them and they all stink." Finally, he said he was very concerned with the welfare of his employees and truly wanted his people to be happy. You could sense gloom, doom, and hopelessness filling the room. However, I was actually happy he said what he did since I have always sold based on relationships and ROH (return on happiness).

Whenever you hear anyone start to talk about the importance of ROI, you should remember the real purchase motivator is ROH. We'll buy whatever brings us the most happiness.

But what is it that makes people happy? According to psychologists, "The happiest people surround themselves with family and friends, lose themselves in daily activities, and, most important, forgive easily. The happiest people spend the least time alone. They pursue personal growth and intimacy; they judge themselves by their own yardsticks, never against what others do or have."[23] I would also add that the happiest people I know are the ones who worry the least.

CONCLUSION

Ordering our thoughts is a normal part of the communication process. Typically, we mention the most important subject first and then move on to issues of lesser priority or urgency. Or we structure our arguments with the most compelling reason at the beginning or end. However, when our mind is presented with a laundry list of thoughts, it attempts to determine which ones are real and true. Metaphors take these individual thoughts and combine them into one contiguous object. These stories connect logical and psychological meaning together. For example, this entire book has been based upon the metaphor of the Heavy Hitter, and this chapter has been a metaphor about metaphors.

As salespeople, we are trying to sell customers one complete package even though we talk about our company, products, features, benefits, and even ourselves individually. Ultimately, we are selling them something much larger—the idea that we can help change their lives for the better and enable them to be a part of something greater than themselves. We know we can make them happy.

Unfortunately, we have been trained to think of customers and ourselves solely as rational decision makers who use logic and reason exclusively. This isn't surprising since we spend nearly the first two decades of our lives in schools that indoctrinate us with the scientific method of investigation and technical theories to explain the phenomena of life. Our training continues throughout adulthood as our employers teach us the processes and procedures needed to fulfill our duties.

We also mistakenly assume that our consciousness is binary by nature and works like a light switch—it's either on or off. We're awake and conscious or asleep in a state of suspended animation. In reality, we experience different degrees and a wide spectrum of consciousness. Normally, we don't even think of our subconscious mind. When we do, we believe there is a clear division between the conscious and subconscious. In fact, they are intimately integrated and in continual contact.

Through sheer conscious willpower, we can temporarily control our personal weaknesses and stick to a diet, manage our temper, and stop other destructive habits. However, the process to create lasting change requires both conscious and subconscious agreement. Permanent change does not happen overnight or with the speed and intensity of a lightning strike. Rather, it takes time for the mind to rewire the existing neural connections and create new pathways. You can actually facilitate this change process with "activation agents." For example, neuroscientists have studied brain scans and found that meditation and prayer actually light up certain areas of the brain that are associated with self-control, attitude, and emotions.[24]

The most powerful activation agent also happens to be the most important persuasion technique. Love is a form of communication entirely its own. Love transmits across every layer of the human communication model and talks directly to the conscious and subconscious minds. Nothing in this world is a more powerful way to communicate than love.

It would be easy enough to end this book by telling you the secret to becoming a Heavy Hitter is to love your customers. However, that's only part of the story. Your parents have considered you a Heavy Hitter for your entire life. Your friends have always thought of you as a Heavy Hitter. Your children think you are a Heavy Hitter, too. Perhaps the only person left to convince you are a Heavy Hitter is yourself.

Why are you in sales? Take a moment and honestly ask yourself this question. What parts do you like and what do you hate? Did you become a salesperson through happenstance or was it a premeditated career move? Are you counting the days until you have enough money to quit or enough experience to move into management? Finally, is this a career you would recommend your loved ones pursue?

The reality is that it is not by accident you are in sales. In fact, you were destined for this profession. While others have chosen life's mundane path, you have selected adventure and chosen to experience the highs and lows of life. Life's far too short to play it safe, and anyone who takes risks is already a success. Today I think about success very differently than I did at the start of my career. Over the years I have learned that the words of philosopher and humanitarian Albert Schweitzer are true: "Success is not the key to happiness. Happiness is the key to success. If you love what you are doing, you will be successful."[25]

Epilogue

THE ESSENCE and purpose of this entire book can be distilled into one analogy—"The Sales Iceberg." The visible portion of the iceberg above the water represents the logic of selling. All salespeople are aware of their products' features, benefits, and specifications. Their companies have identified processes to educate customers about their products and established procedures to determine customers' business qualifications and technical requirements.

However, underneath the waterline is the unseen, intangible part of the sales process that is ultimately responsible for the decision being made. The submerged portion symbolizes the influence of human nature during the sales process. Since most salespeople find the human element of selling to be more complex, unpredictable, and difficult to manage, they don't fully take advantage of customer behavior or they misinterpret and ignore it.

Unfortunately, most companies train their salespeople only on the logic of selecting a product. And like a ship on the Arctic Ocean, salespeople who aren't aware of the part of the iceberg that cannot be seen do not know whether they will survive or perish on the voyage. Meanwhile, Heavy Hitters successfully reach their destination by using intuition to plot a course based upon their customers' behavior.

At the foundation of all sales is a relationship between people. Just as a submerged block of ice can sink a ship, misunderstanding human nature can wreck any business or personal relationship. Of course, many of the concepts covered in this book can also be applied to your personal relationships with your spouse, children, relatives, and friends. Even these relationships require time, effort, and rapport to succeed. You have to wonder how many marriages, friendships, and family relationships have failed because someone wouldn't listen, didn't stay in touch, or couldn't see the other person's point of view.

I have saved perhaps the most important point regarding Heavy Hitters for last. This final lesson about being a Heavy Hitter took me many years to learn. A very good friend of mine, who's made and lost millions of dollars during his lifetime, recently told me, "Never let your successes go to your head, and never let your failures go to your heart." He's right. You will have good quarters and bad ones. You will win large deals and lose them. Hopefully, you will succeed more often than you will fail.

I honestly cannot remember whether the third quarter of 1996 was a good or bad one. I can barely remember what happened just a few quarters ago. However, I do remember that at that moment in time it was the most important quarter ever and my drive to succeed dominated all my thoughts. I also remember that I worked with some very talented people whom I desperately wanted to impress.

As salespeople, our world is structured on a value system that is intimately tied to the production of a single revenue number. We post this number monthly, quarterly, and yearly. This number is how the rest of our world measures our contribution, and it is also how we tend to judge our own worth.

However, you will never be truly happy or satisfied if you measure your self-worth solely by the revenue you generate. You know you are not a good person because you make your number, just as you are not a bad person if you don't. Life is about being with your family and friends and, most importantly, having a relationship with your Creator. These relationships are a true reflection of your life's significance.

And now I would like to have a final word with your subconscious mind. Your genetics may explain your predispositions in life, such as your height and the color of your eyes, but they certainly don't decide your ability to learn something new. Understanding and using these new language models will make you not only a better salesperson but also a better person.

Your brain has a limitless capability. It knows how to absorb seemingly disconnected happenings and translate them into meaningful structured experiences. It has been accumulating these experiences for decades and can create completely new ways to use this information to accomplish what you want so you can get more enjoyment from life.

While some people mistakenly believe they have only one chance to be a success, in fact, life provides endless opportunities to those who allow their subconscious mind to be a positive force in their lives. All you have to do is pay attention to it, just as you would listen to your best friend. It can help you recognize an opportunity and tell you when to take a chance. And as your subconscious mind already knows, you are destined for great things.

I'd enjoy hearing from you. You can contact me at stevemartin@ heavyhitterselling.com.

Notes

Introduction

1. U.S. Department of State, Office of International Information Programs, "Media and Message in America," University of Tampere, http://www.uta.fi/FAST/US2/REF/mediaovv.html (accessed November 3, 2003).
2. James Lindgren, "Hail to the Chiefs," The Federalist Society for Law and Public Policy Studies, http://www.fed-soc.org/Publications/PresidentialSurvey.htm (accessed December 3, 2003).
3. David Moore, "Firefighters Top Gallup's Honesty and Ethics List," The Gallup Organization, http://www.gallup.com/content/login.aspx?ci=5095 (accessed May 21, 2003).

Chapter 1   The Heavy Hitter

1. *Advanced Techniques of Hypnosis and Therapy: Selected Papers of Milton H. Erickson, M.D.,* ed. Jay Haley (New York: Grune & Stratton, 1967).
2. Ibid.

Chapter 2   How People Communicate

1. Trevor Parris, "The Motives behind Marriages," University of Virgin Islands, http://www.uvi.edu/humanities/tparris/eng_201/marriage/Motive.pdf (accessed February 4, 2004).
2. Robert Lee Holtz, "NASA Failures Prompt Vow of Program Reform," *Los Angeles Times,* December 8, 1999.

Chapter 3   How People Are Wired

1. Victoria Neufeldt, ed., *Webster's New World College Dictionary,* 3d ed. (New York: Prentice Hall, 1996).
2. Associated Press, "Physical Therapy Can Help Reset Brain," Yahoo! Health, http://Health.yahoo.com/search/heathnews?lb=s&p=id%3A42089 (accessed June 1, 2003).
3. Bill Walsh with Brian Billick and James A. Peterson, *Finding the Winning Edge* (Champaign, Ill.: Sports Publishing Inc., 1998).
4. William Kelly, "Unraveling the Mysteries of Creativity," *Orange County Register,* March 9, 2003.

Chapter 4   How People Think

1. National Council on Disability, "National Disability Policy: A Progress Report," National Council on Disability, www.ncd.gov/newsroom/publications/progressreport_07-26-02.html (accessed June 15, 2004).
2. Elizabeth Knowles, ed., *Oxford Dictionary of Quotations,* 5th ed. (New York: Oxford University Press, 1999).
3. Johanna McGeary, "Odd Man Out," *Time* (September 10, 2001): 22–32.
4. *Thomas Jefferson: Writings,* ed. Merrill D. Peterson (New York: Library of America, 1984).
5. Nathan Haskell Dole, ed. *John Bartlett's Familiar Quotations,* 16th ed. (Boston: Little, Brown and Company, 1992).

Chapter 5   Finding the Truth

1. Carole Martin, "Nonverbal Communications: Escape the Pitfalls," *Microsoft News Network,* editorial.careers.msn.com/articles/actions (accessed October 15, 2003).
2. Chris Idzikowski, "Sleep Postures and Personality," Neuronic, www.neuronic.com/Sleep_posture_and_personality.html (accessed September 16, 2003).
3. Reuters, "More Brain Power Needed for Mandarin than English," BBC News. http://news.bbc.co.UK/2/hi/health/3025796.stm (accessed June 30, 2003).
4. Richard Stenger, "If End Is Near, Do You Want to Know?" CNN.com, www.cnn.com/2003/TECH/space/02/28/asteroid. alert/index.html (accessed February 28, 2003).

Chapter 6   Choosing Your Battles

1. Health Media Ltd., "Natural Brain Chemicals 'Wipe Out' Bad Memories," American Psychological Association, www.psycport. com/showArticle.cfm? xmlFile=healthmedia_2002_07_31_eng-healthmedia_enghealthmedia_ 062510_22_43134239921_35.xml&provider=Health+Media+Ltd (accessed March 2, 2004).
2. Passages by Sun Tzu are quoted from *The Art of War,* ed. James Clavell (New York: Delacorte Press, 1983).

Chapter 7   Building Customer Rapport

1. John Wildermuth, "Davis' Ratings Dip to New Depths," *San Francisco Chronicle,* www.sfgate.com/cgi-bin/article.cgi?f=/c/a/2003/08/15/MN251071.DTL (accessed November 12, 2003).
2. Hahn Kim Quach, "Schwarzenegger Won with Soft Sell," *Orange County Register,* December 13, 2003.
3. Hahn Kim Quach, "Governor Shapes Deal," *Orange County Register,* December 11, 2003.
4. Quach, "Schwarzenegger Won with Soft Sell."

Chapter 8   Your Two Most Important Customers

1. Niccolò Machiavelli, *The Prince,* ed. Jean-Pierre Barricelli (New York: Barron's Educational Services, 1975).
2. Nathan Haskell Dole, ed., *John Bartlett's Familiar Quotations,* 16th ed. (Boston: Little, Brown and Company, 1992).
3. Andrea Gabor, *The Capitalist Philosophers: The Geniuses of Modern Business— Their Lives, Times, and Ideas* (New York: Crown Business, 2000).
4. Merritt McKinney, "Brain Hard-Wired for Empathy: Study," Yahoo! News, http://story.news.yahoo.com/news?tmpl=story&cid=571&e=5&v=e/mm/2003 1106/hl_mm/brain_empathy_dc_1 (accessed November 6, 2003).
5. Mark Twain, "Mark Twain Quotes," twainquotes.com, http://www.twainquotes .com/profanity (accessed December 21, 2003).
6. John McKay, *McKay: A Coach's Story* (New York: Anthenum, 1974).

Chapter 9   Finding Your Coach

1. Erik Strand, "Wanted: Someone Better than I," *Psychology Today,* September/October 2003.
2. Calvin S. Hall, Gardner Lindzey, and John B. Campbell, *Theories of Personality,* 4th ed. (New York: John Wiley and Sons, 1997).
3. Lawrence Pervin and Oliver John, eds., *Handbook of Personality: Theory and Research,* 2d ed. (New York: The Guilford Press, 1999).

Chapter 10   The Deeper Meaning of Language

1. Laurence Urdang, ed., *The American Century Dictionary* (New York: Warner Books, 1995).
2. George P. Shultz, Foreword to *Reagan, in His Own Hand: The Writings of Ronald Reagan That Reveal His Revolutionary Vision for America,* ed. Kiron K. Skinner, Annelise Anderson, and Martin Anderson (New York: Free Press, 2001), x–xi.
3. Ibid., 18–19.

Chapter 11   Intuitive Persuasion

1. Michael Nash, "The Truth and the Hype of Hypnosis," *Scientific American,* July 2001, 47–55.
2. Kiron K. Skinner, Annelise Anderson, and Martin Anderson, eds., *Reagan, in His Own Hand: The Writings of Ronald Reagan That Reveal His Revolutionary Vision for America* (New York: Free Press, 2001), 377.
3. Ibid., 142.
4. Ibid., 147.
5. Ibid., 329.
6. Ibid., 173.
7. Ibid., 334.
8. Ibid., 50.
9. Ibid., 224.
10. Kenneth S. Bowers, *Hypnosis for the Seriously Curious* (New York: W. W. Norton, 1983).

Chapter 12   Metaphors for the Mind

1. Purdue University, "Using Metaphors in Creative Writing," Purdue University, http://owl.english.purdue.edu/handouts/general/gl_ metaphor.html (accessed March 14, 2004).
2. Mark Sherman, "Obesity May Top Smoking as Top Killer," Christian Broadcast Network, http://cbn.org/CBNNews/wire/040310g.asp (accessed March 24, 2003).
3. George Mason University, "Chemicals Found in Cigarette Smoke," George Mason University, http://www.gmu.edu/student/quitsmoking/chemicals.html (accessed February 6, 2004).
4. Alberta Alcohol and Drug Abuse Commission, "Smoking Is Expensive," http://www.aadac4kids.com/thefacts/smokingfacts/smokingisexpensive.asp (accessed February 7, 2004).
5. Daniel Kahneman, "Map of Bounded Rationality," Nobel e-museum, The Nobel Foundation, http://www.nobel.se/economics/laurates/2002/kahneman-lecture.html (accessed January 5, 2004).
6. Eugene Peterson, ed., *The Message* (Colorado Springs: Navpress Publishing, 1993), Matthew 13:13.
7. Greg Laurie, ed., *New Believer's Bible* (Wheaton, Ill.: Tyndale House Publishers, 1996), Luke 6:43-45.
8. Dave Sharpe, "Effective Communication," Montana State University, http://www.montana.edu/wwwcommd/effectcomm.htm (accessed February 9, 2004).
9. Laurie, ed. *New Believer's Bible,* Luke 6:20-23.
10. *New American Standard Bible* (New York: Thomas Nelson Publishers, 1978), Luke 12:27.
11. Laurie, ed. *New Believer's Bible,* Matthew 19:24.
12. Ibid., Luke 6:24-25.
13. Ibid., Matthew 6:27.
14. Ibid., Matthew 19:19.
15. Public Broadcasting Corporation, "How Does the Autistic Brain Work?" Public Broadcasting Corporation, http://www.pbs.org/kcet/closertotruth/explore/show_ 03.html (accessed June 6, 2003).
16. Laurie, ed. *New Believer's Bible,* Luke 5:4.
17. Peterson, ed. *The Message,* Luke 5:10.
18. Laurie, ed. *New Believer's Bible,* Luke 8:4-8.
19. Ibid., Luke 8:11-15.

20. Gina Keating, "Woman Rescued Hollywood-Style from Fire," ESPN.com, http://dynamic.espn.go.com/outdoors/conservation/news/2002/0905/1427633.html (accessed April 1, 2003).

21. Reuters, "Study: Daily Drink Eases Hypertensive's Heart Risk," Reuters, http://www.reuters.com/newsArticle.jhtml?type=topNews&storyID=4628578 (accessed March 22, 2004).

22. Centers for Disease Control, "Suicide in the United States," Centers for Disease Controls, http://www.cdc.gov/ncipc/factsheets/suifacts.htm (accessed January 12, 2004).

23. Marilyn Elias, "Psychologists Now Know What Makes People Happy," *USA Today,* http://www.usatoday.com/news/health/2002-12-08-happy-main_x.htm (accessed March 24, 2004).

24. Reuters, "Meditation Shown to Light Up Brains of Buddhists," St. Joseph Health System, http://www.stjosephhealth.org/healthnews/reuters/newstory 05220038.htm (accessed August 21, 2003).

25. Albert Schweitzer, "Albert Schweitzer," Wisdomquotes.com, http://www.wisdomquotes.com/002144.html (accessed March 12, 2004).

Bibliography

Alberta Alcohol and Drug Abuse Commission. "Smoking Is Expensive." Alberta Alcohol and Drug Abuse Commission. http://www.aadac4kids.com/thefacts/smokingfacts/smokingisexpensive.asp (accessed February 7, 2004).

Andrews, Robert, Mary Briggs, and Michael Siedel, eds. *The Columbia World of Quotations.* New York: Columbia University Press, 1996.

Associated Press. "Physical Therapy Can Help Reset Brain." Yahoo! Health. http://Health.yahoo.com/search/heathnews?lb=s&p=id%3A42089 (accessed June 1, 2003).

Bowers, Kenneth S. *Hypnosis for the Seriously Curious.* New York: W. W. Norton, 1983.

Boyd, L. M. "There Is Nothing Like a Danish Life." *Orange County Register,* February 27, 2004, Accent 3.

Centers for Disease Control. "Suicide in the United States." Centers for Disease Control. http://www.cdc.gov/ncipc/factsheets/suifacts.htm (accessed January 12, 2004).

Dole, Nathan Haskell, ed. *John Bartlett's Familiar Quotations.* 16th ed. Boston: Little, Brown and Company, 1992.

Elias, Marilyn. "Psychologists Now Know What Makes People Happy." *USA Today.* http://www.usatoday.com/news/health/2002-12-08-happy-main_x.htm (accessed March 24, 2004).

Erickson, Milton H. *Advanced Techniques of Hypnosis and Therapy: Selected Papers of Milton H. Erickson, M.D.* Edited by Jay Haley. New York: Grune & Stratton, 1967.

Gabor, Andrea. *The Capitalist Philosophers: The Geniuses of Modern Business—Their Lives, Times, and Ideas.* New York: Crown Business, 2000.

George Mason University. "Chemicals Found in Cigarette Smoke." George Mason University. http://www.gmu.edu/student/quitsmoking/chemicals.html (accessed February 6, 2004).

363

Hahn, Kim Quach, "Governor Shapes Deal." *Orange County Register,* December 11, 2003, News 1.

Hahn, Kim Quach, "Schwarzenegger Won with Soft Sell." *Orange County Register,* December 13, 2003, News 5.

Hall, Calvin S., Gardner Lindzey, and John B. Campbell. *Theories of Personality.* 4th ed. New York: John Wiley and Sons, 1997.

Health Media Ltd. "Natural Brain Chemicals 'Wipe Out' Bad Memories." American Psychological Association. http://www.psycport.com/showArticle.cfm? xmlFile=healthmedia_2002_07_31_eng-healthmedia_enghealthmedia_ 062510_22_4313423992135.xml&provider=Health+Media+Ltd (accessed March 2, 2004).

Holtz, Robert Lee. "NASA Failures Prompt Vow of Program Reform." *Los Angeles Times,* December 8, 1999, 1.

Idzikowski, Chris. "Sleep Postures and Personality." Neuronic. http://www.neuronic. com/Sleep_posture_and_personality.html (accessed September 16, 2003).

Kahneman, Daniel. "Map of Bounded Rationality." Nobel e-museum, The Nobel Foundation. http://www.nobel.se/economics/laureates/2002/kahneman-lecture.html (accessed January 5, 2004).

Keating, Gina. "Woman Rescued Hollywood-Style from Fire." ESPN.com. http://dynamic.espn.go.com/outdoors/conservation/news/2002/0905/1427633. html (accessed April 1, 2003).

Kelly, William. "Unraveling the Mysteries of Creativity." *Orange County Register,* March 9, 2003, Accent 3.

Knowles, Elizabeth, ed. *Oxford Dictionary of Quotations.* 5th ed. New York: Oxford University Press, 1999.

Laurie, Greg, ed. *New Believer's Bible.* Wheaton, Ill.: Tyndale House Publishers, 1996.

Lindgren, James. "Hail to the Chiefs." The Federalist Society for Law and Public Policy Studies. http://www.fed-soc.org/Publications/PresidentialSurvey.htm (accessed December 3, 2003).

Machiavelli, Niccolò. *The Prince.* Edited by Jean-Pierre Barricelli. New York: Barron's Educational Services, 1975.

Martin, Carole. "Nonverbal Communications: Escape the Pitfalls." *Microsoft News Network.* http://editorial.careers.msn.com/articles/actions (accessed October 15, 2003).

Maslow, Abraham. *Toward a Psychology of Being.* 2d ed. Princeton, N.J.: Van Nostrand Reinhold, 1968.

McGeary, Johanna. "Odd Man Out." *Time,* September 10, 2001, 22–32.

McKay, John. *McKay: A Coach's Story.* New York: Anthenum, 1974.

McKinney, Merritt. "Brain Hard-Wired for Empathy: Study." Yahoo! News. http://story.news.yahoo.com/news?tmpl=story&cid=571&e=5&v=e/mm/20031106/hl_mm/brain_empathy_dc_1 (accessed November 6, 2003).

Moore, David. "Firefighters Top Gallup's Honesty and Ethics List." The Gallup Organization. http://www.gallup.com/content/login.aspx?ci=5095 (accessed May 21, 2003).

Nash, Michael. "The Truth and the Hype of Hypnosis." *Scientific American,* July 2001, 47–55.

National Council on Disability. "National Disability Policy: A Progress Report." National Council on Disability. http://www.ncd.gov/newsroom/publications/progressreport_07-26-02.html (accessed June 15, 2004).

Neufeldt, Victoria, ed. *Webster's New World College Dictionary.* 3d ed. New York: Prentice Hall, 1996.

New American Standard Bible. New York: Thomas Nelson Publishers, 1978.

Parris, Trevor. "The Motives behind Marriages." University of Virgin Islands. http://www.uvi.edu/humanities/tparris/eng_201/marriage/Motive.pdf (accessed February 4, 2004).

Pervin, Lawrence, and Oliver John, eds. *Handbook of Personality: Theory and Research.* 2d ed. New York: The Guilford Press, 1999.

Peterson, Eugene, ed. *The Message.* Colorado Springs: Navpress Publishing Group, 1993.

Peterson, Merrill D., ed. *Thomas Jefferson: Writings.* New York: Library of America, 1984.

Public Broadcasting Corporation. "How Does the Autistic Brain Work?" Public Broadcasting Corporation. http://www.pbs.org/kcet/closertotruth/explore/show_03.html (accessed June 6, 2003).

Purdue University. "Using Metaphors in Creative Writing." Purdue University. http://owl.english.purdue.edu/handouts/general/gl_metaphor.html (accessed March 14, 2004).

Reagan, Ronald. *Reagan, in His Own Hand: The Writings of Ronald Reagan That Reveal His Revolutionary Vision for America.* Edited by Kiron K. Skinner, Annelise Anderson, and Martin Anderson. New York: Free Press, 2001.

Reuters. "Meditation Shown to Light Up Brains of Buddhists." St. Joseph Health System. http://www.stjosephhealth.org/healthnews/reuters/newstory05220038.htm (accessed August 21, 2003).

Reuters. "More Brain Power Needed for Mandarin than English." BBC News. http://news.bbc.co.UK/2/hi/health/3025796.stm (accessed June 30, 2003).

Reuters. "Study: Daily Drink Eases Hypertensive's Heart Risk." Reuters. http://www.reuters.com/newsArticle.jhtml?type=topNews&storyID=4628578 (accessed March 22, 2004).

Schweitzer, Albert. "Albert Schweitzer." Wisdomquotes.com. http://www.wisdomquotes.com/002144.html (accessed March 12, 2004).

Sharpe, Dave. "Effective Communication." Montana State University. http://www.montana.edu/wwwcommd/effectcomm.htm (accessed February 9, 2004).

Sherman, Mark. "Obesity May Top Smoking as Top Killer." Christian Broadcast Network. http://cbn.org/CBNNews/wire/040310g.asp (accessed March 24, 2003).

Skinner, Kiron K., Annelise Anderson, and Martin Anderson, eds., *Reagan, In His Own Hand: The Writings of Ronald Reagan That Reveal His Revolutionary Vision for America.* New York: Free Press, 2001.

Stenger, Richard. "If End Is Near, Do You Want to Know?" CNN.com. http://www.cnn.com/2003/TECH/space/02/28/asteroid.alert/index.html (accessed February 28, 2003).

Strand, Erik. "Wanted: Someone Better than I." *Psychology Today,* September/October 2003, 23.

Sun Tzu. *The Art of War.* Edited by James Clavell. New York: Delacorte Press, 1983.

Twain, Mark. "Mark Twain Quotes." twainquotes.com. http://www.twainquotes.com/profanity (accessed December 21, 2003).

Urdang, Laurence, ed. *The American Century Dictionary.* New York: Warner Books, 1995.

U.S. Department of State, Office of International Information Programs. "Media and Message in America." University of Tampere. http://www.uta.fi/FAST/US2/REF/mediaovv.html (accessed November 3, 2003).

Walsh, Bill, with Brian Billick and James A. Peterson. *Finding the Winning Edge.* Champaign, Ill.: Sports Publishing Inc., 1998.

Wildermuth, John. "Davis' Ratings Dip to New Depths." *San Francisco Chronicle.* http://www.sfgate.com/cgi-bin/article.cgi?f=/c/a/2003/08/15/MN251071.DTL (accessed November 12, 2003).

Glossary

Agreeableness One of the factors in the five-factor model; it describes how well people get along in group settings and their level of independence.

Anchor The conscious, premeditated association of a specific feeling to an object.

Auditory A person who processes information primarily using the auditory word catalog.

Belonging needs People's natural disposition to want to be part of a group in order to share similar interests and values, a sense of community, and affectionate relationships.

Benefaction The desire to achieve personal goals that contribute to one's well-being, such as happiness, esteem, power, or wealth, which influences the way the customer behaves during the sales cycle.

Coach A friend and ally within the customer's company who provides accurate information about the sales cycle and promotes the Heavy Hitter's solution.

Congruence Truthful communication defined when all layers of the human communication model are in agreement.

Conscientiousness One of the factors in the five-factor model; it describes a person's degree of diligence and ability to complete tasks.

Conscious mind The part of the mind that a person controls.

Content layer The actual words spoken during the course of a conversation.

Cowcatcher The beginning sentences of a metaphor that are intended to grab the listener's attention.

Customer placebo Misleading information presented by the customer to nonfavored vendors, such as false buying signs and a display of more product interest than actually exists.

Enterprise sales The sale of complex products and solutions to multiple people or multiple groups of people in an organization. These sales are typically large purchases that involve electronics and equipment or the creation of new ideas, license agreements, and partnerships.

Esteem needs The need to be deemed an expert and the need for power or position.

Extroversion One of the factors in the five-factor model; it describes a person's capabilities to build and manage relationships.

Five-factor model A formal model for classifying personality types that includes five personality factors: negative emotionality, extroversion, openness, agreeableness, and conscientiousness. Each of these factors has six facets, and each facet has a low, medium, and high measurement.

Flashbulb episode An emotional, physical, or cerebral experience that is so overpowering that it is permanently imprinted in one's short-term memory.

General word A word that is nonspecific in meaning and requires the use of operators to achieve a specific interpretation.

Heavy Hitter A successful salesperson.

Hook The main point of a metaphor that delivers a conscious and subconscious message.

Human communication model The layers of verbal and nonverbal communication (including the phonetic, content, purpose, word catalog, internal dialogue, and physical layers) used by people to convey and interpret thoughts, personality, and experiences.

Hypnosis A communication model for describing how thoughts can be structured and words communicated to produce desired responses.

Incongruence Misleading communication where layers of the human communication model contradict each other.

Internal dialogue The never-ending stream of communication inside the mind that represents honest, unedited, and deep feelings.

Intersecting activities Interests, hobbies, and personal pursuits by which people display their personality types, word catalog wiring, and value systems.

Intuitive persuasion The strategy to instill a message in the customer's mind by sensing all the data emanating from the customer, comparing the current scenario to past situations, creating a deep receptive state, and guiding the customer's internal dialogue.

Kinesthetic A person who processes information primarily using the kinesthetic word catalog.

Leading The process of influencing another person's actions by purposely changing yours.

Linkage The connection of two nonrelated messages together in order to have the second message more readily accepted by the listener.

Marking Using body language and speech to highlight spoken words so that they are remembered by the subconscious mind.

Martin Curve A theory that explains that 10 to 15 percent of everyone you try to sell to will not buy. Also, 10 to 15 percent will give you all the buying signs but never buy anything.

Maslow's hierarchy of needs The theory explaining that human beings want to satisfy an ever-escalating set of needs, which begin with biological deficiencies, ascend through social requirements, and ultimately culminate in the fulfillment of deeper spiritual needs.

Metaphor A single story that conveys different lessons and multiple meanings. Using metaphors is a special intuitive persuasion technique to change a customer's attitude and behavior.

Mirroring The conscious act of modifying your behavior to fit into your surroundings.

Models Descriptions and representations of how systems work.

Negative emotionality One of the factors in the five-factor model; it describes a person's tolerance for stress, anger, and worry.

Neurolinguistics The study of how the brain uses and interprets language.

Neutral wording The presentation of ideas and thoughts without any reference to word catalogs.

Openness One of the factors in the five-factor model; it describes whether a person prefers a familiar environment with defined daily routines or seeks variety and is open to new experiences.

Operator An additional word that is added to a general word to more accurately convey meaning.

Pacing The natural process of adjusting your tempo to your environment.

Persuasion The process of building personal relationships with customers and always acting in their best interests by understanding their needs, wants, thought processes, and personalities; the act of building mutual trust by demonstrating your technical and business competence; and the ability to speak in the spectrum of languages customers use both logically and emotionally.

Phonetic layer The enunciation and vocal sounds of the actual words being spoken.

Physical layer Also known as body language, the nonverbal communication emitted by a person's body posture.

Physiological needs Basic needs that are necessary for survival such as food, air, sleep, and shelter. For Hitters, physiological needs include the stability of their company, the competitiveness of their product, and the soundness of the marketplace.

Primary word catalog The default or main mode of communication (either visual, auditory, or kinesthetic) that a person is most comfortable using and uses most often.

Purpose layer The intentional assembling of words to selfishly communicate an idea or experience.

Rapport　A special relationship between two or more individuals based upon harmonious communication.

Receptive state　The positive environment that enables a message to be accepted and remembered.

Safety needs　Needs that establish stability, such as home, family, and religion. In sales, safety needs include information on how to compete with other vendors and the competency of the Hitter's manager.

Sales intuition　The ability to read and anticipate a customer's actions beforehand.

Search loop　A person's unsuccessful search for information by repeatedly accessing each of the word catalogs.

Selection pressure　The pressure on the salesperson to promptly answer the customer's question in order for the response to be perceived as truthful.

Self-actualization　The personal maturity that is achieved after all physiological, safety, belonging, and esteem needs have been satisfied.

Subconscious mind　The part of the mind that a person doesn't control but that still collects information and is capable of influencing behavior. Also referred to as the unconscious mind.

Technical specification language　The androgynous, nonpersonal, and technical communication that is one of the primary languages the customer speaks.

Triangulation　The process of identifying and validating information by using different sources.

Turning point　The critical moment in the sales cycle where the deal momentum changes.

Unverifiable statement　A statement that elicits skepticism since the internal dialogue does not accept it as being true.

VAK count/VAK keyword count　Tally of a person's use of visual, auditory, and kinesthetic keywords in order to determine his or her word catalog wiring.

Verifiable statement A statement that the listener will accept as true after it is validated by the internal dialogue.

Vignette Short interactions of dialogue between the Heavy Hitter and the customer, usually about one topic or conversational theme.

Visual A person who processes information primarily using the visual word catalog.

Word catalog The mind's method of gathering information, accumulating knowledge, and recording experiences based upon one of three senses—visual, auditory, or kinesthetic. The word catalog is also responsible for the association of psychological meanings to words.

Word catalog wiring The mind's ability to use a unique combination and amount of the visual, auditory, and kinesthetic word catalogs.

Index

About the Author

IN ROLES ranging from salesperson to vice president, Steve Martin has been personally responsible for over a quarter of a billion dollars of high-technology sales while working for leading-edge Silicon Valley companies over the past 20 years.

He began his career programming computers as a teenager in the late 1970s. Through working with computers, he became acutely aware of the preciseness and structure of language. In addition, programming is built upon "models," verbal descriptions and visual representations of how systems work and processes flow. Models enable repeatable and predictable experiences.

Early in his career, he was also introduced to the concepts of neurolinguistics, the study of how the human brain uses and interprets language. When he transitioned his career into sales, he realized that the language his customers used was directly related to their behavior. He could build models to create successful relationships based upon a customer's language, personality, and thought process. Without any sales experience to speak of, he was the number one salesperson in his company for the following four years.

Steve went on to be a top sales producer for a billion-dollar software company and was promoted into management to imprint his "selling model" on other salespeople within the organization. As vice president of sales, Steve successfully trained his salespeople in the principles of *Heavy Hitter Selling*. As a sales trainer, he has helped thousands of salespeople become Heavy Hitters. Today, Steve remains an avid student of neurolinguistics and human nature during the sales cycle. After countless customer meetings, he still enjoys the exhilaration and satisfaction of a successful sales call.

Steve Martin trains the sales organizations of companies all around the world. He doesn't just present information and tactics; he demonstrates them in a highly interactive environment that emulates a typical sales call. It's an educational, entertaining, and enlightening experience. Additionally, Steve consults with companies to help them find the answer to the fundamental question, "Why aren't we selling more?" For more information, please visit www.heavyhitterselling.com.